Bone Voyage

Bone

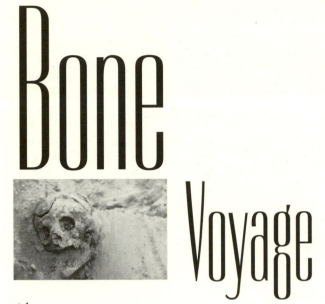

Voyage

A
Journey
in
Forensic
Anthropology

Stanley Rhine

University of New Mexico Press, Albuquerque

Library of Congress Cataloging-in-Publication Data
Rhine, Stanley.
    Bone voyage / a journey in forensic anthropology / Stanley Rhine.
       p.   cm.
    Includes bibliographical references and index.
    1. Forensic anthropology. I. Title.
   ISBN 0-8263-1967-x (cloth)
   ISBN 0-8263-1968-8 (paper)
   GN69.8.R45   1998
   614'.1—dc21   98-23459
                                                          CIP

Contents

Illustrations

Preface

It seemed that whenever there was a truly weird phone call received in the Department of Anthropology office at the University of New Mexico, it would be routed to the Osteology Laboratory of the Maxwell Museum of Anthropology. This tradition extends back at least to the early summer of 1974, when the phone rang and the bemused department secretary asked me if we could help. A six-year-old light aircraft crash had just been discovered in a wilderness area in the northern part of the state, and the Federal Aviation Agency was sending its crack anthropological crash investigator Dr. Clyde C. Snow in to identify the four skeletonized bodies that had been recovered. They needed space to lay out the bodies. Could we be of assistance?

Could we! This sounded like an interesting break from routine. The next morning a half-dozen State Policemen trooped into the lab, each with a garbage bag full of . . . well, various things. Snow was also there, raring to go. I had heard him give a paper at a physical anthropology meeting a couple of years earlier. Its topic was the survivability of passengers in an aircraft crash, and it was one of the more interesting papers that year. Now he was here.

Snow appeared in the same stocky, shambling, slow-talking guise as he did at the meetings. With his head stuffed securely into his collar and heavy-lidded eyes peering intently through half-glasses, his movements through a room could be traced by the fitful trail of cigarette ash following behind him. Never in a hurry, he was given to punctuating his speech with colorful metaphor, much of which was a shade too colorful to repeat in church. When I asked if he would mind if I watched, he replied, in effect, " . . . if you want to hang around, you're going to work." By that time, the Maxwell Museum of Anthropology (for which I was assistant curator) had assigned a work-study student, Nancy Akins, to the lab. She and another museum helper, Kathryn Linn, also a former osteology student, pitched in as well. Guessing that there was at least three days' work in front of us, Snow and his instant helpers opened the bags, removed bones, clothes, sticks, rocks, the occasional stray aircraft part, and whatever else had been picked up at the scene.

The crash scene had been visited by the State Police, who recovered the remains. As far as we were able to reconstruct the search later, each officer must have been given a large garbage bag and directed to pick up whatever looked important. It seemed as if they had struck out, crossing, recrossing, and crisscrossing each others' paths around the scene. If we could have diagrammed their trails from above, we would probably have had a reasonable approximation of Brownian movement. As a consequence, there was no necessary relationship among the contents of any one bag, and a given sack might contain parts of all four people who were aboard the plane. Since the police officers were inexperienced in looking for bones, they did not find them all. While smaller bones might have been completely eaten by carnivores, others had certainly been dragged off for considerable distances and overlooked.

As the recovery team had made no notes about where the bones were picked up, our immediate task was to separate these thoroughly scrambled (commingled) remains back into the four discrete units that had represented those people in life. This was made more complicated by the fact that all four of those aboard the light plane that had been missing so long were males. All were between the ages of twenty-six and thirty and between five feet eleven inches, and six feet one inch tall. The picture this invoked was that of four totally indistinguishable pals, as alike as peas in a pod, grinning in Xeroxed fashion from an old preflight photo. This friendly little scenario might not, however, have been correct. Someone who was supposed to have gone on the flight might have gotten sick or busy, or an extra passenger may have been added at the last minute. One of the people believed to have died in the crash could still be alive and have assumed a new identity—unlikely after all this time, but nevertheless possible.

Although it sounds as if the skeletons were impossible to separate, the task proved rather straightforward. Of course, separation could not be based entirely on color or condition. A bone or an entire arm or leg might have been dragged off some distance by a predator less interested in a tidy scene than an easy meal. Thus, the leg bones of one person might be dried, bleached, and cracked by six years of exposure to the elements, while his pelvis, for instance, might be clean and pristine, having been left to decompose and skeletonize slowly, protected by its location within the crumpled fuselage.

When Snow left to run down dental records, x-rays, and records of hospital treatment of the four men, the three of us patiently continued the meticulous matching of bones on the basis of size, weight, muscularity, congruity across the joint surfaces, and so on. To a degree greater than we had anticipated, each of the four crash victims slowly began to emerge as an individual. With the sorting completed, Snow used the records he had obtained to begin the task of identification. With dental x-rays, he demonstrated how skeleton No. 1 was actually Wright Onmann. The match was perfect. One by one, names were placed with each of the others, except for the last. No dental records or x-rays of any sort could be found. Then came a lucky break—literally.

About two years before the plane crash, one of the passengers had broken his tibia (shin). There were no x-rays, but the description of the fracture found in his medical records matched precisely the bone callus that could be seen on the anterior (forward) margin of a fragment of tibia less than six inches long. We could tell what bone this fragment was from and knew that it was crossed by a fracture that had taken place in the last few years before the crash. This information allowed us to make the final identification. Until that time, we had not known where to put that mending piece of bone. This fragment of tibia might have gone with any of the others whose legs were incomplete, but since the other identifications had been made positively, it could not go with any of them. Therefore, it had to be a part of the last John Doe skeleton and, if so, John Doe No. 4 was no longer John Doe.

We felt good about having helped Snow accomplish this three-day task in a day and a half, and having made positive identifications on all four crash victims. Before he left for home, Snow told me that if I wished to be involved in forensic work in the future he would contact Dr. James T. Weston, chief medical investigator of the year-old statewide death investigation unit. Should other bone cases show up to darken Weston's door, he might call me for assistance.

Other cases did indeed show up, and in a few months Weston called me regarding what was to be the first of hundreds more cases over the next twenty years of forensic anthropology in New Mexico. What follows here represents mostly that experience, with interesting examples drawn from elsewhere to fill in some facts on the broader practice of forensic anthropology. Rather than recounting the triumphs of forensic anthropology from a personal standpoint, this book attempts to set forth a few cases with the purpose of drawing a larger series of lessons from them. In so doing, the reader should be able to glean something of both what forensic anthropologists do and how they do it. It does not, however, fully represent the range of conditions under which forensic anthropologists operate nationwide, nor does it attempt to offer a comprehensive literature review.

Many names appear in the following pages. With few exceptions, which are noted, I have chosen to alter the names of case subjects in the interest of protecting their relatives from unnecessary pain and suffering. The loss of a loved one is one of the most traumatic of life's events, and in many instances here the details of the subjects' deaths are graphic enough to run the risk of reopening wounds in family members that can never fully heal. No purpose would be served by using the victims' real names.

Though these victims' deaths were sometimes at far too young an age and often through no fault of their own, they may still teach us some valuable lessons. To borrow the phrase seen occasionally in medicolegal work, *"Hic locus est ubi mortui viveuntes docent"* (this is the place where the dead teach the living). Although the names have been changed, the cases are real, and even if I am guilty of having audaciously fabricated occasional bits of conversation and may also have infrequently engaged in the slightest hint of embellishment, the facts of the cases are as true as memories, notes, and old case files allow. My hope is that those who have had some involvement with these cases will not react to their presentation here as explorer and mountain man Kit Carson did when told of some of the lurid adventures attributed to him, "It may be true, but I ain't got any recollection of it."

All other names appearing throughout this book are real. Not only are those of the anthropologists real, they belong to a fine group of people with whom I have greatly enjoyed associating. These have been invaluable colleagues, friends, and teachers, and this book could never have been written without their suggestions, ideas, and encouragement, though none of us was aware at the time that any of their intellectual pollination would blossom forth in this fashion. They deserve more recognition than they have received for their dedicated hard work. It is particularly appropriate to note here the pivotal influence of one of the pioneer forensic anthropologists, the legendary Dr. Alice Brues, who became my advisor at the University of Colorado.

A hearty thanks is offered to the New Mexico Office of the Medical Investigator (OMI). The understanding and cooperation of four chief medical investigators, dozens of dedicated forensic pathologists, scores of deputy medical investigators, and all of the other folks associated with the OMI made two decades of forensic anthropology possible. They also made it very enjoyable and rewarding in terms of experience and opportunity. Without the entry into the world of legal medicine afforded by the OMI, my life would have been vastly different and much less interesting.

Several people have been kind enough to read portions of chapters of this work in the interest of accuracy. Specifically, Walter Birkby, Homer Campbell, Diane France, Eugene Giles, Madeleine Hinkes, Ellis Kerley, Vernon McCarty, Patricia McFeeley and Ross Zumwalt all read chunks and made valuable suggestions. Ted A. Rathbun was asked to review the manuscript by the University of New Mexico Press and made many useful suggestions. Western historian Durwood Ball, transmuted by unkind fates into an editor for the University of New Mexico Press, struggled mightily against an overly wordy manuscript. Only a few of the good parts suffered banishment by his busy pencil. Copy editor Louise Cameron clarified meanings and saved me from many an infelicitous construction. What remains before you now has reached its present state due to the involvement of these people, who may now consider themselves properly thanked. Those errors of fact and interpretation that remain must be credited to the limitations (or stubbornness) of the author.

I have also benefited from the insights and perceptions of life gleaned from a number of fine people with whom I have been privileged to share some of life's experiences. Of major importance has been the encouragement, advice, and suggestions of my wife, forensic anthropologist Sue Jimenez, who, among other things, plowed through the entire manuscript. Knowledgeable and helpful dentist Stephen Wagner has long been a resource (and trusted dentist) for denizens of the lab. The late William L. Minear, a retired orthopaedic surgeon, took to visiting the lab frequently, spreading both enjoyment and his intimate knowledge and appreciation of bones to all of those who passed through there. Nor could this acknowledgment be complete without mentioning the many students who have also passed through the lab doors over the years. It has been the long-standing practice of the University of New Mexico's Maxwell Museum's Laboratories of Physical Anthropology to involve students in ongoing forensic casework as a means of enhancing their education. The "we" that crops up so frequently in what follows is usually in reference to their presence and involvement. It is a cliché that a teacher learns from his students. It is also true. I have certainly learned as much from them as they have from me. Their constant questioning and probing causes one to ask how one really knows something, and how well one knows it. On more than one occasion, they have brought me up short with their opinions and observations. This interaction helps to instill some of the caution so important in forensic work. So to all of those who have contributed in various ways to my education, and thus to this volume, a belated but heartfelt thanks.

Introduction

A Funny Thing Happened on the Way to the Morgue

Anthropologists do indeed get strange assignments sometimes. The strangest of these usually fall within forensic anthropology, the analysis of skeletal remains in a medicolegal context. A question that is often asked is "Why *forensic* anthropology?" It is the anthropologists who have studied human skeletal remains in detail, and it is they who can best evaluate them in a forensic context. Indeed, their inclusion in a medicolegal investigative team can save authorities time, effort, and even embarrassment.

An example will illustrate this point. Deputy sheriffs scoured a ditch a few miles south of the city limits of Albuquerque, New Mexico, in a valiant effort to find the body of Natalie Attyred, reported by an informant as having been dumped there. The sheriff of an adjacent county was on hand, standing on a ridge next to the ditch, directing his troops who slogged determinedly up and down the channel. Their efforts were augmented by the aquatic rescue team that had been called in to plumb any large pools of water. All of this frenzied activity caught the attention of a passer-by who informed the local sheriff of this incursion into his territory. Eventually, units of the State Police and the Albuquerque Police Department (APD) also cruised by to see what all the excitement was about. The only thing this massive expedition lacked was a forensic anthropologist.

The Office of the Medical Investigator (OMI), a statewide investigative agency located in Albuquerque, was belatedly alerted to this search, which the sheriff was sure was about to turn up a body any minute. The chief medical investigator dispatched one of his investigators and the forensic anthropologist to the scene. As the deputies continued their probing of three-inch-deep sandbars on the bottom of the concrete channel, searching for the body, there were discussions about who had jurisdiction. This rather heated exchange was interrupted when a deputy scurried up the hill, the carnassial tooth of a dog clutched in his hand. "Is it her?" he breathlessly implored.

If you have never looked in the mouth of a dog, the carnassial is the carnivore's equivalent to a human's molar tooth. It is a relatively long, narrow tooth, with the jagged contour of a Pike's Peak. By comparison, humans have rather square, slightly lumpy, but quite dull molars. No, the tooth did not belong to the missing woman. Even the dogged determination of the deputy could not make it so. Had the forensic anthropologist not been on hand to make this instant identification, the search might have continued for hours in the hope of locating the rest of the (nonexistent) body. Furthermore, a quick look up and down the ditch told the anthropologist that there were only a couple of places with sand deep enough to cover a body, although in fact the deputies persisted in probing and shoveling even the shallow pockets of sand.

Forensic anthropologists identify bones. They also assist in the recovery of bodies and perform many other tasks having to do with human remains in that interesting intersection of medicine and the law. A well-thought-out plan for recovering a body should include a forensic anthropologist, who can bring his or her expertise to bear. Given the conditions at the ditch, a half-hour search by two knowledgeable people could have located a body, if one were there. Instead, the search consumed hours of time and involved dozens of people. Somehow the news media missed this one—an excellent example of how not to conduct a recovery effort.

The fascinating field of forensic anthropology is only about twenty-five years old, but immense public interest has already led to the writing of a number of interesting books on the subject. Each is recommended to those with an interest in the topic. The title of Christopher Joyce and Eric Stover's treatise on the globe-trotting forensic exploits of Clyde Snow, *Witnesses from the Grave* (1991) clangs like the slamming of the door of a body storage unit. While providing some background on Snow, the book concentrates on his recent excavation and identification work in Argentina. Douglas Ubelaker and Henry Scammell's *Bones: A Forensic Detective's Casebook* (1992) features Ubelaker's forensic anthropological work out of the Smithsonian Institution. The Smithsonian's long-standing ties to the FBI nets Ubelaker interesting cases from all over. The late William Maples and Michael Browning's *Dead Men Do Tell Tales* (1994) sets up the essential truth of forensic anthropology in its title. While concentrating on

Maples' work in Florida, the book also covers a number of his famous-people cases from around the world.

With so many good books already available to students and followers of forensic anthropology, why still another? For many years I taught a sophomore course, "Forensics and Crime," at the University of New Mexico. An introduction to medicolegal investigation, it touched on the range of investigative and analytical techniques of forensic medicine, and, like most people teaching such courses, I would on occasion toss in a few examples of forensic scientists at work. Intrigued by the anecdotes, students often asked "Why don't you write a book?" After some years, I also began to wonder why I didn't. Consequently, if this turns out well, I owe those students a debt of gratitude.

Recently I heard a colleague proclaim that all of the best cases have been done. On the contrary, every day holds the possibility of enthralling new cases, with enough twists and turns to satisfy even the most jaded specialist. The most experienced forensic anthropologists have some marvelous tales to tell, as the exploits of Snow, Ubelaker, and Maples clearly show, and their fund of fascinators is nowhere near exhausted. Many other vastly experienced forensic anthropologists have committed only a few of their most intriguing cases to paper. Even forensic anthropologists with only a few cases under their belts have interesting stories to share and useful conclusions to draw from them. We should hope that the examples presented here might cause them to uncap their pens or to limber up their keyboards to add to our stock of shared information.

In reading the Maples and Browning book, I was impressed by the solemnity and seriousness of forensic anthropology. They and many other authors make the point that forensic anthropologists (and other forensic specialists) explore the realm of the dead, and the remains that we analyze are due our respect. They were, after all, not very long ago, just as human and just as alive as any of us.

This theme of appreciating the human context of the bones we deal with was wonderfully illustrated by Loren Eiseley in his book *The Unexpected Universe* (1969). Eiseley recalled an incident in his life ("Anthropologists sometimes get strange assignments," he later mused) when he stepped down from a train that had stopped near a junkyard in which fires flickered. Approaching one of them, he engaged in conversation a man who was forking discards from the nearby city onto the fire. At one point, the worker hoisted an old radio onto his fork and flipped it into the flames. Eiseley noticed the tubes and wires dangling inertly from it and thought to himself that at some time, perhaps the 1920s, voices and music had blared from it. Back on the train, the image of the damaged and lifeless radio conjured up in Eiseley a recollection of having fitted a seared and scorched skullcap back onto a skull. It, too, was like some fine machine irreparably broken, he thought—"Now, where were the voices and the music?"

This is the sort of thought, albeit not usually put as eloquently as only Eiseley could, that comes into the minds of others who work with human bones. Eiseley's question might also, in some sense, be the question that all forensic anthropologists most want to answer: where are "the voices and the music"? The accumulation of bones that each anthropologist faces at the beginning of a case was once a living, breathing, thinking being, and it is the anthropologist's task to build up a reliable image of who and what he or she was—to find the voices and the music. The anthropologist is aided in this task by the fact that the bones themselves can speak to those who have learned to listen.

Most of us have grown up with cartoons in which the characters literally bounce back from physical stresses that would at least seriously maim and probably kill any real biological organism. While we chortle at the amazing immortality of Wile E. Coyote in his never ending quest for a roadrunner dinner, continuous exposure to such stimuli, combined with a general ignorance of anatomy and physiology, probably renders us increasingly immune to violent spectacles. We expect real bodies to bounce too, but they splatter instead. Al Capp's cartoon send-up of Dick Tracy, Fearless Fosdick, developed clean see-through holes when shot, but real people bleed and die. Injury and death may be thought to be amusing in the abstract, but they never are in the concrete. Not only is the life of a sentient being cut short, but the deceased person's relatives and friends have had their lives sundered as well. Even those who we might dismiss as depraved and with no redeeming social virtue (to paraphrase the Supreme Court) are loved or admired by someone, and that person's life is also impacted by the death. As a spokesman for a national funeral director's association observed, " . . . death, especially to the person who has just experienced it, is not funny."

Still, while not chuckling at the misfortune and demise of others, the circumstances under which these occur or are discovered may occasionally offer some diversion. Nor is gallows humor unknown among those whose occupations bring them into the proximity of the grim reaper. In fact, some have expressed the opinion that to be successful as a forensic anthropologist, one must have a viewpoint that is slightly askew from the norm. Things that others would find horrifying, repulsive, and stomach-wrenching are, to the forensic anthropologist, perplexing yet fascinating and intriguing. Of course, when birds of a feather flock together they invariably tell stories of mutual interest, and when the birds are forensic anthropologists, their tales often take on a bizarre, even macabre quality. It is wise to keep voices low in a restaurant to avoid creating a "dead zone" around the dinner table.

An Enchanting Land

Most of the "action" to be recounted on these pages has to do with forensic anthropology that takes place in New Mexico, the "Land of Enchantment." Just to put things into context, it will help to have a vision of New Mexico before your eyes. Contrary to the impressions of many people (including some of the newer residents), the "sentinel of the desert," the tall multiarmed saguaro does not grow in New Mexico. While most of the southern and eastern parts of the state can properly be classified as desert, much of it sprinkled with a variety of cacti, the state contains great varieties of landforms and environments.

Four physiographic provinces terminate in New Mexico: the eastern third of the state is part of the Great Plains; the Southern Rocky Mountain province dangles its southernmost extension in a narrow tongue down just past the state capital of Santa Fe; the southeastern fifth of the Colorado Plateau extends over the northwest corner of the state; and the southwestern quarter, along with the southern and middle Rio Grande Valley is made up of the easternmost part of the Basin and Range province (Hunt, 1967). This 121,365-square-mile state is the fifth largest and fourth highest of the United States, with elevations ranging from 2,817 feet to 13,160 feet, and averaging 6,100 feet. The annual precipitation ranges from under eight inches to forty inches (Beck and Haase, 1979), with temperatures typically running between −30 to over 120 degrees Fahrenheit. It is a very sunny state, with as much as 3,700 hours of sunshine a year in the southwest part. The state's largest city, Albuquerque, even holds a record as the sunniest city, where the sun shone every day for 779 consecutive days between December 16, 1961 and February 2, 1964 (Burdett et al., 1990). February 3 was cloudy.

This is probably more than you ever wanted to know about New Mex-

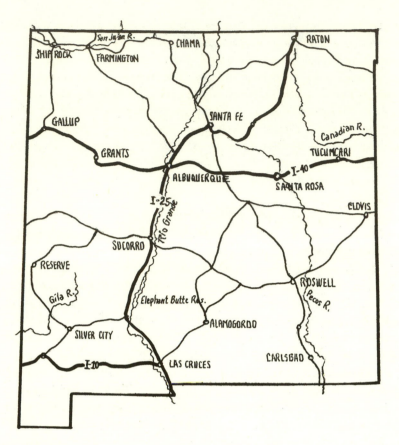

New Mexico
(Map drawn by Stanley Rhine)

ico, but it is important to get a feel for its geography, since in such a varied landscape conditions vary widely with the time of year and location. This has a significant effect both on the survival of people and what happens to their bodies after death, an important factor in forensic anthropology.

New Mexico has been (and is still) occupied by a succession of peoples. The first humans to invade the soil that is now New Mexico emigrated from Asia over a period of thousands of years beginning more than ten thousand years ago. Nineteen pueblos and seven reservations are still occupied by their kin. Next to come were the Spanish, in 1539. By 1609, when they established the hamlet of Santa Fe as the seat of colonial government, Spanish hegemony reached over vast areas of both North and South America, but in 1680, simmering Pueblo resentments about their treatment at the hands of the interlopers boiled over. The successful Pueblo Revolt drove the Spanish down the Rio Grande to El Paso. After several attempts, New Mexico was finally reclaimed for the Spanish king and the Catholic Church by don Diego de Vargas in 1692 (Chilton et al., 1984). In 1776, Franciscan Father Dominguez left Santa Fe to search out an overland route to California, in the interest of opening this vast area to the teachings of the church. At the same time, some 1,600 miles to the east, a gaggle of unruly colonists was declaring its independence from the English king.

When Mexico won its independence from Spain in 1821, the outpost of Santa Fe became the center of government in Mexico's northernmost provinces. However, legal authority rested lightly on the shoulders of residents as the territory was far from Mexico City. Then, stepping into this governmental vacuum with the wind of manifest destiny at his back, General Stephen Watts Kearny led his U.S. troops into the Santa Fe plaza, claiming the territory for the United States in 1846. That cheeky move was never challenged. Still, more than a half-century passed before New Mexico was admitted as the 47th state in 1912. Since then, descendants of the original Indian occupants, the Spaniards, the Anglos, and small contingents of Asians and Blacks, in every combination imaginable, have been joined by a post-World War II invasion of flatlanders and a more recent backwash from California. This has lent an incredible richness and variety to life in the state. It has also made the problem of identifying unknown bodies more difficult.

A third of the state's 1.5 million residents reside in metropolitan Albuquerque. As a consequence, with dependence on agriculture, stockraising, and mineral extraction as base sources of income, New Mexico remains a poor and rural state. Augmented in the last five decades with marked impact in the scientific-technological and tourist businesses, the state offers an array of varied scenic and cultural attractions. Despite its status as the birthplace of the nuclear age near Alamogordo in 1945, New Mexico remains with one foot firmly planted in the quieter, more rural nineteenth century. In time, even some of the more recent arrivals begin to operate at a more languid pace. Now, having established some feel for the territory, we may see how forensic anthropology plays out within its borders.

1

A Premature Funeral

Bones and Fire

On June 4, 1959, Forest Service lookouts reported smoke rising from what was assumed to be a small forest fire just east of the Arizona state line, among the 8,000-feet peaks of the San Francisco Mountains of southwestern New Mexico. A firefighting crew dispatched to the scene discovered no forest fire, but an automobile burning furiously on the side of a gravel forest road. Dousing the flames, they found a mass of burned flesh, a skull, some other bones, and some teeth resting inside the burned-out hulk.

The car was found to belong to a Mr. Armando, well known in the lightly populated region. His fiery demise prompted the organization of a six-person coroner's inquest in Catron County. According to former Catron County Sheriff and now Washoe County (Nevada) Coroner Vernon McCarty, the "six responsible citizens" required by 1950s New Mexico law were most easily found by the justices of the peace at a local bar. McCarty observed that an insufficiency of able-bodied citizens could be remedied either by visiting several such spots or by prolonging the official quest at one of them for as long as it took to empanel the necessary six people.

The resulting coroner's jury in this case was made up of ranchers, Forest Service firefighters, two bartenders, and a service station attendant. It concluded that the remains were "badly burned and charred beyond positive identification," according to the *Albuquerque Journal* for June 17, 1960. Nonetheless, an identification was made by Armando's two brothers-in-law and the district attorney, apparently functioning in his multiple roles of death investigator and skeletal "expert." That it *was* Armando was attested to the by the fact that the human skull was accompanied by some impressively large upper incisors. These prominent choppers had conferred upon the victim the name "Squirley," by which he was known throughout the area.

The Funeral

Funeral arrangements were speedily made, a bountiful feast prepared, and a coffin procured to hold the few pitiful charred remains of Squirley. Providing him with all the trimmings, this rather large send-off attracted relatives and friends from miles around to the site of the ceremony in Albuquerque. The metal sealer casket (which alone cost $1,510), publication of death notices, use of the chapel, and other personal services ran the bill up to $2,055.50—a lot of money for the funeral of a resident of rural New Mexico in 1959.

Just as the family was settling into its mourning, the hungry, haggard, legally dead Mr. Armando wandered into a forest logging camp not far from Reserve, New Mexico. This was a mere five miles from the remote spot near the boundary of the Apache and Gila National Forests where he had "died" only a few days before. The loggers notified one of Armando's brothers-in-law, who called the sheriff, who picked him up. Weak from exhaustion, Armando told of wandering around for five days before finding the logging camp.

Taken to the hospital in mile-high Reserve, Squirley told Sheriff Barney Hickson that everything had been going fine until an electrical fire broke out under the dashboard of his car. In addition to his prospecting equipment, he had been carrying dynamite caps. Prudently deciding on a hasty exit, he dove out through the window, "falling down a hill, getting up and running as the car went off the road, and hitting his head," related Hickson. For the next couple of days, things were pretty hazy, but Squirley slowly regained his grip on reality and started for his mother-in-law's ranch. He made it only as far as the logging camp before collapsing.

Who Was Buried in Squirley's Coffin?

The discovery that the recently deceased was in fact alive and well came as joyful news to his family, but it did pose a particularly disconcerting problem. If Armando was still alive and well, who had they just buried? It seems that the Socorro County District Attorney had always harbored some doubts about the identification of the body as he had asked the family to delay burial. Captain E. A. Tafoya, head of the State Police criminal investigation division also said, "We never were satisfied. We knew they weren't fresh human bones." So did Squirley. He told Sheriff Hickson that the bones recovered from his car were an old Indian skull he had found, a porcupine he had shot, and some calf bones.

By this time, people were becoming somewhat testy about the whole business. The court was understandably curious about the real identity of the remains in Squirley's coffin and speedily approved an exhumation. This time, to avoid further confusion, the burned bones were sent to an anthropologist at the University of New Mexico in Albuquerque.

As the 1950s slid into the 1960s, the field of forensic anthropology had still not been officially invented, so the task of identifying these bones fell to an old-school anthropologist of broad learning and great experience. Although his research interest was African ethnology, his varied accomplishments included teaching the Anthropology Department's human skeleton class. Rising to the challenge, the professor quickly realized that there was a particularly inhuman quality about these bones. In short order he was able to identify most of the bones as having formerly belonged to a cow, the skull as that of an ancient human, and the front teeth as having belonged in the partially fleshed porcupine torso. So the remains were not Squirley at all, nor even a doppelganger, but a chimera consisting of one part human and several parts not.

There was some speculation that Armando, banking on the dental features that he shared with porcupines, had attempted an insurance fraud, but since no insurance claim was ever filed, the Sierra County grand jury's attempt to indict him for fraud was dismissed. So too were the charges of illegally transporting explosives. Then, a year after Squirley's spectacular but unfulfilled demise, the Garcia Mortuary sued Mrs. Armando, as she was disinclined to pay the more than $2,000 bill for a funeral for her very-much-alive 43-year-old husband, especially since at no time had he been dead or had any part of him ever been buried. Attorney Edward Apodaca told the court, "I don't know if a case of this type has occurred anywhere. . . . I find no case where a porcupine has been given the ritual of burial as human remains." It was certainly a lot of money to shell out to temporarily plant a porcupine, but Mrs. Armando was judged liable for the costs. She never came up with the money, but Squirley held on to the coffin, assuming that there would eventually be some further use for it. Featured prominently in the decor of the Armando living room, it finally came into use again, making Squirley one of the pioneers of New Mexico recycling.

First of all, a small plea for compassion is in order. This incident took place in a more innocent age, when things were usually assumed to be as they appeared. It probably never occurred to the able sheriff to seek outside expert help in identifying the fragmentary, charred remains found in Squirley's burned-out truck. After all, the district attorney and the victim's own brothers-in-law all recognized them as Squirley.

The recovery of the burned remains was probably somewhat casual and very incomplete. In many jurisdictions such searches are still poorly carried out today. Indeed, at mid-century it was roundly assumed that a skeleton could be completely destroyed in a fire. But as Dr. William M. Bass has pointed out (1984a), this is not the case. Uneven heating and expansion of the marrow and the bone itself will cause it to shatter. Heating the skull will cause it to explode like an egg left too long in a microwave oven. Even the intense heat produced by a crematorium is not sufficient to destroy bones completely. In fires of the temperatures and durations normally seen in structures, for example, the soft tissue is slowly consumed leaving only rather small fragments of bone. The sooner the fire is extinguished, of course, the more of the body will survive. Vehicular fires are usually of such relatively short duration as to be less destructive than a crematorium.

Destruction of Bodies by Fire

As a fire starts, the outer layers of the skin begin to burn away and the heat of the fire begins to dry and contract the muscles. Since the flexor muscles (the muscles that bend the arms, legs, fingers, and toes) are more massive and powerful than the extensors (the muscles that straighten them out), the limbs are pulled into the "pugilistic position," like the crouch of a boxer, a sort of fetal position with bent legs and arms and a curved back. At this stage, the body is thus slightly curled up, with most of the outer layers of skin burned off. Clothing, particularly heavy clothing, offers enough protection that patches of skin may remain. This is the amount of destruction seen in self-immolations, many vehicle fires, and some quickly extinguished house fires. As the body is transported to the autopsy facility, some of this charred outer layer spalls off to reveal bright red muscle tissue beneath. At autopsy, though surface features have been destroyed, organs may be removed and samples of tissue, urine, blood,

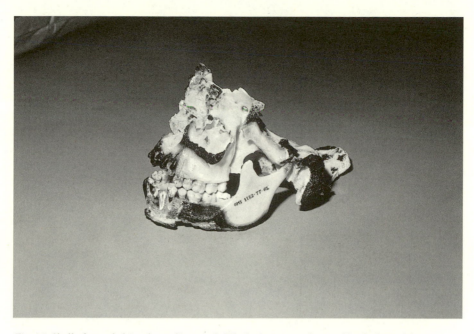

Fig. 1.1. Skull of a truck driver burned in a crash. The braincase was shattered by the heat of the fire. Parts of the skull were left unburned, protected by thicker layers of soft tissue, while the front of the mouth and incisor teeth were greatly damaged.

and vitreous humor (the fluid of the eye) may be taken in the normal manner.

In a fire of longer duration or higher intensity, temperatures will rise enough that the fluids present in the skull vaporize. The pressure inside the skull continues to build since its only outlets are plugged by various soft-tissue structures. The pressure finally increases to the point when the vessel can no longer hold, and the skull explodes. This explosion flings pieces of the vault of the skull some distance from the body, leaving the bones of the skull base and the face more or less intact. Exposed only a little longer, however, the relatively thin layers of soft tissue are burned off the face, and the flames may severely damage some of the underlying bone structure (Fig. 1.1).

At this stage, the lips have dried, pulled back, and mostly burned away, exposing the front teeth directly to the heat and flames. However, the mass of the tongue and cheek muscles continue to protect the cheek teeth (pre-molars and molars) from the fire. Even at this stage, the pelvis is still pro-

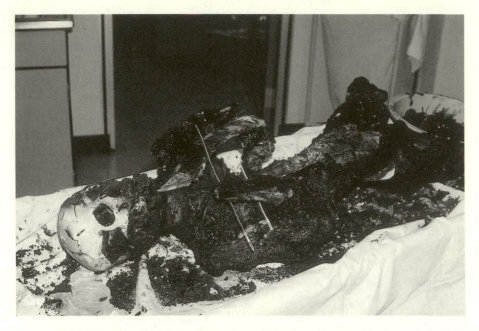

Fig. 1.2. Remains of a woman who was shot and then burned in a van. The intact skull reveals that it had suffered from blunt trauma before the fire. Two probes indicate the direction of bullets through the thorax.

tected from the fire by its surrounding mass of muscle, and there are still large amounts of muscle left on the legs and perhaps the upper arms. If the body is recovered at this stage, the autopsy can still reveal a great deal of information about the victim by way of extracted fluids and removed organs. Toxicology may still be done from these fluids or from a section of removed muscle. Since the molars and premolars have been protected by the tongue and cheek muscles, they can be charted to effect an identification. Vehicle fires rarely contain enough fuel to continue burning beyond this level of destruction (Fig. 1.2).

If the fire continues, most of the internal organs are lost, and the ribs are burned down to short stubs protruding from the spine. The lower legs and arms are destroyed and only about half of the length of the upper arms and legs remains. An inch or so of charred bone is left protruding from the ends of the limbs. The pelvis is still largely intact, but if the fire continues, all of the soft tissue will eventually be destroyed and even the largest bones will usually be reduced to grayish white splinters no more

than three or four inches long. It is only by careful, meticulous searching that one can recover these very tiny fragments of bone. (For another
description of the destruction of bodies by fire, see Glassman and Crow
[1996].) A forensic anthropologist with lots of time to spare and several
graduate students with like amounts of time and a desire to glue every last
little piece back together could probably do so, but the task can be daunting.

It is important to note here that although a body that has been burned
in this fashion is in some sense destroyed, the skeleton is not. It is simply
reduced by the fire to small pieces. Indeed the precise properties of these
pieces can reveal important information about the duration and/or nature of the fire itself, so helping investigators in their quest to discover
what took place. While Bradtmiller and Buikstra (1984) observed some
increase in the size of elements of bone microstructure with burning,
Nelson (1992) found the opposite. Nelson suggests that the difference between the two experiments is due to differences in the amount of burning and posits that bone may expand slightly before it shrinks. This would
suggest a mechanism by which bone exposed to heat shatters. As the bone
heats up, its high moisture content causes it to expand. Continued heating and expansion fragments it. Having shattered and with its moisture
content reduced, it shrinks as it cools, the shrinkage perhaps amounting
to somewhere between 3 and 5 percent.

This is just the sort of knowledge and perspective that an experienced
forensic anthropologist would have brought to the analysis of the bones
in Squirley's car. Those bones didn't look as if they had been subjected to
intense fire, and therefore there should have been a great deal of muscle
still present on them. Moreover, dried bone, such as that of the Indian
skull Squirley dug up, does not fracture in the same way as fresh bone
when exposed to fire. Bones from bodies burned in open fires show a considerable amount of transverse cracking (across the shafts of bones), while
dried bones show predominately longitudinal (lengthwise) cracking (Fig.
1.3)(Baby, 1954). This difference may be due to the greater amount of expansion a fresh bone undergoes because of its entrapped moisture, but
the physics of this differential expansion remains to be worked out. In
any case, it is clear that a forensic anthropologist called to the scene could
quickly have determined that these particular remains did not add up to
a body that had burned in Squirley's car.

Thus, a careful search of any scene, whether the inside of a vehicle or
a structure, is imperative. Such a search will produce a massive number

Fig. 1.3. A fragment of long bone burned in a body, showing the curved fractures commonly seen in bones burned in flesh. Old, dried bones tend to crack longitudinally. (Photo courtesy of the Office of the Medical Investigator, Albuquerque, New Mexico)

of fragments. From these, complete bones can be reconstructed. Those bones can then be analyzed in the normal fashion of forensic anthropology and solid conclusions drawn. This is, make no bones about it, an exacting and tiresome process.

Color is not a useful criterion as adjacent parts of the same bone may be quite different in color, having come to rest in an oxidizing/reducing microclimate that is slightly different from one just a few inches away. One therefore begins by sorting fragments according to size and shape, putting pieces with a larger diameter, such as would be found in the humerus, the femur, and tibia (the bones of the upper arm and the upper and lower leg), in a different pile from those with a smaller diameter, such as might be found in the radius, ulna, and fibula (the smaller bones of the forearm and lower leg). Those can be separated from flat bones, which would be found in the skull vault and parts of the pelvis. Eventually, some of them will begin to fit together so that after many hours of sorting, fitting, gluing, and mumbling, whole bones—or ones complete enough to

Fig. 1.4. Calcined and fragmented skeleton of a man burned to death in an intense house fire. A hurried recovery and subsequent transportation to the autopsy facilities contributed to the fragmentation of the bones. Note that the bones vary in shade from black to a calcined white.

measure—will begin to emerge from the hopeless-looking pile of black-to-gray-to-white rubble (Fig. 1.4).

Even further down on the scale of burning are what have become known as "cremains." These are the small fragments and powder remaining after a body has been cremated. As we have already established, even the prolonged high temperature of the crematorium's retort is not sufficient to destroy bones. When the door is opened, the shapes of the bones are instantly recognizable though they have been cracked, distorted, and sometimes fragmented by the heat. The high temperatures have also driven off the organic material, so that the bones have become very friable and will crumble if not handled with great care. Most crematoria now process the remains further by putting them through a grinder which reduces them to fragments only a few millimeters long. Forensic anthropologists have been called upon to pick through such shards in a number of civil suits. Though identifications cannot usually be made from such tiny fragments, it is sometimes possible at least to recognize certain bits as being human. Cornell forensic anthropologist Dr. Kenneth A. R. Kennedy (1996) discusses a case in which he was able to determine that the cremains presented to him in two urns were consistent with two children, one a neonate and the other a 3½-year-old. He was even able to show that one urn contained a mixture of two children by measuring the thickness of skull fragments and the sizes of other bone splinters to make his determination. Even the weight of the burned skeleton (Trotter and Peterson, 1955) can provide some information with Warren and Maples (1997), showing a correlation between weight and both sex and stature. Maples features an informative discussion about the nature and analysis of cremated bone in *Dead Men Do Tell Tales* (1994).

Teeth, though cracked and with enamel spalled off, can be recognized as human, and some dental appliances can survive the ordeal of cremation. It is with such material that identifications can be made. Surgical staples, orthopaedic devices, staples used to hold the crematorium's cardboard container together, and other such items will also survive the protracted high temperatures, but such larger artifacts are culled before the grinding takes place.

The ground bone is placed in an urn and delivered to the next of kin. Some people thus end up spending years on the mantle, perhaps being brought forth for special occasions. In other cases, relatives wishing to carry out the deceased's last wishes or hoping to find a pleasant place for him or her to "spend eternity" empty the urn in a favorite place, such as (in New Mexico) a picnic grounds next to the mountains north of Albuquerque or one of the prehistoric buildings in Chaco Canyon in the western part of the state. Park rangers making their rounds will often find a fresh little pile of cremated bone fragments in a corner or a niche in one of the ruins. They carefully scoop them up and send them on their way back to the OMI. Not many people make two postmortem visits to the OMI, however.

The forensic anthropologists in the western United States have been meeting every summer since 1981. One of our traditional morning exercises since our meetings were moved to near Nevada's Lake Mead is to hike up in the hills behind our meeting place to see how many additions have been made to the accumulation of cremains from prior years and how they are progressing. There is a grand sweeping view of the sere, serrated mountains and blue sparkling Lake Mead, but it is doubtful that the cremains pay it much attention.

Some Other Burned Body Cases

In some instances bodies are not burned so completely that the medicolegal community customarily refers to them as "crispy critters." In one such case, a motorcyclist faced with crashing into a truck ahead of him attempted to beat the odds by laying his bike down on the pavement. Sometimes this tactic can turn a potentially fatal accident into one resulting in major injury only, but it didn't work this time. Friction with the road tore his gas tank loose and ruptured it, spreading gasoline over the machine, the road, and the rider, and igniting a blaze. The amount of fuel was so limited that tissue damage caused by the fire was, from an anthropological perspective, minor, but, in combination with his other injuries, fatal. A positive identification could quickly be made from dental records.

More extensive burning was seen in a 1990 case from near Roswell, New Mexico. Located on the high plains on the east side of the state, Roswell became a popular watering hole for cowboys driving cattle up the Chisum Trail and through the town's wide main street in the 1870s and 1880s. It has since settled into the less uproarious existence of a regional trading center and home of the New Mexico Military Institute. About fifteen miles east of town, a footlocker was discovered smoldering under a bridge by three fellows heading off to fish the Pecos River. Seeing a blackened blob lying next to the smoking footlocker, one of them kicked it, and as it rolled away they could all see it was a human skull. They called the police. A closer look into the charred footlocker revealed a partially burned body. At autopsy, the upper part of the body of the approximately twenty-year-old female was found to be badly burned and the skeleton considerably damaged by the fire. The legs and feet, however, were almost intact but greatly decomposed. It is unusual to find a combination of decomposition and burning. This made it clear that she had been dead for several days prior to the attempt to dispose of her body by burning.

Despite great efforts by local authorities, this woman has never been identified. Roswell, also the site of Robert Goddard's pioneering liquid-fueled rocket experiments in the 1930s, has gained a certain notoriety as the much ballyhooed site of the crash of an alien spaceship in 1947. The small, large-eyed bodies of the crew are said to have been quickly spirited away by the army for autopsy at some secret location. Roswell now commemorates this infamous event with a Main Street Museum and an annual celebration that draws believers and the bemused curious from half a continent away. Although the New Mexico OMI is prepared for any contingency, somewhat whimsically even providing a space in their reports for "extraterrestrial," there would appear to be no doubt that this still-unidentified body did not arrive from some far-off galaxy, either in a spaceship or a footlocker. Still, one might occasionally wonder why identification eludes this Roswell body after a half-dozen years.

Even more extensive burning was seen in a case from 1994. Sixteen-year-old Frank Jones had disappeared from his home in Albuquerque, and efforts to find him proved fruitless until, after a few days, the burned-out hulk of a car was found in an adjacent state. The car was the same make and model as that owned by Frank, and its New Mexico license plates matched the number shown in state records for Frank's car. In the trunk was what remained of a badly burned human body, which was taken to a nearby medical examiner's office for identification.

The medical examiner and his local anthropologist concluded that the burned remains were those of Frank Jones. However, the identification was not positive, and the FBI was not satisfied that the examination had been sufficiently rigorous. The very brief anthropology report stated that the remains belonged to a sixteen-year-old Hispanic male without offering any grounds for those conclusions. When the body arrived at the New Mexico OMI, it was in a much more fragmentary condition than it had been when found, due in part to the autopsy and in part to the 300-mile postmortem journey of the very friable burned bones. We had to compare details of the remains before us with those that could be seen in the accompanying autopsy photos to ascertain that we were in fact dealing with the same body. The chain of evidence was presumably uninterrupted, but we wished to verify it for ourselves since the condition of the remains appeared so different.

While the skull appeared essentially intact at autopsy, it was now a pile of blackened bone fragments. T. L. McCabe, a graduate student in forensic anthropology, began by separating, identifying, and laying out all of the bone fragments in anatomical order, and over the next couple of days, another graduate student, James Dawson, laboriously reconstructed the charred and blackened skull. With that accomplished, a dozen features emerged that did indeed lean towards the conclusion that this was the skull of a Hispanic individual.

The original anthropology report set forth only one observation on which the age was based, and because of subsequent damage to the burned bones, we could neither verify nor refute it. Close inspection of the fragments of burned bone did, however, uncover ten points of skeletal maturation which consistently pointed to an age between about fifteen and twenty years, nicely bracketing the age of sixteen and a half of the presumed victim. The best pelvic indicators of sex were either absent or too damaged to evaluate, but we found the measurements of long bones (bones of the arms and legs) and the general robusticity of the skeleton to be consistent with the assumption that the victim was male.

The original report concluded that there was insufficient remaining skeletal material from which to estimate stature, but we were able to measure three bones, from which we managed to get consistent estimates that the stature fell between five feet six inches and six feet, with the most likely stature being around five feet nine inches to five feet ten inches. Jones was five feet, nine inches tall.

An x-ray of the skull taken at the original autopsy was compared with one taken antemortem, in 1989, at Albuquerque's Lovelace Hospital. Though the skull had been so badly damaged by the fire that a perfect match could not be made, the pattern of the frontal sinus seen on those two x-rays compared favorably.

Given this accumulation of data—agreement of the skull x-rays, our estimation of age, height, sex, and race—we too concluded that the remains were consistent with the missing Frank Jones, but we could not make a positive identification. Given the state of the remains, and since the only dental records for Frank dated back to his primary dentition (baby teeth), a dental identification was not possible. Nonetheless, given the consistency of the anthropological findings, the circumstances of his disappearance, and the fact that the burned-out car was his, Frank's family accepted the identification.

Working after classes at the University of New Mexico, it took us nearly two weeks to sort, reconstruct, analyze, and report on these remains. The original anthropology report was not so much wrong as it was deficient in detail. Much more could have been learned if the autopsy had been done right the first time, since a second one always has less to work with (see chapter 5). Though we had conducted a far more searching analysis than had originally been done, nothing we did was exceptional, and if as much effort had been put into the first examination, a positive identification might have resulted.

It was disappointing that despite all of our work we could not make a positive identification, but we felt that the effort was worthwhile. For one thing, it was a clear reminder that a great deal of information can be gleaned even from bodies greatly damaged by fire and subsequently degraded further by transportation and autopsy. In addition, it was a useful demonstration for those who felt that there was nothing to be learned from further analysis of the body. It was also a small help to the family to know that no effort was being spared to establish beyond doubt that these remains belonged to their son.

Since exposure to fire gradually reduces the amount of soft tissue available for analysis, the forensic anthropologist (whose focus is on the skeleton) becomes increasingly important in the investigation of burned bodies. As the burning becomes more severe, so the input of the anthropologist becomes ever more critical to the resolution of any case.

Human Versus Nonhuman Bones

Squirley's premature funeral provides a reminder that the first job of the forensic anthropologist, as Stewart (1979) has observed, is to ascertain whether the remains in question are human. This sounds too obvious even to need mentioning, yet it is an important consideration among forensic anthropologists (Angel, 1974; Brooks, 1975), and much time and effort will be saved if that question is answered up front. Nonhuman remains are not of medicolegal significance: the case can be closed with no further investigation. Moreover, if an investigating agency invests a great deal of time and effort looking for the murderer of a four-legged ruminant, embarrassment is inevitable as the news media reveals them to have been off on a wild goose chase. Or a wild porcupine chase (to further muddy the metaphor).

Although the average physician is well versed in anatomy, that expertise does not extend to the myriad details of skeletal variability and interpretation that are the stuff of forensic anthropology. Lacking a familiarity with morphological variability of skeletons, physicians sometimes mistakenly assign human status to skeletons that have never walked upright, or misinterpret the features of ones that have. It is an inescapable conclusion that the person who is trained and experienced in the detailed analysis of bones should be the one who identifies them. Of course, that person is the forensic anthropologist.

Not long after Mr. Armando wandered through the Catron County forests, a physician performed one of Albuquerque's traditional summertime rituals. He was out digging in his backyard, probably in preparation for some house remodeling or to enhance his garden. In the process, he discovered what he thought was a partial human skull. Such findings are not uncommon in this part of the world where the benign soil preserves skeletons for centuries. He proudly bore his find to the Anthropology Department at the University of New Mexico for verification and elaboration. He was directed to the late Dr. Harry Basehart, the same anthropologist who was consulted in the Squirley case. Basehart turned the specimen over in his hands, slowly withdrew the pipestem from between his teeth, and, with a friendly smile tugging at the corners of his lips, suggested heading down to the basement.

A huge rack of drawers in one dingy hallway contained the comparative skeletal collection. Sliding open a drawer labeled "Turkey Bones," he reached in and extracted one—a pelvis. Ever the gentleman, he slowly rotated the two identical specimens before the physician, one in each hand. He gently suggested to the discoverer that instead of a human skull, he had dug up "the pelvis of some large avian species." Concluding their consultation, Basehart asked for his visitor's business card. He was not trying to find a family physician, but to ensure that if a personal medical emergency should develop he did not make the mistake of consulting a physician who could not distinguish between a human skull and the south end of a northbound turkey.

Several years after this visit, in 1973, the New Mexico OMI was established by the legislature, replacing county coroners with an Albuquerque-based chief medical investigator. This new position was occupied by a forensic pathologist charged with monitoring and investigating deaths statewide. The system was up and running by the middle of the year. There was a lot of adjusting to be done, as law enforcement agencies that had been used to carrying out independent investigations were now required to inform the OMI of the discovery of a body and to put their work at the scene on hold until the arrival of OMI's investigator.

One of these cases, however, was just too juicy to pass on to the OMI. A hiker reported seeing a skeleton on the mesa west of Albuquerque. The sheriff sent his deputies to the scene, where they found skeletonized remains, most of the bones held together by desiccated tendons. The torso was separated from the extremities, and the skull was missing. According to the new law, the OMI investigator should have been called immediately to the scene by the sheriff, but he apparently decided that he could handle the initial steps in this important case himself.

The remains were shown to a local physician, who decided that they were about the right size for a twelve-year-old. At this point, the sheriff's office calmly surveyed the facts of the case and apparently progressed through the following train of thought: "There is no head, the limbs have been separated from the body, and the doc says it's about twelve years old. It must have been a twelve-year-old kid who was murdered and dismembered. . . . No, more likely it was a twelve-year-old *girl* who was murdered and dismembered. . . . No, it must have been a twelve-year-old girl who was raped, brutally murdered, dismembered, and spread out over the west mesa."

With the case formulation complete, the sheriff informed the media, who ran with these "facts" to blast the populace of Albuquerque with stories on television, on the radio, and in print about this poor, innocent twelve-year-old girl who had been brutally raped, murdered, and dismembered on the west mesa. The media seem to take particular delight in disseminating news of other peoples' suffering and so played this story to the hilt. It was the lead item on the local television newscasts, earned banner headlines in the papers, and occupied some small part of the public mind for days.

Finally, after three days of milking the story for all it was worth, the sheriff turned the remains over to the OMI in Albuquerque. One of the OMI pathologists looked at the skeleton, counted the ribs, and was quoted in a tiny item in the next day's paper as saying "It's got too many ribs to be human, so it has to be either a bear or an ape." This conclusion really piqued my interest. Somehow it did not seem to be beyond the bounds of possibility to conceive of some person in Albuquerque so bereft of the trappings of civilization and humanity as to rape, murder, and dismember a poor innocent twelve-year-old girl, but to imagine that someone would have raped, murdered, and dismembered an *ape?* With apes as common in New Mexico as liberals in Catron County, it would probably be difficult to find one to rape, even if one were set on it.

Branching out from teaching in the Anthropology Department and watching over the skeletal collection at the Maxwell Museum at the University of New Mexico, I had been involved in forensic anthropology for the previous couple of years. The next day, I was summoned to the OMI to look at the skeleton. It was a bear. One hopes that had the skull been present, the sheriff or the physician might have recognized that it was not human.

Laid out on a table at the OMI, the bear skeleton was small and young, as evidenced by unfused epiphyses, meaning that the bones were still growing. For some reason, nobody had actually taken the time to look closely at the skeleton. Like so many people, they probably thought that there was little to be learned from a pile of bones. Had they looked closely, they might have noticed that there were no terminal phalanges—the tips of the toes (and claws) were missing. There were also delicate scratch marks on the ends of the middle phalanges (the central joint) of the paws and more scratches on the uppermost remaining neck vertebra. What had obviously happened was that someone had shot a young bear somewhere, got its carcass that far, and skinned it out (along with the skull and claws). He or she was probably sitting at home on a new bearskin rug watching the media frenzy in amusement.

The human skull is so distinctive that virtually everyone can recognize it as such. The postcranial bones (everything else on the body) are more difficult (see chapter 3), but much easier with one of the classic references, such as *Mammalian Osteoarchaeology* (Gilbert, 1973) (Fig. 1.5). When discussing human versus nonhuman, by the way, it is surprising how many people (including many who should know better) carelessly say, "human versus animal." The sense of this dichotomy is that humans are not animals. If that is so, then humans must belong to the plant kingdom. Some who so thoughtlessly rain down this taxonomic ruin on our species are professors who have, perhaps, been lulled by the somnolence of their students into believing that since they appear to be incapable of movement they must be begonias. Not so. They are indeed animals, a fact betrayed by anatomy at every level, from the cell to the skeleton to the whole organism. Thus, a gentle nudge to correct usage: human vs. nonhuman, if you please.

A FEW FINAL OBSERVATIONS

These accounts are by way of illustrating the importance of involving a forensic anthropologist at the earliest stages of a death investigation involving a skeleton. As the person most familiar with human bones, he or

Fig. 1.5. Human and nonhuman skulls.

she is in the best position, first, to determine whether the bones consti-
tuting a case are in fact human and, thereafter, to interpret the clues those
bones hold.

If the anthropologist ascertains that the remains are not human, then
of course the investigation is closed since the case has no medicolegal
significance. Historic or prehistoric skeletons, even if otherwise fascinating and informative, are not of medicolegal significance either. If, on the
other hand, the remains are found to be contemporary human, in New
Mexico the OMI is required by law to investigate all cases in which a person dies while not under the care of a physician (that is, when the family
physician has not seen the deceased so recently as to know that the death
was expected); cases in which the death is unattended; and cases where a
person has died as the result of violence, as the result of a vehicular accident, while in custody, where drugs may have contributed in some way,
or where there were "suspicious" circumstances. In addition to these situations, in which the law requires intervention by the OMI, the OMI has
a certain amount of leeway in interpreting the statute so that any case

deemed worthy of investigation is sure to receive it. (One would expect to find a similar list of conditions requiring investigation at any medical examiner's office across the country.)

Increasingly, death investigations are being put into the hands of designated experts. Had a car been found burning alongside a road in New Mexico even a few years after Squirley's was discovered, the sheriff would have been accompanied to the scene by the local deputy medical investigator. The latter would have shipped the remains to the central office of the medical investigator, who would have called in the forensic anthropologist. The bones would have been determined not to be of medicolegal significance, the funeral called off, and this story would never have been brought to my attention by Vernon McCarty, then the chief deputy medical investigator in Albuquerque, who thought we should write it up some time and with whom I discussed it for years.

A resident of Catron County, McCarty had the distinction of becoming the youngest person elected to the post of county sheriff there. Upon taking office, he was handed a court order to seize the personal property of Mr. Armando, to sell it at public auction, and to apply the proceeds against the $2,055.50 still owed by the Armandos for his premature funeral twelve years earlier. Cordially received by Squirley himself, it soon became evident that McCarty was just the next in a long line of sheriffs to attempt the collection. "I've been expecting you," he told McCarty with a toothy grin. "Every time they elect a new sheriff in this county, the lawyers run that judgment back through just to see if there is anything to collect." Living in a house that was owned by someone else and driving a car that was registered to another, Armando's personal possessions were insufficient to pay the judgment.

In 1973, McCarty moved north to Albuquerque to become the chief deputy medical investigator to the late Dr. James T. Weston at the newly created OMI. He remained conscientiously and effectively occupying that post until 1979, when he was appointed coroner for Washoe County, Nevada, where he remains doing his typically thorough work today. In my early days at the OMI, I learned a great deal about what good investigation is from him.

Why Forensic Anthropology?

From the foregoing, it can be appreciated that forensic anthropologists approach the skeleton from a different intellectual compass heading than physicians. Able to estimate age, sex, race, and stature, and to draw some conclusions regarding diet and nutrition, the forensic anthropologist is also familiar with the nature of bone injury and aspects of determination of cause and even manner of death. Forensic anthropology is, thus, an important adjunct to legal medicine. Where bodies have been degraded by fire or the passage of time, a forensic anthropologist's perspective can be invaluable because all or a portion of the soft tissue has been destroyed and investigators are dependent on information that can be gleaned from bony matter only. This focus on the skeleton can be important not only when skeletonization and decomposition have taken place, but also in cases of incineration and mummification. Given their broad experience in the analysis of prehistoric, historic, and contemporary remains, forensic anthropologists can also provide insights on pathologies, pseudopathologies, damage occurring to the bone ante-, peri-, and post-mortem, and even on the time since death.

The forensic anthropologist brings to such work a vast experience with the analysis of dried bone. Most have trained by analyzing hundreds of prehistoric burials, historic burials, and contemporary remains, and have thus seen, through a unique window of time, the effects of long-term, intermediate, and short interment of bone. They have also seen the effects of differing soil types, soil pressures and staining, and disturbance. They know the osteological impact of carnivores and rodents, and the results of inexpert recovery techniques. They have seen the trajectory of the skeleton through its growth, maturity, and decline. Though pathologists, radiologists, orthopedists, and others deal with bone in their own more limited contexts, anthropologists alone deal with the full range of dried bone specimens, from the fossil hominids of 4 million years ago to the John Doe whose badly decomposed body was discovered yesterday.

Forensic anthropologists also offer assistance in the recovery of remains at the scene, and they are particularly useful when bodies have been buried, when remains have been scattered, or when dismemberment of fresh bodies has occurred as a result of predator activity or airplane crashes. They work with burned bodies and can be useful when people perish in dwellings, public buildings, or vehicles of all sorts.

In short, a forensic anthropologist has much to offer every major medicolegal investigative unit.

2
Picking up the Pieces

Search, Discovery, and Recovery of Bodies

If at First You Don't Succeed . . .

In July 1988, 19½-year-old Leticia Garcia was reported missing in Santa Fe. Her vehicle was later found several miles from her home. It contained her purse and some personal belongings, but a search of the immediate area uncovered no sign of Leticia herself. On January 22, 1989, a resident of a mobile home near the intersection of Old Las Vegas Highway and Bobcat Crossing found a skull and part of a femur that had been brought into the yard by the family dog. The Las Vegas Highway leads from Santa Fe to the older, smaller, and less glitzy Las Vegas that is located on the high plains of New Mexico, some fifty miles east over Glorieta Pass. Las Vegas, New Mexico, was an important way station on the Santa Fe Trail and later on the route of the Santa Fe Railroad. Now settled into the twentieth century with Highlands University and the Armand Hammer United World College, it had a lawless renown at one time, with the help of the likes of Billy the Kid, Bat Masterson, Doc Holliday, and Wyatt Earp.

The skull and femur were duly brought to the OMI in Albuquerque for analysis. Santa Fe authorities were convinced that this was the missing Ms. Garcia, and very much hoped that our conclusions would mirror theirs. The anthropological analysis, however, was equivocal. In trying to establish the sex of the remains, we discovered that measurements put the skull into the overlap range or just over the line on the male side, so that, metrically speaking, sex was not determinable with confidence. The large features and heavy bone of the skull, along with the fact that the brow ridge was rather prominent, suggested that the remains belonged to a male. On the other hand, the femur showed a rather delicate linea aspera (a raised ridge for muscle attachment on the back of the bone), which is a female trait, but this is not much on which to base an estimate of sex. Such measurements as could be taken from the femur were not helpful either. Since it had been gnawed at both ends, we could not make a tight stature estimation. In theory, a forensic anthropologist could have eyeballed the femur, made a pretty reasonable guess at its length, and come up with a stature estimate from that, or stature could have been calculated from formulae designed for use with incomplete bones (Steele, 1970). If either one of those estimates was large enough, the balance would have weighed towards the remains being male. However, estimating height from incomplete bones generates a larger range of error than an estimate from complete bones. Tantalizing though this kind of guesswork is, it is fraught with problems. Getting just one measurement wrong can corrupt the result completely, and while one wishes to do everything possible, poor data produce ambiguous results. No conclusion is better than an untrustworthy one.

Our, albeit tentative, conclusion that features of the skull suggested that it was probably male did not accord well with police expectations. Our analysis of the skull did, however, point quite unequivocally to the probability that this person was Hispanic, since traits typically scored as both white and Indian were combined. (This sounds much simpler than it really is, as the traits we evaluate can combine in a variety of ways.) All of the adult teeth were present and complete, and other features were consistent with the assumption that these bones came from a young adult. The basioccipital synchondrosis (the junction of the sphenoid and occipital bones on the base of the skull) was fully fused. In their useful summary of skeletal aging of Korean War dead, McKern and Stewart (1957) showed that in males this fusion is well under way by the age of seventeen and complete by twenty-one. Hence, since there was not even the slightest trace of a fusion line left in this skull, we placed the age in the mid-twenties to make sure the range was broad enough to include the missing person.

No male in his mid-twenties was missing, and police continued to believe that the skull was Ms. Garcia's in spite of what the forensic anthropologist thought. Since our hypothesis that the remains were male was tentative, it was viewed with a degree of skepticism. Additional bones would have to be located before we could resolve the issue one way or the other. When the weather moderated, a search team using cadaver dogs, discovered a significant cache of bones. They found vertebrae, ribs, a clavicle, a radius, an ulna, a scapula, a sacrum, an ilium, a tibia shaft, a quantity of long blond hair, and numerous articles of clothing. Relatives identified the clothing as belonging to Ms. Garcia. In some jurisdictions, this might have been enough evidence to declare the body identified.

SOLIDIFYING THE IDENTIFICATION

The OMI wanted to do more in this case, however. A search for dental records turned up nothing until weeks after the identity had been established anthropologically. (OMI's forensic odontologist, Dr. Homer Campbell, was then able to confirm her identity on dental grounds.) The only medical record that could be found at the time of the discovery was a lateral skull and neck x-ray taken when Ms. Garcia suffered a whiplash injury a year before her death. We had to try to squeeze an identification out of that one x-ray.

Of course, one particularly troubling matter remained: were these recently discovered bones from the same person as the skull, or did they belong to someone else? Although we now had a number of bones representing most of the body, they certainly did not constitute a complete skeleton, yet since there was no duplication, all of the bones *could* belong to a single individual. Moreover, the color, condition, state of skeletonization, nature and extent of carnivore damage, and sizes of the bones recently discovered were all consistent with each other and with the skull and incomplete femur brought in by the dog.

The antemortem x-ray showed an unexpected and fortunate (for us) anomaly. Ms. Garcia had a most uncommon condition: a congenital fusion of the second and third cervical vertebrae. They had been welded by nature into a solid mass with no movement between them. Among the vertebrae discovered at the scene were fused second and third cervical vertebrae. With that match, it became highly probable that the skeletal remains were indeed Ms. Garcia. But what of the skull? Was it also hers?

The general contours and specific features of the skull seen in the antemortem x-ray were consistent with those seen in the postmortem skull x-ray taken at the OMI. The frontal sinus (the air pocket in the frontal bone above the nose) can be seen in x-ray looking rather like a flock of little bunny ears protruding up behind a head of cabbage. The shape of the sinus is thought to be so individual that it has been used for years by forensic anthropologists for identification (Ubelaker, 1984). Since this was a lateral x-ray, however, that sinus was not visible. Nonetheless, it seemed to us that if the frontal sinus can be used, other sinuses might also profitably be compared. Fortunately, the antemortem x-ray clearly showed the mastoid sinus (the air pockets in the lump of bone that extends down be-hind the ear), and a comparison with the postmortem x-ray taken at the OMI revealed exactly the same pattern of air cells. Combing the litera-ture, the forensic pathologist assigned the case, Dr. Kris Sperry, found a single reference (Cuthbert and Law, 1927) showing that the mastoid sinus has been used previously in skeletal identification, even if—from the lack of subsequent use—it appears that those doing radiographic identifi-cations seldom have to reach quite so far down into the hat to produce an identification. There are many easier and more common ways to make an identification, but if none of these can be used due to the nature of the skeletal remains or the antemortem records, unusual measures are called for. Any atypical procedures, however, must be firmly based on osteolog-ical reality: figurative pulling of rabbits from hats for ID purposes is not permitted.

At this point we judged that all of the bones found were most likely from a single individual. Using the x-ray taken of Ms. Garcia before her death, we could now show that since the pattern of the mastoid sinus matched, the skull was hers and that the fused neck vertebrae were also hers. Therefore, we concluded, this incomplete skeleton was the missing Ms. Garcia.

Since the identification seemed secure, no further work was required, but I was curious to see how far we could go with this incomplete skele-ton. While we had the opportunity, I decided to make a couple of addi-tional comparisons. The middle meningeal artery that feeds blood to the brain leaves an impression on the inside of the skull. Its pattern is so vari-able that it is also useful as a means of identification. The pattern seen on the antemortem x-ray precisely matched that seen postmortem. The highly individualistic pattern of the skull sutures also matched. Thus, two addi-tional, if small, bits of data added to the strength of our conclusions.

There were some matters that had caused us problems in identifying the remains as Leticia in the first instance. Final stature estimates matched Ms. Garcia's profile. One of the recently discovered bones yielded an es-timate of 160.24 cm (±4.24 cm) or sixty-three inches, give or take a cou-ple of inches. A missing person flyer for Ms. Garcia gave her height as sixty-three inches. Although the features of the skull were weakly mas-culine, such features might also be found in some females. The recovered pelvic bones were typically feminine in the contours of the subpubic angle, the greater sciatic notch, the auricular surface and in the curvature and proportions of the sacrum. Since the pelvis is always a more reliable indicator of sex than the skull, changing the attributed sex to female seemed correct.

Everything now fit very nicely except for the age. The estimate given at first was mid-twenties, yet she was only nineteen and a half. An error of five years or so is considerable but probably within acceptable limits, even at this age. Could the age range be narrowed somewhat? Although other factors of bone maturation and general appearance had been considered, the fusion of the basioccipital synchondrosis was the principal factor in the original estimate. Since the age estimate had been based on the working hypothesis that the skull was male, the age could be too high, as skeletons of males mature more slowly than those of females. By nineteen and a half years, then, females might already show full fusion.

Unfortunately, there were no immediately available data on the age of basioccipital fusion for females. It was therefore necessary to plow through the records of the Maxwell Museum's sizable collections of documented and forensic skeletons to search for some. Each of the eleven females under the age of twenty-five had been examined to determine the state of basioccipital fusion. Drs. Walter Birkby, at the University of Arizona, and Richard L. Jantz, at the University of Tennessee, each had information on additional cases, resulting in a total of twenty-four females of known age between thirteen and twenty-five years. Included in this sample were two cases of complete basioccipital fusion by the age of thirteen—much earlier than expected. In fact, only two cases (one at age thirteen and one at age twenty) had open synchondroses. Consequently, based on this small sample, a female at age nineteen and a half could reasonably be expected to have a fully fused synchondrosis.

Having established that we were dealing with the remains of Leticia Garcia, the next item was determination of time since death. She had disappeared in the height of summer, when decomposition would be rapid. Based on observations of the rate of skeletonization accumulated in prior cases in New Mexico, and comparing those with cases seen in Arizona (Galloway et al., 1989), as well as with the effect of carnivore activity seen in the Pacific Northwest (Haglund, Reay, and Swindler, 1989), a period of six months seemed entirely acceptable.

What the Bones Tell Us

Here is a case in which the hunches of the investigators were right, but any identification must be based on solid evidence. Here, the determination to locate more remains paid off with the discovery of the additional bones and clothing, which—although they did not by themselves constitute a positive identification—helped considerably in resolving the matters of sex and stature. In the end, the family was still not satisfied with the small number of bones recovered and visited the scene to find more. However, none of the ones they found was human, so the investigators apparently did a good job of finding everything that remained of the young woman. One of the potential problems with cases involving incomplete remains is that bones dragged some distance away by predators and not found today might be found by someone else—weeks, months, or even years from now. At present, only the long memories of the people who have worked on previous cases keeps such stray material from ending up as a new John or Jane Doe.

Certainly one important moral of this story is that the forensic anthropologist cannot analyze skeletal material that he or she does not have. Recovery is thus the essential first link in skeletal analysis. If no more than the skull and femur had been found of Ms. Garcia, the identification could still have been made on the basis of the skull x-rays and a dental comparison, but would that comparison ever have been made when the operating hypothesis was that the remains were probably male rather than female? Perhaps not.

The Garcia case also reminds us that one of the persistent problems in the identification of the skeletons of the young is that they are less likely than older people to have undergone medical treatment. Until and unless a person seeks treatment for a broken bone or some other ailment, no medical records will exist. Youngsters and even young adults are infrequently x-rayed and as a consequence useful antemortem records will rarely be found for children. We were fortunate that the OMI investigators were able to ferret out, first, the skull x-ray that made identification possible and, later, the dental x-rays that confirmed it.

This case (Rhine and Sperry, 1991) also illustrates the willingness of the OMI to encourage a continued exercise of curiosity beyond the critical matter of identification. However, none of this work is really extraordinary. Forensic anthropologists are often challenged by their cases to probe into the misty realms of the unknown. The work recounted here consumed many hours of looking at other skulls, required library and lab work and the cooperation of others. But such challenges also provide forensic anthropologists with an opportunity for testing assumptions and validating methods. Taking these small steps into the unknown leads to new discoveries about the skeleton. You might think that over four hundred years of detailed studies of human anatomy would leave little left to discover, but this is patently not so. Many details of skeletal anatomy and development remain to be uncovered.

Looking in All the Wrong Places

Between a Rock and a Hard Place

Air Force Lieutenant Davidson Rock made a phone call to a friend from a street phone on September 16, 1979. Suddenly the line went dead and, as it turned out, so did he. Nearly three months later his body was found, and immediately jurisdictional questions popped up. Since the murder had been committed—or at least the abduction had taken place—in Albuquerque, the Albuquerque Police Department (APD) thought it should have a role in the case. As the body was found in Sandoval County, the Sandoval County Sheriff also wanted the case. So did the Military Police and the Office of Special Investigation representing the interests of the Air Force. The matter was finally settled when investigators determined that the body lay just below Mesa Gigante, twenty-three miles west of Albuquerque, and therefore part of the Laguna Indian Reservation. It thus became an FBI investigation.

The question of jurisdiction is important since one agency must assume responsibility for collecting evidence and working up the case. In New Mexico the OMI has jurisdiction only on state- or privately owned lands, but the bodies found on federal lands or in FBI jurisdictions such as Indian reservations usually wind up at the OMI anyway. It has the trained people and proper facilities for conducting medicolegal autopsies.

In this instance, there was not much of a problem with recovery of Lt. Rock's remains. The body had been left lying on its back on the surface of the ground, no attempt having been made to bury or hide it. Predators had discovered the body well before people found it, and the critters had done a good bit of gnawing on the body. The soft and easily chewable muscle and organs of the abdomen were easily accessible to dogs and coyotes. Rapid late-summer decomposition, combined with the effects of predation, soon exposed the vertebral column. Each pair of vertebrae in the lower back is held together by an area only about the size of a silver dollar, and in this case, the combination of decomposition and predation,

Fig. 2.1. The remains of Lt. Rock. He was shot and then his thorax was dragged away from his decomposing body by predators. (Photo courtesy of the Office of the Medical Investigator, Albuquerque, New Mexico)

along with a little gnawing of the vertebrae, had effectively detached the upper part of the body from the lower. At that point, the head, torso, and arms were dragged off from the pelvis and legs (still in their Levi's). That the torso had been moved was obvious from the drag marks still visible on the dirt leading away from the pelvis and legs (Fig. 2.1).

The OMI investigators speedily accomplished the recovery by slipping the two parts of the body into a body bag, sealing it, and delivering it to the Albuquerque OMI. In addition to need for positive identification, another important matter was whether Lt. Rock had been shot at the scene or elsewhere. There were three small-caliber bullet holes in his head, all with entrances on the right and two with exits on the left. The wounds were clearly visible at the scene; the body had lain out long enough to expose most of the bones of the skull. One projectile remained in the skull. If Lt.

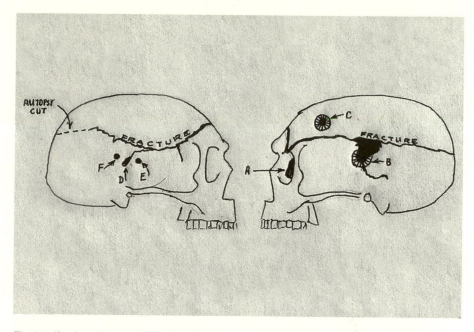

Fig. 2.2. Sketches of the skull of the body shown in fig. 2.1, which were included in the anthropology report. They show the locations of gunshot entrance and exit wounds. Note the external beveling of the exit wounds seen on the left side.

Rock was shot at the scene, investigators might find other projectiles in the soil beneath the head (Fig. 2.2).

After federal, county, city, and Indian authorities consulted over how to proceed and who should investigate, an FBI agent excavated the ground in the area beneath where the skull had lain, to a depth of about two feet. No projectiles were found. The next day, the FBI, APD, and Laguna Police returned to the scene for more digging, but still no projectiles were found. A third search by the APD and personnel from Kirtland Air Force Base, located bullet casings and one live .25 caliber round about a mile from where the body was discovered. They may or may not have been connected to the murder. A fourth search, about a week after the discovery of the body, using a metal detector and a screen, found nothing. Even though metal detectors can miss small objects, investigators concluded that Lt. Rock had not been shot at the scene, but somewhere else.

While conferring with a just-arrived member of the Air Force's Office of Special Investigation, we noted that the closely spaced entrance wounds suggested that Lt. Rock had not been moving or in a car when he was shot, as had been supposed. On the contrary, we hypothesized that he must have been still, perhaps lying on the ground with the left side of his head in contact with the earth, when the shots were fired into the right side of his head. We surmised that the body had thus been prone (on the stomach) when shot. Since the body was discovered lying supine (on its back), we concluded that it had been rolled over from where it was shot. Previous investigators had dug in the area directly beneath where the head was found, but what we really needed to do was dig where the head actually was when Lt. Rock was shot. The Air Force investigator and four forensic graduate students returned to the scene almost three weeks after the body was discovered. Digging in the spot likely to have been under Lt. Rock's head when he was shot, rather than where the head had been found, they quickly located a projectile.

CONFUSION AT THE SCENE

The initial stages of this investigation illustrate well the problem of having too many people at a murder scene. While there are some advantages in having numerous investigators from whom to draw ideas, too many fertile minds can create rather than dispel confusion. At a scene, enthusiasms tend to race around like unbridled ponies. The more people present, the more such enthusiasms multiply. It is difficult to do good, thorough, and calmly thought-out work at crowded scenes.

Digging under where Lt. Rock's head was lying did nothing more than provide the excavators with a bit of futile exercise. In this case, then, the problem lay not in the recovery of the body, but in finding other evidence connected with the cause and manner of death. Other cases have presented much more formidable challenges. The most difficult involve search in addition to recovery.

SEARCH . . .

Another example of looking in the wrong place began with the arrival of some sheep bones at the OMI. They had been found by one of the investigators, who thought they were probably not human but brought them in just to make sure. The bones generated a great deal of interest because, we soon learned, of a report claiming that a body had been dumped near where they were found. This was next to a road in Torrance County, south of Interstate 40, about forty miles northeast of the center of the state. It therefore seemed like a good idea to get some more information and put forensic anthropology on the trail.

After much discussion between the OMI and the State Police, who had assumed jurisdiction, we got permission to search. The targeted location was that which had produced the sheep bones. We arrived at the designated spot, ten miles south of Interstate 40, on the morning of July 21, 1987. Converging on the scene were two State Police cars, the OMI investigator, and three carloads of media people. The informant sat quietly in one of the police cars. While everyone else was trying to decide what to do, our group of four anthropologists stepped through the fence to search an area about a half-mile square. We returned to find that everyone had moved up the road to where the body had "really" been dumped. We joined them at what we were assured was the place, only to be told that the informant had changed his mind again. We searched the area anyhow, our reward being several cow bones.

Sitting by the side of the road eating lunch, we learned some additional facts by listening to the officers chat. The missing person, Mandy Lyn, had been abducted from Albuquerque a year and a half previously. Her two abductors (of whom the informant was one) commandeered her car, bound her, stuffed her into the back seat and drove off on Interstate 40 towards Oklahoma. It was early in December 1985, after dark, and snowing. A few miles from Clines Corners, the kidnappers hit the exit for State Highway 3, and having decided to get rid of the woman they turned off and drove, according to the informant, about ten miles. (Ah ha! So this is why we had come exactly ten miles before beginning the search.) They pulled over to the side of the road, bundled Ms. Lyn out of the back seat, took her under a tree just off the east side of the road, strangled her, and left her body crumpled beneath the juniper. They got back into the car and resumed their journey to Oklahoma.

About two and a half miles south of the interstate, the road made a slight curve where it passed between two abandoned stone buildings. One of the officers said, "He [the informant] remembers seeing those two buildings." For the first time since the search began, the pieces seemed to fall into place: A year and a half ago, these two men had turned off of the interstate and onto a side road they had never traveled on before. It was dark and snowing. In the back seat was a woman they were about to kill.

With its scattered low trees and limited visibility, one place in that area must have looked pretty much like any other to them, and given their mental state, they were probably not watching the odometer very closely. Bearing these facts in mind, it seemed possible to me that the ten miles the informant thought they drove might mark the end of the search area but not its focus. Since he remembered the stone buildings, it seemed logical to go back and make a fresh start there.

Instead, the rest of the afternoon was spent in sashaying back and forth on the road as the informant picked first one spot then another as "definitely" the place where he and his partner had left the body. We finally retired to our truck as people wandered back and forth in an increasingly desperate attempt to find something. One of the State Policemen finally said he would spring for a steak dinner if that would improve the informant's memory; another thought the informant's sense of geography was inexact, doubting that he could locate a certain rather sizable part of his anatomy in the dark. The anthropological contingent arrived back in town convinced that we should have started a search at the stone buildings.

To that end, the forensic anthropologist asked for permission to return two days later to check out that area, pointing out to the OMI that a well regulated and organized line search with a few knowledgeable bone people should prove effective. The State Police agreed on the condition that we meet with them and other searchers early the next morning in a restaurant in Moriarty, some forty miles through Tijeras Canyon, out on the high plains east of Albuquerque.

Seated at a table in a crowded room, our crew of five experienced bone people was told that it was to be under the direction of State Police Officer Globe, who informed the group that he had attended a course on search and rescue and knew exactly how the operation should be conducted. We were instructed to merge into the two dozen people present: Albuquerque Search and Rescue, a cadaver dog team with two bloodhounds, and other State Police. This was a far cry from the cozy little search we had envisioned. Moreover, though I suggested we start at the stone buildings, Officer Globe regarded searching eight miles farther north to be a waste of time. Since the search two days ago had turned up absolutely nothing, it was his intention to return to exactly the same spot and try again. He was sticking to the informant's somewhat flexible recollection of where he and his partner had left the body.

Based on prior experience with the condition of skeletal remains after extended exposure, I sought out Officer Globe again to explain that since the missing Mandy Lyn had been dead a year and a half, the remains would have been disturbed by coyotes, dogs, and other carnivores. Various parts of the body would have been pulled off, two hundred to three hundred feet or more. By this time, the exposed bones would be essentially free of soft tissue and bleached white by the sun. There would be such a contrast between the bones and the red soil that they would be visible at a great distance. In fact, I suggested, the country was so open that they might even be spotted from a low-flying plane. It was patently obvious that the woman's remains were not where we had spent all day looking before, so I proposed, once again, that we go back to the last thing the informant remembered—the two stone buildings—and search south from there, spaced out fifty to a hundred feet. But it was Globe's show. The informant said ten miles, so ten miles it was.

With a certain "here we go again" resignation, we drove east another thirty-three miles, and turned south onto the narrow two-lane blacktop of New Mexico Highway 3. From here our caravan continued precisely ten miles and stopped. The informant sat unhappily handcuffed in the back seat of one of the State Police cars, contemplating the sparse bunch grasses and evergreens scattered across the red soil spread before him once again. We stepped off the road, spaced ourselves about twenty-five feet apart and slowly began walking. We took great care to make sure that the line remained straight, as Globe directed us from the highway. This, as he had explained, was a "strip search," though happily not the kind of strip search that police usually engage in. He claimed that such searches yield a 95 percent probability of finding a body. He neglected to mention that that estimate depended upon the body being there.

Since the land was so open, we could have spaced out with fifty to a hundred feet between us and would have found anything that was there in a single pass. However, our leader pointed out that he had been trained in recovery, and it was clear that he was not about to alter his way of doing things because some professor thought there was a better way. In fact, the technique he espoused is typically used to assure good coverage of an area, and it would have been appropriate for a heavily vegetated region, a thick eastern forest, an area of dense brush by a river, or a corn field. But this was none of those environments. The map depicts this area as blank, yet it is far from empty. The Pedernal Hills is an area of gently rolling ground with occasional small escarpments and outcrops. The twelve to fourteen inches of annual precipitation there supports sparse, low trees, each separated from the next by fifty feet or so with scattered grasses under foot. The soil is very red. We should have been able to spot bones from a considerable distance.

After pacing off a very deliberate quarter-mile, we stopped, wheeled, and passed back over the same area. Then, coming back at it from 90 degrees, we wheeled a final time, making one last pass. By this time we had probably left a footprint on every square foot of ground and would surely have found Ms. Lyn, even if she were attempting to elude us.

The chance discovery by two roving officers of some duct tape of the sort that had allegedly been used to bind the victim was enough to shift our attention northward. Two passes over that area, however, turned up nothing more of interest. What to do next? Globe seemed to be unsure. We spent the next hour or so wallowing around, a solution in search of a problem. Various searchers, apparently having nothing better to do, wandered aimlessly back over the area we had already covered. About this time it began to rain. Finally, Globe decreed the search at an end. I asked if he would mind if we came back later on our own. He considered this for a moment, then gamely announced that it was all right, since he didn't think we could "mess anything up." Rather than walking back to the cars by way of the road, our anthropology team spread out and walked the area in between the two isolated intensively searched areas and then continued some distance north in the drizzle. We found nothing. This bit of ground had now been pretty thoroughly covered.

On the drive back to town, we all resolved to return the following Saturday, when we would start at the stone buildings and work back south, spacing out with seventy-five feet between us; we apprised the OMI of our plan. By the time Saturday arrived, however, I had decided not to spend another day away from home, but the graduate students—Bryan Curran, Stuart Boydstun, Steven Churchill, Paula Ivey and Marsha Ogilvie—were salivating at the prospect of the search and were anxious to go on by themselves. They had all spent many hours poring over human skeletons, were good at identifying them, and knew what to look for and how to look for it. About nine o'clock that morning, the phone rang. They had found her— only about ten minutes after they started at the stone buildings. We drove out to the scene, arriving before most of the authorities. After calling me, the students had called Officer Globe to announce their find (Fig. 2.3).

Globe was not about to engage in another fruitless trek out onto the

Fig. 2.3. Aerial view of scene in Pedernal Hills of eastern New Mexico, where the body of a woman murdered one and a half years earlier had been dismembered and scattered by predators. The arrow points to the skull.

plains, and he refused to budge until he heard officially from the OMI investigator. The investigator was called. He drove the forty miles or so to the designated spot, leaned over the fence, and called, "You got her?" They called back, "Yep." "O.K.," he said, "I'll call the State Police." The nearest phone being some six miles away and the scene being more than sixty miles from Santa Fe and Albuquerque, it was after noon before everyone arrived. In the meantime, the students had flagged and mapped the bones, which were spread out for some three hundred feet from where the body had lain, so that the police could photograph them prior to their actual recovery and ultimate delivery to the OMI.

One of the local television stations had picked up the police radio message and arrived at the scene by helicopter just after we did. I was taken aloft for a quick rotary wing tour of the scene, confirming that the remains could be seen from the air. Scattered bones had indeed been bleached by the sun and were clearly visible from a few hundred feet up. An air search would have found her (Fig. 2.4).

Fig. 2.4. Bleached lower leg bone from the body shown in fig. 2.3. It is still articulated with a foot that was protected by a shoe. The body had been left under a tree a year and a half previously. A pin flag placed by the anthropology crew facilitates mapping the precise location of this and other body parts.

ORGANIZING A SEARCH

There are several conclusions to be drawn from this tale. For one thing, if we had known all of the facts before we began and had been allowed to contribute to the decisions setting the rules of the search, the body could have been found within fifteen minutes. What input we were allowed was not taken seriously because of the tendency of law enforcement personnel to take statements quite literally (here, the word of the informant). The officer in charge had all the information we had—and more—and should have been able to apply the same logic as we did, but for some reason he did not.

Second, although it is wise to have a plan in place before arriving at a scene and it is important to have only one person clearly in charge, one should be flexible enough to modify the plan when topography or circumstances suggest another one. Furthermore, rather than simply demanding that an operation be done "my way," the person in charge should consult in advance with others to see if there are useful ideas that can be gleaned from their experience.

Third, while there should always be a sufficient number of people to accomplish the job, having too many can make control difficult. This search could best have been conducted with no more than a dozen people. There is, after all, a major difference between searching for someone presumed to be alive and someone known to be dead. If alive, time may be of the essence, since the missing person may be sick, injured, dehydrated, or comatose. Searching for someone who is dead can be slower, more deliberate, and done without the confusion that multiplies logarithmically as the number of searchers goes up.

Fourth, when useful expertise is available, it should be exploited. As bones were found during the search described above, people would break out of line to show them to one of the anthropologists, much to the consternation of the director. But that allowed them to find out immediately whether something should be flagged or the search halted. If the remains had been confirmed as human, it would have been necessary to stop everyone, show them what had been found, and—based on that find—tell them more precisely what else to look for.

Most field investigators have not been trained in the details of skeletal recovery. This is not surprising, since the recovery of a skeletonized or partly skeletonized body is an unusual event for most of them. Just to put this all in perspective, let's take a typical year—say 1989. In that year there were 5,868 deaths in the state of New Mexico (OMI, 1989). A total of 4,193 of those fell under the jurisdiction of the OMI; of these, 29 percent, or 1,228, were autopsied; of these, sixty-two cases received anthropological attention. While this is quite a respectable annual number of cases for forensic anthropology, it amounts to only 1.5 percent of the total caseload. Moreover, in 1989, only fifteen of those sixty-two cases involved any sort of recovery effort, about 0.3 percent of the total, or one out of every 279 cases. Assuming that each of the investigators has an equal probability of being called on every case, using 1989 as a guide he or she would average about thirty-eight cases a year. If recovery cases are also equally distributed, there would be about seven years between each one for every investigator (again using the 1989 figures as a benchmark).

The average investigator therefore has very little chance of working on a case where recovery is an issue. With little experience—and little possibility of getting any—he or she will inevitably fail to recover some bones when finally assigned a recovery, simply because of failure to recognize them as bones. He or she may also be handicapped by the belief that there is little to be learned from "just bones" anyhow, and may not want to bother with picking up little pieces.

Forensic anthropologists do not just analyze bones; they can be of great help in the recovery of human remains at the scene. Buried or partially buried bodies and burned remains are particularly amenable to anthropological recovery techniques, which have been finely honed through he decades by archaeologists. Forensic anthropologists use them to good advantage.

To Excavate is to Destroy

Sometimes, the recovery problems in forensic work can be formidable. If the discovery and recovery of remains on the surface is difficult, finding buried ones is even more so. Many of these cases turn on the word of an informant. Most of the recollections of just where a body was buried on a dark, moonless night, three years previously, are a bit fuzzy. Few murderers or their accomplices take time to triangulate the spot exactly. Technology provides a possible answer to the problem of locating graves with ground-penetrating radar (GPR). Under certain conditions, GPR may be used to determine where a body is *not*, while it can also show indications of recent disturbance that might harbor a body (Miller, 1996).

On rare occasions, the informant knows exactly where the body is. Two young fellows were walking over an area of broken ground in what is sometimes called "the far northeast heights" of Albuquerque. It is cut with innumerable arroyos feeding Pino Canyon and the Cañon de Domingo Baca, along which small scattered cottonwoods patiently wait to capture the occasional cascade of rain water on its way downhill toward the Rio Grande. The undulating desert land also supports scattered grasses, small bushes, prickly pear, and cholla. While this area is now dotted with expensive homes, fifteen years ago it was the residence of jackrabbits and horny toads. Dropping down to the base of a small wash, the two explorers noticed what they thought might be a human leg bone protruding from the top of the bank. They carefully triangulated the location, determining to inform the police when they reached home.

But everyone knows how it is with good intentions. One intends to do something, but then life intrudes and what should have been done today gets put off until tomorrow. In this instance, several tomorrows passed, which blurred into weeks, then months. Finally, the hikers went to the police, who conducted them back to the scene. Much had changed since they were last there. A long earthfill flood-control dam now crossed the area. Triangulating their position anew, the bone finders were certain that the exact spot where the bone had lain was now right in the middle of the freshly completed dam, about fifteen feet from its top.

The OMI investigator was called to the scene on this April, 1982 morning and a lively discussion ensued about what should be done. In the end it was decided that there was no alternative. The explorers were positive that they remembered the spot exactly, and on the chance that there might be something there, it was necessary to dig. Archaeologists are fond of saying that to excavate a site is to destroy it, but few of them ever have had a chance to destroy a just-built dam in the process.

Arrangements for equipment were made and we arrived at the scene on a Saturday morning to find a front-end loader waiting. Consulting one last time with the informants, the operator stationed his machine in front of the dam and raised the bucket as high as it would go. With the engine snorting, the dam destroyer surged ahead, lurching up the slope and expertly shaving the first few inches off the top. With watchful eyes stationed on both sides of the excavation, we carefully observed the fresh cut as the backhoe do-si-doed back and forth, dumping the spoil dirt at the side and returning to delicately shave off another few inches of dam. About ten feet wide at the top, the earthfill dam quickly widened out as it went down, so that each pass became longer and longer (Fig. 2.5).

As the backhoe slowly chewed its way toward the bottom, it started to look as if we weren't going to find anything. What does one say under the circumstances—"Sorry that we just destroyed your dam and didn't find a body"? Were we going to have to move over one bucket's width and repeat the process day after day until the entire dam had been flattened?

Then, just a couple of feet above the base of the dam, the side of the bucket exposed the unmistakable outline of a thin wooden coffin on the south side of the cut. It had just clipped off the coffin's end. Typical of inexpensive coffins, the lid had collapsed. The dirt above it indicated that it had been undisturbed and that by the greatest of luck the dam had been built right on top of it. A small backhoe was brought up to the top of the dam, and it began working its way down. After a morning's work, the

Fig. 2.5. Earthfill dam near Albuquerque being trenched to locate a body allegedly buried at its base. The bucket of the front-end loader is under the vigilant eye of forensic anthropologist Madeleine Hinkes in case anything should be found. After each cut, the walls are inspected.

bucket had reached close to the top of the coffin and the shovels were brought out.

By early afternoon, we had dug down to the top of the coffin, in the process locating a second coffin a couple of feet away. Removing loose dirt from the collapsed lids, we were rewarded with the sight of one plastic body bag in the first one and two in the second. Whatever these three bodies were, the fact that they had been placed in body bags and buried in coffins (we found a slightly rusty steel marker in front of one of them) meant that they were not of medicolegal significance. The police and the OMI investigators melted away, but we returned the next morning to complete the recovery.

While cleaning up the skeletons back at the OMI, we discovered a small blizzard of saw cuts peppering the skeletons. Each had been "autopsied," but in a strange manner. One had sections cut out of the back of the vertebrae. Another had several holes drilled in the skull. All had had the tops of the skulls sawn off. There was even a small-caliber bullet hole in the

Fig. 2.6. Skeletonized remains found in a coffin at the base of the dam shown in Fig. 2.5. Note autopsy cut on forehead.

skull of one (Fig. 2.6). After many days of puzzling over where these bodies could have come from, the head of the Anatomy Department speculated that they must have been used for some surgical practice prior to the founding of the medical school. He suggested that they had eventually been handed over to a mortuary for burial, but rather than pay for expensive cemetery plots, the mortuary simply took the coffins way outside the city and buried them. The city limits were now beginning to catch up. Maybe there are still others lurking quietly out there somewhere.

THE VALUE OF INFORMANTS

This case demonstrates that law enforcement should not simply give informants with a wild story a pat on the head and send them home. The two explorers were right that they had seen a human bone, and, unlike the Oklahoma informant, they knew exactly where. Although it turned out otherwise, the remains they saw could have belonged to a murder victim. The authorities must investigate every report.

Forensic Anthropology after Dark

When on duty, investigators are on call twenty-four hours a day. For the rest of us, most of the time, things are never so urgent that they can't wait until the following day, but every now and again it is necessary to respond immediately. Sometimes it's just a matter of trying to be helpful, such as the time when a phone call came in just as I was preparing to lock up the lab for the night. An investigator had been called out to the Old Town area of Albuquerque. (This was originally the site of the small eighteenth-century Hispanic settlement that gradually developed into the huge metropolitan area of Albuquerque. Old Town has evolved into a tourist mecca, where visitors to the city come to purchase rugs, jewelry, pottery, and myriad handcrafts of diverse origins).

Some workers who were digging adjacent to Rio Grande Boulevard on the edge of Old Town to place a restaurant sign had struck bones and called the police. They called the OMI, and the investigator, having peered down into the four-foot-deep hole, decided that the bones were probably not human. The options were to post an officer at the scene until the bones could be investigated in the morning, dig the bones up right then and take them into the OMI where they could be evaluated the next day, or call the forensic anthropologist and try for an immediate evaluation. In the end, they opted for the latter, as it would bring much faster results and cause less difficulty than the others.

The scene had been cordoned off with the usual yellow crime scene tape, behind which two officers and the investigator waited. It was not even necessary to climb down into the hole to see that the last time these bones had been above ground, they were surrounded by a cow. The tape came down, the officers left to continue their patrols, and the rest of us went home. Quite a few forensic cases end abruptly when it can be shown that they have no medicolegal significance and that the medical investigator's jurisdiction can be terminated. Even if the cow was murdered, such events are not within the jurisdiction of the medical investigator.

On more than one occasion, developments in a case have meant calling a forensic anthropologist in just as the sun is beginning to ease down behind the extinct volcanos that form the western skyline of Albuquerque. With the cool of evening creeping silently over hill and hollow, an infectious enthusiasm for digging—usually in response to a report of a body being buried "around here somewhere"—seems to reach a crescendo. However, no matter how enthusiastically we all swung shovels, such efforts never seem to produce bodies.

A MOONLESS RECOVERY

The report of the discovery of a body is something else. One evening, just as the stars were winking into view, I received a phone call from an investigator in the south valley. Two boys had been playing along the banks of an irrigation ditch when they discovered a piece of pottery, which they took home to their mother. She went back with them to the ditch bank, and there they found bones beginning to erode out. The police were called and were met at the scene by the OMI investigator. In his service with the OMI, he had seen many enough long-term burials to recognize this one immediately as prehistoric, but he called in just in case.

Kathryn Linn and I went to the scene with shovels, screens, trowels, dental picks, string, and the rest of the usual equipment in case some action was required. The investigator's judgment was quickly shown to be correct. The bones were completely free of soft tissue, stained a dark color by long exposure to the soil, and accompanied by additional undisturbed pottery fragments from an undoubtedly prehistoric time. The remains were therefore of no medicolegal interest: we could just write this one off and return home, or we could learn something more about life in those ancient times by excavating the skeleton the next morning. However, the investigator and the two officers present were all certain that if we simply walked away from it or put off recovery until tomorrow, the bones would be dug up and on someone's living room shelf by sunup. Feeling an obligation to posterity, we elected to remain and recover the burial in the interest of examining it for whatever light it might shed on living conditions in that area some seven hundred years earlier.

The investigator departed and the two officers gamely drove around to the other side of the ditch, stationing their vehicles so as to bring their headlights to bear on the scene of the crime, now metamorphosed to scientific excavation. At various times over the next four hours, they would be called away, sometimes singly and sometimes together. The experience of removing a skeleton on a moonless night, alternately working in shadows thrown by headlights from the opposite side of a ditch or by feel alone is one to be savored but not necessarily repeated. But the officers stuck it out to the end, and when it was all finished we were able to add a little more information to that which had already been accumulated from a large site that—we were later told—was nearby.

A VAST CROWD

The next nocturnal dig was on a warm summer night a couple of years later. It was prompted by the discovery of the body of Ms. Pat Tela, a 23-year-old woman who had been missing from her home in Albuquerque for about a week. The frantic parents had tried everything and finally resorted to a psychic, who declared that the body would be found near a popular picnic area at the base of the mountains north of town. A large search party found nothing but the clean bones of quadrupeds. Since Ms. Tela had been dead a relatively short time, the body would have been well into decomposition but would be a long way from being reduced to clean bones. The searchers were, nonetheless, sufficiently excited by these discoveries to redouble their efforts, the logical discontinuity between clean nonhuman bones and decomposed human bodies somehow fueling their ardor for the search. In the meantime, a cyclist was exploring the hilly area at the eastern edge of town, the mouth of Tijeras Canyon, where Interstate 40 climbs out of the Rio Grande Valley by twisting back and forth between the bases of the Sandia and Manzanita Mountains. By luck, the area that he had chosen to explore was the right one. His quest for the body of Ms. Tela was rewarded with an unpleasant odor carried past his nose by the late-afternoon breeze.

He called the police, and soon they and the OMI investigator were at the scene. It looked to them as though someone had dumped the body there and covered it with a few inches of dirt. The investigator did not have a shovel in his car, but he did have a cellular phone. He called a fire station about a mile away and asked if it had a shovel. Of course it did, and the firemen said they would bring it right out. Fire Department protocol requires a call to headquarters to let them know of any mission. A fire truck and chief's car bearing the shovel raced to the scene, siren blaring and lights flashing. Their radio message was picked up by the news media, who made it to the scene nearly as fast. The investigator poked the shovel into the mound and wrenched a couple of bones free from the body. He thought they looked human. Next he called the duty pathologist, Dr. Kurt

Nolte, who told him to secure the scene for an early-morning recovery. The last red rays of the setting sun were just then gently caressing the Sandia Mountains looming over the scene, reminding anyone who was paying attention why the Spanish explorers thought they resembled watermelons.

But nobody was looking at the sunset, and word of the find continued to spread. Ms. Tela's disappearance had been the subject of considerable media attention, and everyone concluded that it was she who had been found. Those with spare time on this warm late-June evening began to flow to the scene, becoming a pool of onlookers lapping at the edge of the hollow in which rose the mound of dirt secreting the body. As the sun went down, the pool of both on- and off-duty law enforcement people became a sizable lake. Motorists and an increasing crowd of other curious onlookers washed up on the fence next to the adjacent Interstate 40 entrance ramp. Pushed by the police, who very much wanted to dig up the body, the investigator concluded that it was time to contact the forensic anthropologist, but he was not sure how to do so. Someone suggested looking in the phone book, but that idea was rejected. "He wouldn't be in the phone book," scoffed one of the officers present. Finally someone looked.

The phone rang at about half past ten. I was told that I would be getting a call soon, asking me to come out. They also called the duty pathologist again, but he repeated his desire to do the excavation in the morning when there would be sufficient light to do it properly. This sage advice fell on deaf ears, however. The police were determined to have the body recovered. Finally, at nearly eleven o'clock, the phone rang again, and I was given directions on how to get to the scene. I arrived about twenty minutes later to find a mob of people enjoying the spectacle. A long line of cars was parked on the edge of the Interstate 40 ramp, and hundreds of people and news cameras were lined up against the fence overlooking the scene. Roads leading to the scene were blocked by a phalanx of police cars with flashing lights. About two hundred feet back from the body stood a multitude consisting of uniformed police, detectives, and other police in mufti. The district attorney and a number of assistant district attorneys were in the crowd. The woman's father had arrived. The police department's crime van was there, and the landscape was littered with parked police cars, most with engines running and headlights on. The static bark of police radios echoed around the scene. It began to look as if the whole force was there.

They were anxious to do the job (or, actually, to have someone else do it)—and right then. Five of us traipsed quietly in single file down into the dark hollow and toward the mound about 200 feet from the law enforcement brigade. On its top lay the bones turned out three hours earlier with the shovel. With the hot weather, the body had already decomposed so much that the shovel had peeled the bones clear of surrounding soft tissue. A substantial-looking police flashlight illuminated them as we hunkered down quietly in the dark. By luck, the bones that had been exposed were the right innominate (part of the pelvis) and femur (the upper leg bone). From a distance of ten feet the innominate's wide subpubic angle and deeply billowed pubic face were clearly visible. There was no way to tell from that distance who she was, but the features clearly showed that the remains were those of a young female. I said as much. There was silence. Then, in a hushed voice, the chief detective observed, "Wow! That must be why you get paid the big bucks!" With a small smile of self-satisfaction invisible in the dark, I thought, "Yes, I guess that's why." A few weeks later I discovered that the *retirement* pay of such high-ranking detectives was larger than my salary as forensic anthropologist, curator of the Maxwell Museum, and professor of Anthropology at the University of New Mexico.

We made our way back up to the dozens of waiting law enforcement people. The police promised us floodlights powered by the crime van's generator to continue the recovery, and when we called him, the chief medical investigator, Dr. Ross Zumwalt, agreed that given the situation and with portable lights, a recovery could be accomplished without losing evidence. The lights were rigged, the generator cranked up, and the work begun. In order to ensure that nothing was missed, the two investigators and I carefully dug around the body to define its position. It soon became evident that it was unclothed. Working first with a shovel and then a trowel, the body was carefully dug under, uncovered, and gently levered into a body bag with its load of surrounding dirt, ready for delivery to the OMI for an autopsy the next morning. As the body was being carried uphill to the waiting ambulance, I continued to trowel through the area under which the body had lain. Other than the expected products of decomposition soaking into the soil and my pants, nothing further was to be found. At the autopsy the following day, the body was quickly identified, on dental grounds, as the missing Pat Tela.

Under normal conditions, nocturnal excavations are to be avoided, but it seemed in this instance—with so many people and so much equipment present and enthusiasm for the project running so high—the best course was to dig. This willingness to proceed also seemed to create an aura of goodwill between the police and the OMI, an important consideration where jurisdiction over scenes is shared. Despite the unusual conditions, there was no hint that any evidence was lost. Nonetheless, given the choice between recovering a body in the dark or waiting until the next morning, Nolte's first instinct was absolutely right: it is always better to wait for good light.

If You Don't Have It, You Can't Analyze It

In forensic work you never know what you are going to find, but you do know that it will be interesting, even if it does not have medicolegal significance. From the relatively mundane discovering of skeletons in coffins to piecing bodies back together after the explosion of a fireworks factory (Bass and Rodriguez, 1986), the forensic anthropologist can be of help in resolving problems of identity and assessing the trauma that has occurred. However, the accuracy and speed of one's conclusions are dictated to a large degree by the amount and quality of evidence at hand.

If remains are recovered by a forensic anthropologist, the chances of a thorough recovery are much enhanced. The general rule in skeletal biology is "If you don't have it, you can't analyze it." It is not very profound but completely true. Every forensic anthropologist charged with the analysis of skeletonized human remains has experienced the frustration of having to draw conclusions from incomplete evidence gathered by others. Every forensic anthropologist has also probably seen investigators bringing in a set of remains in which every one of the twenty-four suprasacral vertebrae (the flexible part of the spine above the pelvis) except for one has been found. It is invariably one right in the middle of the spinal column that is missing. Why? What other (perhaps critically important) bones were missed? Did those at the scene just not recognize them? Did they think they probably weren't bones, or weren't human ones and just didn't bother to pick them up? Good field recovery is the critical element in any analysis, and having a forensic anthropology team at the scene is one way of assuring that everything that is there to be found *is* found and brought back.

In some locations and during some seasons the decomposition and skeletonization of bodies can be very rapid. Under a different set of conditions, bodies can be preserved for centuries by mummification, and skeletons for even longer. In such situations, the investigator never knows whether he or she is dealing with a recent homicide, a Civil War soldier, or a prehistoric Indian. It is, therefore, always a good idea to call for anthropological assistance.

Anthropological Scene Search

Forensic anthropologists have generally been trained in archaeological survey techniques, which have been devised to find traces of humans, their activities, or habitations on the surface of the ground. Archaeologists are trained to be aware of small fragments of bone and stone, as well as vegetational and ground-surface changes indicating the presence of structures, or other human activities, including locations of graves.

Adapting these techniques to medicolegal situations requires that those charged with the scene search be familiar with the appearance of bone, be able to recognize bones from bone fragments, and be knowledgeable about the effects wrought on human remains by the passage of time in a particular location—in other words, taphonomy, scavenging patterns, the infestations of insects, and so on. A vast number of factors can impinge on bone-varying greatly from one environment to the next, and the forensic anthropologist must be prepared for them all (Haglund and Sorg, 1996). Even skilled police investigators and highly competent searchers can miss important indicators of the presence of remains, or fail to recognize a portion of the remains simply because they are not familiar with the details of human skeletal anatomy. Clearly, such searches can benefit from the application of a trained anthropological eye.

An ideal situation is one in which the investigators maximize the potential of evidence recovery by calling for anthropological help in retrieving remains that are buried, partly buried, dispersed, or burned, or in any circumstance in which recovery may be difficult or tricky. In most cases, recovery can be delayed for hours, or even a day or more. The skeleton won't get a bit deader if it lies out there one more night. Of course, in a few instances, as illustrated earlier, immediate recovery is necessary because of construction, an aircraft crash, or some other highly charged circumstance, but it is usually advisable to wait for the anthropologist.

AT THE SCENE

The precise details of a search will be determined by the conditions. Where vegetation is sparse, different techniques are called for than would be the case in wet country with high grasses, bushes, and thick growth. Searching in mountainous territory offers its own challenges. The best general technique is that used by the State Police officer discussed earlier, in which a line of searchers, keeping in voice and visual contact, moves slowly across an area. At the end of a pass the line moves over, typewriter carriage fashion, and heads back toward the jumping-off place. At every step, the eyes sweep the ground, looking for unusual shapes, shadows, and contrasts. If all of the searchers know in advance exactly what to look for, the search may be conducted quickly and effectively, but if not or if ground conditions tend to blend with the object of the search, progress can be very slow. It is important to take whatever time is necessary and not to hurry a search. In some instances, the searchers may have to double back across the same area at 90 degrees to ensure complete coverage and to take advantage of working with the sun at an angle rather than working toward it. Where the contrast between the ground and the search objects is low, it can be advantageous to schedule the search for early in the morning or late in the afternoon, as longer shadows can help to distinguish objects from their background.

Photography and Mapping

Before beginning any recovery, the scene should be photographed completely, and measurements should be taken from a common reference point. Archaeologists establish a single measurement point, usually at the edge of a site, called a "datum point." This is marked with a post or flagged stick. It is located on a map, and all measurements are based on that point. They also grid off a site with tape or string, making each grid anywhere from 1 m (about a yard) square to 3 m (about ten feet) square, depending upon circumstances. This is a more elaborate procedure than is usually required for forensic work, but essential in a complex scene such as the Galaxy crash in Reno (see chapter 10). Even scratching lines in the dirt will help to locate things. In the best of all recovery worlds, everything is charted on the map before anything is moved or removed.

The secret of success in recovery is to take enough time to do the job right. Once done, it can never be repeated. If it is done properly, the people back at the lab will be able to put the whole scene back together again from the notes, maps, and photos. This will make a firm reconstruction of the situation possible, assuring that the proper conclusions are drawn and adding credibility to the case, should it go to court.

RECOVERY OF BURIALS

The skills of the anthropologist are of particular importance in cases where remains have been buried, as it is essential to recover every bit of human remains and other evidence. Most forensic anthropologists have participated in archaeological excavation and are aware of how those techniques can be adapted to the recovery of burials in a forensic context (Morse, Duncan, and Stoutamire, 1983). The work of Clyde Snow in Argentina (Joyce and Stover, 1991) vividly illustrates how meticulous excavation combined with a trained anthropological eye can yield clues missed by others.

The full and proper recovery of a burial requires not only painstaking digging technique (moving from shovels to trowels and brushes), but also a careful sifting of dirt to find everything. Many archaeologists favor a sharpened, round-pointed shovel to slice off about a centimeter or two of dirt at a time, moving across the entire excavation grid, and then down a like distance. In looking for buried remains, most investigators start to dig as if intent on reaching China. They put in a series of "postholes," usually piling backdirt up close to the hole. They then have to move the same dirt two or three times as the hole enlarges. Digging a small deep hole may be good exercise, but it is poor recovery technique. Excavators should work over an entire area, going down one arbitrary shallow level at a time, throwing backdirt into a screen at the edge of the excavation area for sifting. The growing pile of spoil dirt should be kept far enough from the excavation so that it will not slump into the hole or have to be moved as the hole is enlarged.

When a body is located, a shovel can be used carefully to remove the excess dirt at the margins, but a trowel and brushes should be used to finish removing the dirt. It sounds as if this would take ages, but in practiced hands a trowel can move a huge amount of dirt very quickly. Every bit of dirt taken from close to the body should be screened to make sure that no evidence is lost, and a sample should be retained for possible later analysis.

PACKING FOR SHIPPING

Once the material has been recovered, it must be moved to the laboratory for analysis. It is unfortunate, but true, that skeletons can be seriously damaged during transportation. In extreme cases this sort of damage can be so great as almost to destroy the remains. It is useless to spend hours carefully recovering a burial, only to throw the bones into a beer carton in the trunk of a patrol car. Bouncing out over rough roads creates bonemeal in the trunk and bad tempers in the lab.

The easiest packing procedure is to wrap each bone in newspaper and then additional crumpled paper to isolate each bone from the others. The principle is to keep the bones from bouncing against each other. Cotton should never be used for packing. It is expensive and it can be very time-consuming and difficult to get off of the bones once they have arrived in the lab. Styrofoam and other kinds of effective packing material can be used, but newspaper is readily available, cheap, and works well.

LABELING

The chain of evidence must be established at the scene and maintained intact from that point on. The best method is to label paper bags with a soft pencil. If they get wet, ink will probably run and the information would be lost. Each bag should be labeled with the case number or a control number. Location information should also be included on the bag as it may be important for reconstructing the scene later. Boxes and all containers should be labeled so that there is no question about the chain of evidence and where everything was found. Bags should be stapled closed and boxes taped. Items and procedures required for finding, recovering, and transporting human remains are based on good common sense. There is nothing "high tech" about any of this. It is just a matter of being careful and—very importantly—working slowly. It is always advisable to involve a forensic anthropologist at an early stage of the operation.

3

The Skeleton in the Closet

The Flow of Information to and from the Forensic Anthropologist

"We have a case for you to look at," the voice on the other end of the phone tersely said. That was the way it usually started. After a couple of years, investigators from the OMI in Albuquerque had learned that forensic anthropologists prefer not to be told anything in advance about a case. (It is best to cultivate and nurture one's ignorance so as to avoid having one's perceptions clouded by knowing what the investigators think .) The OMI is only about a half-mile away from the University of New Mexico main campus, across Lomas Boulevard on the Medical School campus. The walk was usually pleasant for graduate students and me, anticipating what might be waiting. Sometimes it was a pile of bones that turned out not even to be human; sometimes it was a prehistoric burial discovered in the process of digging a ditch or adding a room to a house. Most often it was something of forensic interest. This was definitely one of the latter, a skeleton found in a closet.

Decomposed bodies usually announce their presence well in advance of visual contact. Stepping into the OMI, it was usually not necessary to walk through the vestibule, past the row of offices, through the body receiving area, and into the autopsy suite to know that a decomposed body was waiting there. Its odor hit you the minute you stepped in the building. However, no such hint permeated the air this day. None of the office staff was wearing that slightly pained expression which typically signaled the presence of a decomp in the rooms beyond.

Nonetheless, laid out on the autopsy table was someone who had not been found immediately. In fact, it had been quite some time since this person last walked into a room. Some of the bones were visible through a rather thin veil of slippery, greenish brown soft tissue. But there was almost no odor. Strange. Lying beside the body was a tangle of gummy

53

Fig. 3.1. Nearly skeletonized remains of Hans Zopf as found in a closet in a garage. The body had been wrapped and covered with mothballs. (Photo courtesy of the Office of the Medical Investigator, Albuquerque, New Mexico)

newspapers and clothing, all of which was speckled with little white spheres.

The pathologist explained that the body was received wrapped up and packed in mothballs. Clearly visible in the right side and left rear of the skull was a pair of holes, looking suspiciously like gunshot wounds, but an analysis had to wait until the bones were clean. There is a danger in jumping too hastily to conclusions. It was a simple matter to strip the soft tissue from the bones. Many of them just lifted out of the encumbering soft tissue, almost clean. The body had been recovered a couple of hours earlier from a closet in a garage. Wrapped up like that and placed carefully in a closet in the garage with the door nailed shut from the outside, suicide seemed an unlikely explanation. What had happened (Fig. 3.1)?

A Self-Inflicted Gunshot Wound

According to the most reliable of informants—the wife of the decedent—one day in the mid-1970s, she returned home to find her husband dead of a self-inflicted gunshot wound to the head. He was lying on the floor at the foot of their bed. Rushing to him, she cradled his punctured pate in her arms until his body began to grow cold and stiff. There was no one to mourn with her, since her husband was born in Nazi Germany and had no relatives living in the United States.

Finally, realizing that his relatives would have to be notified, she roused herself to action. She wrapped a bedspread around her husband's head and dragged him out of the bedroom, across the driveway, and into the garage. She levered his body into a closet at one end of the garage and poured formalin (something the average Ms. Fix-It always has in her garage) over the head. Over the next couple of days, she wrapped his body in various pieces of clothing and newspapers and shoveled in a lifetime's supply of mothballs to make sure he would be in good condition when the relatives arrived.

Having tucked him in quite thoroughly, she nailed the door shut and departed for Germany in search of her husband's next of kin. The search was difficult and time consuming but ultimately successful. Yet none of the relatives seemed to be particularly moved by the poor gent's sudden and unexpected death. Crestfallen, rejected, and numb with shock, she returned to the United States, determined to lose herself in her art as a means of escaping from the pain of Hans Zopf's sudden and unscheduled departure.

Some individuals spend an inordinate amount of time on a voyage of personal discovery, an open-ended and extended quest in search of themselves. Here was someone attempting exactly the opposite, to lose herself—an effort which, with the passage of time, proved to be fabulously successful. So successful was she in her reverse quest that it was not until one day when she was sculpting a hand that she suddenly realized was that of her dear late future ex-husband (they were in the process of divorcing when he shot himself) Hans that she was jolted back to reality. Stunned by Hans' sudden but off-hand reemergence into her life, she related this painful discovery as well as the whole story of Hans' abruptly truncated life to her therapist. After considering the implications of what he had heard, the therapist suggested that it might be a good idea if she were to inform the police of Hans' untimely demise.

She agreed, and it was thus, in 1977, that she stepped off the airplane from California, where she had managed to lose herself for three years, and into the arms of the Albuquerque Police. They conducted her to her house, where they were met by the medical investigator. Piles of boxes were moved away from the closet door, the nails pulled, and the lovingly wrapped but decomposed and mostly skeletonized remains of Hans were ushered back out into the world. We know all of this because the future ex-wife told us—in some detail.

The Autopsy

At the OMI, we found that what was left of the body was wrapped in multiple layers of clothing, in which could be detected the faint aroma of mothballs. The bundle was carefully unwrapped, yielding slabs of decomposing tissue sagging off the bones. After photographs and the other formal requirements had been met, the remaining flesh was slid off the bones so that they could be analyzed.

The skull did indeed exhibit a single gunshot wound of entrance on the right inferior temporal (just in front of the right ear), and a larger, externally beveled exit wound on the occipital, just superior to the superior nuchal line and to the left of midline (just to the left of the middle of the back of the head). Since the soft tissue on the skull is quite thin, it tends to disappear rather quickly. With the loss of that soft tissue over the intervening three years, the investigators were deprived of the opportunity to see the stippling and dissection of the skin (Di Maio, 1985) that would be expected with a contact wound. If it could be confirmed as a contact wound, suicide would be a possible manner of death. While not the most common location for a suicidal gunshot wound, it could be managed. Contrarily, had the skin been present and failed to show the usual signs of a contact wound, that would have suggested that the shot was fired at short range by someone other than the victim. Someone could have held a pistol up just in front of the right ear, pulled the trigger, and watched as the bullet, blood, and some of the brain emerged from the left lower back part of the head. Still, a suicidal person determined to make things difficult for an investigator might manage to pull the trigger while holding the gun some distance from his or her head. The best evidence—the body itself—could thus not directly answer the question of who committed the murder. After three years, testing for primer residue on the hands of the victim or the wife would have revealed nothing, so the matter of "Who dunnit?"—of critical importance here was left unresolved. In other words, on the basis of the evidence extracted from an analysis of the skeleton, the wife's story could not be disproved. About all she could be charged with was not reporting a death (Figs. 3.2, 3.3).

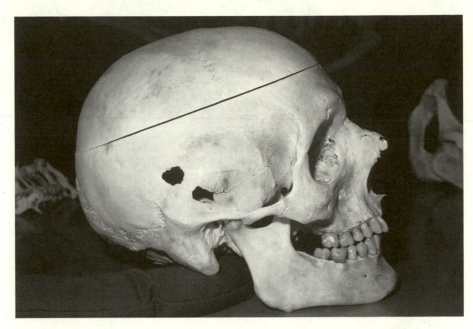

Fig. 3.2. Right side of the skull of the body shown in fig. 3.1. The upper defect is a rounded entrance wound. The irregular hole below the entrance wound was probably caused by a secondary impact of the semiautomatic pistol on recoil. The straight line above the entrance wound is an autopsy saw cut.

Some days after the autopsy, the wife, Gunny, generously donated the skeleton of her late future ex-husband to the Maxwell Museum's documented collection of human skeletons.

A Self-Inflicted Gunshot Wound . . .

Several years after the discovery of Hans, a woman returned to her home to find her husband dead of a self-inflicted gunshot wound to the head. The police were called to the scene immediately this time, but they seemed disturbed by the fact that the entrance for this self-inflicted wound was on the occipital (the back of the head), with the exit on the frontal (right between the eyes). While inconvenient and difficult, a determined suicider could shoot himself or herself in the back of the head, aiming the weapon to effect an exit in the front. It is not, however, the common thing to do, as Eisele and his colleagues have shown (1981). Police were also baffled that the weapon that had produced this "self-inflicted" gunshot

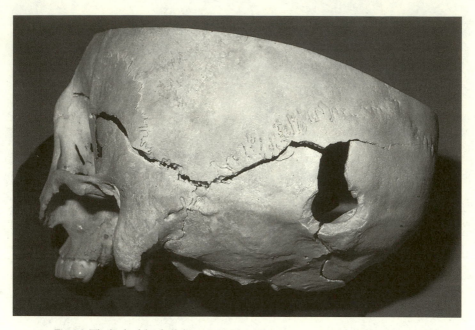

Fig. 3.3. The back of the skull shown in Fig. 3.2. The exiting projectile produced the beveling seen on the bottom of the exit wound and its upward elongation, as well as the fracture leading away from the exit wound.

wound was not in the victim's hand. Nor was it to be found lying on the floor, nearby, as they might have expected, nor anywhere in the room, nor in the house, nor—even—in the same county.

Acting on an anonymous tip, the police proceeded (which is what police do) to a bank in an adjacent community, where they found a recently fired gun in a safe-deposit box that had been rented just days previously. There were some suspicious circumstances surrounding the records of the rental. On the form filled out to rent the box, the date had been erased and an earlier one substituted to make it appear that the rental began on the day before instead of the same day as the demise of the victim. The form contained two names. One was Marion Haste, the wife of the most recently deceased gentleman, the innocent and unsuspecting Macon. The other was that of the victim's mother-in-law—none other than Hans' wife, Gunny.

A microscopic comparison was made of marks left by the barrel on the bullet recovered at the scene with those left on a test bullet fired from the weapon found in the safety deposit box. This comparison made by tool marks examiners of the Albuquerque Police Department showed that the two bullets had emerged from the same gun. Hence, this was the weapon that had abruptly ended Macon Haste's life. The police, smelling several rats and remembering the unforgettable mothballed Hans, pursued the prosecution of the case with vigor. Macon was murdered. Due to the efforts of the law enforcement agencies, mother and daughter have been assigned cozy little barred rooms at one of New Mexico's limited-egress residences.

Finally, after sixteen years, the case is closed. But wait! Not quite so fast. Marion's husband Macon may not have been such an innocent himself. He was recently implicated, in a postmortem sort of way, by a former lady friend, in the murder and burial of a high-school girl in the mountains a few miles west of Denver, near Idaho Springs. Attempts to locate the decade-old grave, said by one of the investigators to have started with teaspoons and escalated to backhoes, have so far been unsuccessful. In their zeal to find the body, they have even uprooted and torn out hundred-year-old trees.

When confronted with the nicely preserved complete skeleton of Hans, in good condition other than the bullet hole in its head, I immediately hoped to add it to our then minuscule collection of documented skeletons. The future ex-wife Gunny being agreeable, a document was drawn up and signed, but there was a catch. She insisted on "visiting rights" and came to see him several times. With those visits it became clear to me that unlimited visiting rights to skeletal remains are not the best idea since sliced bread.

Since that time, the Maxwell Museum's documented skeleton No. 17 has been joined by more than two hundred others that arrived as a result of their requests or the wishes of their survivors, by consignment of relatives who wanted nothing further to do with the recently deceased, from people wishing to avoid the high cost of a funeral and burial, or in some cases by donation from the medical investigator when no next of kin could be located, even after a thorough search.

Documented Collections

The Hans case came along just as we were beginning to build a documented collection of skeletons at the Maxwell Museum. Documented collections are those in which the identities of the remains are known. Not only the name, but the really important matters such as age, sex, race, height, cause and manner of death, and something of the person's medical history are included. From such skeletons we learn most of what we

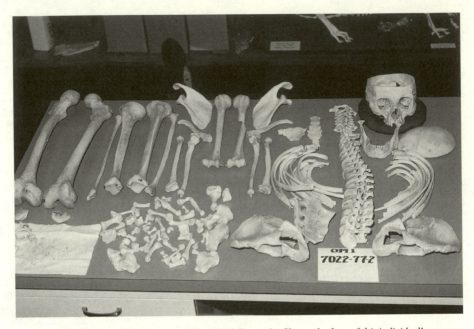

Fig. 3.4. A complete documented human skeleton. On file are the facts of this individual's age, sex, race, stature, cause of death and other particulars.

really know for sure about human bones. In analyzing them, the practiced osteologist can determine with great accuracy the specifics of that individual, but unless his or her identity can be documented, we can never be absolutely sure that the conclusions we have drawn about a skeleton are correct (Fig. 3.4).

The Smithsonian Institution inherited a magnificent resource, the Terry Collection, which is a group of some 1,600 skeletons of individuals collected in St. Louis up until World War II. The Cleveland Museum of Natural History has a similar collection, the Hammon-Todd Collection. These are of critical importance in basic osteological research as both are made up of known individuals. Forensic anthropologists and other osteologists turn to such collections when they wish to find out something about bones. This is not to say that important findings cannot be extracted from skeletons whose identities are not known. To the contrary, most of what we know for certain about the way people lived in prehistoric times has been learned from a study of their skeletons.

Archaeologists may probe the artifacts and architecture of ancient times, and from such probing much can be learned, but if we wish to learn about the people themselves, we must eventually study their skeletons because that is all that is left of them. Forensic anthropologists have invariably spent a part of their professional existence doing just that. Familiarity with a people of another time and another place is osteologically broadening, just as travel is culturally so—if one undertakes the journey with an open mind. The current desire of many native peoples to see the skeletons of their ancestors reburied out of reach of Anglo anthropologists is understandable on one level, but it deprives them of the opportunity to learn things about their ancestors that they can learn in no other way. It is sad if one believes that the remains of one's ancestors are being studied by outsiders primarily to burnish their own reputations and only secondarily to add to our store of knowledge, but it is sadder still to think that those ancestral voices will be forever muted by reburial. It is through research on skeletons that we come to understand something of what it was like to have been alive in a place and time other than our own. Not to conduct such research is to deprive ourselves (and others as yet unborn) of the opportunity to look through a unique window into the past—deliberately to chose ignorance over knowledge, a choice that flies in the face of what it means to be human.

Documented skeletons are a particularly valuable research asset. When one looks at an unknown skeleton, one may only attribute qualities to it. One does not know for sure, for example, what the sex is. There are numerous features that one may inspect, briefly alluded to in chapter 4, that will probably resolve that question, but in a more exact sense, one's assumptions are just that. Most osteologists hold that the probability of sexing a skeleton correctly is perhaps over 99 percent if most of it is present, but 95 percent if only the pelvis has been found. With the skull alone, the probability drops to about 90 percent. It is, thus, through the use of skeletons in a documented collection that one can deal with the most fundamental of epistemological questions in osteology: how do we know what we know? The accumulation of documented skeletal specimens from different geographical regions is therefore a most laudable goal, even if building a collection is also a slow and difficult process.

Every Skeleton is the Same, Every Skeleton is Different

General texts about human skeletal anatomy (Bass, 1987; Shipman, Walker, and Bichell, 1985; Steele and Bramblett, 1988; White and Folkens,

1991) can teach us much about the shapes of bones. They offer firm grounds for distinguishing a humerus from a femur and telling left from right, and explain other useful analytical steps. They can do this because any one skeleton is like every other. And yet, at the same time, it is possible to assert the opposite: that each skeleton is different from every other. In fact, these contradictory statements are both true. Let me explain.

When you have seen one skeleton, you have "seen 'em all." They all have the same bones, shaped the same ways, located in the same places and doing the same things. That is why a thoracic vertebra is a thoracic vertebra is a thoracic vertebra. The vertebral column, the segmented spine with the head sitting on the top end and you sitting on the bottom end, is made up of five types of vertebrae. Those in the chest are the thoracic vertebrae, the twelve segments making up the middle part of the spinal column in humans. Vertebrae have a specific series of roles to play: each is a miniature red blood cell factory; each acts as an anchor for the ribs, which in turn offer support and protection to the internal organs; each provides a rigid framework upon which to hang various organs. Like the other bones of the body, a vertebra can supply calcium to any other place in the organism that is in need. Bones also act as points of origin and insertion for muscles that make movement possible.

Between every adjacent pair of vertebrae is a sort of mushy fibrous disc that allows each vertebra a slight amount of motion on its neighbor. The cumulative motion between all vertebrae makes it possible for us to bend over and touch our toes or for a dog to lick its nether regions. The constraints of function, in combination with a long (and continuing) evolutionary process, determine the shapes of those bones before birth. The bipedality of humans calls forth shapes differing slightly from those needed for the quadrupedality of most other animals. All members of the sub-phylum *vertebrata* have vertebrae, the ones in the middle of the spinal column always being recognizable as thoracic vertebrae, regardless of whether you are talking about a mouse, humans, or *Seismosaurus*. However, like all other bones, those vertebrae have their own specific shapes. Those shapes differ from the corresponding bones of other mammals since they are all under the control of genes, which themselves have been altered over the eons to facilitate the performance peculiar to the species within which they reside. That sameness is what allows us to reach into a pile of jumbled human bones and pick out the thoracic vertebrae, or the fourth left rib, or any other bone we may target for that matter.

On the other hand, every skeleton is different. That is, the precise details of their shapes, sometimes the foramina, the aricular surfaces, and of course their dimensions, are all variable. Being male means one thing skeletally, while being female means something else. The bones are the same and their basic shapes are the same, but females tend to have slightly smaller vertebrae than males. The forces generated by our movements place stress on the vertebrae (as well as on the other bones), causing them to adjust to those stresses by means of an electrically moderated deposition of new bone and removal of old. Consequently, each skeleton is adjusted to the specific needs set by the posture and activity of its owner and operator. The bones generate those minute electrical charges as a result of stresses placed on them because of the nature of activity (Iscan and Kennedy, 1989). In this way each skeleton is "fine tuned" to the needs of its owner and operator. We are only at the beginning of discovering how the interpretation of those morphological nuances can reveal the way in which an individual used his or her skeleton.

Moreover, a person may inherit from a parent or parents a disease that can drastically alter the shape and affect the function of the skeleton. Some diseases capable of altering bone can be acquired during life (Ortner and Putschar, 1985). Some of these, such as torticollis (wry neck), may be evident to casual observers in life and to forensic anthropologists in the skeleton, and they can aid in the identification of an unknown body (Klepinger and Heidingsfelder, 1996). As we go through life, our skeletons respond to the incessant tuggings of attached muscles fighting to overcome the effects of gravity and inertia, and they may suffer additional stresses peculiar to our lifestyle or occupation. The effects of these strains, such as those resulting from citrus harvesting (Wienker and Wood, 1988) may be recognizable in the skeleton. Some stresses exceed the bones' strength and elasticity. When its elastic limit is reached, a bone fractures. Once again, the electrically mediated processes step in to dissolve the old bone and lay down the new, but even the most expertly set bone will show signs of its having been broken, and that idiosyncratic feature is clearly useful in making an identification from skeletal remains.

Thus, it is possible to assert that all skeletons are at once alike and different. Their sameness allows us to identify a thoracic vertebra whenever we see one and to distinguish between the skeletons of humans and those of other animals. It allows us to apply what we find in one skeleton to others across the vastness of space and time. As Smithsonian forensic anthropologist Dr. Douglas Owsley says, "We apply what we learn from archaeological excavations to criminal cases and vice versa" (Royte, 1996). Their differences allow us to distinguish not only between you and Felix the cat, but between you and your cousin Felix. Every encounter with a skeleton illuminates those differences, though the best way to comprehend them is through research in a documented skeletal collection.

The Informant

In many cases, bodies would never have come to light had the police not been led to the scene by an informant. For instance, Hans might have remained hidden until long after the cows came home had Gunny not spilled the beans. Luckily, informants often do come forward.

In the case discussed in chapter 2, the search and the subsequent recovery would have been impossible without the cooperation of an informant. The woman had been abducted from her apartment complex by two men who decided that they needed her car more than she did. A year and a half later, they were stopped in Oklahoma, where they had been living during the intervening period. They were driving the victim's stolen car with expired New Mexico license plates. They were stopped on some minor traffic violation, but when the officer noticed that the license had expired he called it in and was rewarded with the information that the car's owner had also apparently expired, that the car had been stolen, and that the men were wanted in New Mexico. While jailed, one of them broke down and promised to lead officers to the place where he said his companion had murdered the woman and they had left the body.

Coyotes, buzzards, maybe ranch dogs, and other carnivores would have quickly found her. They would have dragged arms, legs, the skull, and other bones off for some distance. Since she had been missing for a year and a half, the sun would have baked off what the critters didn't get, so that her bones would be essentially free of soft tissue, bleached white, but with the surfaces not yet peeling and flaking away as would happen with longer exposure. That was exactly what we found, the white of the bones glinting against the red of the soil—perfectly visible and very obvious. You did not have to be a forensic anthropologist to see them. But you did have to have an idea where to look. No prudent person would set out to search the eastern half of this 121,365-square-mile state in the hope of finding someone who had disappeared a year and a half earlier.

The informant can thus play an important role in narrowing down search parameters. In another decade or so, the bones of this woman could have been so badly eroded and reduced by the relentless sun and the procession of rain, snow, and the occasional heedless cow stomping on them that a positive identification would not have been possible. Like many things forensic, finding them when we did was partly a matter of good luck.

More Bodies

As winter descended in far eastern New Mexico, deciduous plants had shed their leaves and ice formed at night along the banks of the Canadian River. Other than that, the land looked little changed from August, the browns and reds of the landscape hardly betraying the approach of Christmas, except to the practiced eye. That another brown Christmas was nigh, however, was clear from the usual fanfare blaring from the speakers of radios and televisions, and from the holiday ornaments draped from light poles and in store fronts in this town of about six thousand established just after the turn of the century not far from the Texas border.

One child, galvanized to action by this late-seventies Christmas blitz, undertook to search the house from stem to stern in the hope of finding where his presents were secreted. Ascending quietly to the attic, the youngster soon spied an old dusty trunk off in a corner. His eyes lit up like a Christmas tree, and, pushing a couple of items off the top, he lifted the creaky lid. A decidedly non-Christmassy bundle, a somewhat elongated 1½-feet-long blob wrapped loosely with cloth, lay on the bottom. It was definitely not a pony, but it must be for him. What could it be? Enthusiastic little fingers deftly unwrapped the bundle to reveal . . . a dried and somewhat yellowed baby mummy. Surprise! The usual scenario ensued: the mother phoned the police; the police and OMI investigator came to the house; the body came to the OMI.

The body was indeed that of a human infant. The house having only recently been occupied by the present family, its members were both shocked and bewildered that their attic contained this unofficial Sears, Roebuck & Co. sarcophagus. The isolation of the infant's tiny body from most of the external agents of decay, flies, and other insects, in what could have been a very warm environment, caused the small mass to desiccate naturally, turning it into a mummy. From x-rays we could judge that it was full term, but at this late stage, the pathologists were unable to determine whether the infant had been born alive. Neither was it possible to determine the cause or the manner of death. City Police could not find the last people who had lived in the house or any indication that anyone who had lived there had given birth to a baby that was not accounted for.

Under the right conditions, even the bodies of adults can be mummified. Adults, of course, will have left a trail behind, which can usually be sniffed out and followed by determined investigators to an identification. But this baby eluded all attempts at identification. So rather than there being any grand conclusion, this tale drifts off quietly into the land of insolubility. There is, however, one man in far eastern New Mexico who, recalling his escapade, probably warns his own children against searching for Christmas presents.

Informants need not always be human. Many cases come to the attention of investigators when dogs bring home bones to gnaw on. In the Bobcat Crossing case discussed in chapter 2, a family dog brought home a skull and a femur. But unfortunately, even though investigators kept a watchful eye on Bowser, the dog apparently decided that he had already gotten the best bones and never returned to the cache.

Two young fellows wandered into my office one day not long after I arrived at the University of New Mexico. Clenched tightly in the hand of one was a somewhat bedraggled and very greasy-looking grocery store paper sack. They wanted to know if the bones inside were human. (This was the first of many such incidents. The finders of bones invariably display mixed feelings: hoping that they will be human and yet fearing that they might be. There is always a bit of a thrill if they are, and relief— tinged with disappointment—if they are not.) Reaching into the bag, I extracted a very greasy distal tibia and fibula from which was suspended the better part of a foot, all held together by desiccated tendons. It was human and far from fresh. With its dark-brown color, sticky greasiness, and stringy tendons it looked, smelled, and felt like an old anatomical specimen. I pointed out saw marks across the tops of the lower leg bones, indicating that this lower leg had been sawn off of the rest of the body. The young men were visibly shaken. This was more than they had bargained on. Beyond saying that their dog had brought it home, they suddenly became reluctant to provide any information about who they were or where they lived. My advice was to call the police to see if anyone could shed some light on how this leg had walked out of wherever it had been. As an anatomical specimen, it was not of forensic significance, but it is quite uncommon—and was therefore interesting—for such preserved body parts to show up in the mouth of a dog. Being rather small and delicate, it didn't fit the classic frontier story of the mortician sawing off the legs to make the body fit in a coffin he had in stock. Besides, it had been too saturated with formalin to be anything other than an anatomical specimen. The youths left hurriedly, leaving me to wonder to this day just where that leg came from.

In another example of the importance of an informant, this time a human one, a man who had been killed about three years previously was recovered thanks to an informant's cooperation. The victim, Max Zilla, was sitting in a pickup when at least two and perhaps more of his former friends fired into it. There had been some rising feeling of unhappiness over the fact that Max had become excessively friendly with the wife of one of the other fellows. This culminated in some bad blood, which resulted in the letting of same. The body was hauled out miles from the small northwestern New Mexico town where the murder took place and buried in sand at the base of a rock.

The State Police had been working diligently on Max's disappearance, and a trooper had tracked down one of the participants in his murder, who had moved to West Virginia. The officer began to lean on him—not an easy task over the phone—and eventually convinced the suspect that it would be an excellent idea if he were to return to New Mexico's continental divide country some day soon and point out the spot where the body was buried. He agreed to do so. Now all they had to do was get this guy to the scene and dig up the body. But as good as the police were at digging up informants, they had had no experience in digging up bodies. The lab phone rang one day in January of 1981. They wanted help in digging up a body somewhere out of town, but they weren't saying where. This is exactly the opportunity that forensic anthropologists hunger for: to get out in the open air to recover a body. That the State Police had asked made it that much better. If they wanted help digging up a body, they had it.

The whole maneuver was kept strictly secret. The police were concerned that if any of the other participants heard of the impending arrival of Bill Canary who was about to sing for them, lead was likely to fly. Being in proximity to Canary meant that a carelessly aimed projectile might come to rest in themselves, a prospect they did not entertain with any obvious enthusiasm.

On the appointed early-February day, forensic anthropologist Madeleine

Hinkes and I drove to a small Sandoval County town, the name of which was revealed to us in the last phone conversation, to meet the officers and their informant. Joining them in their vehicle, the officers took the front seats, an arsenal spread out on the floor at their feet; the two forensic anthropologists shoehorned themselves into a very narrow back seat with Canary, shovels, screens, and other equipment crammed into the remaining space. Within a few miles we left the narrow paved road ("Pray for me," says a locally favored bumper sticker, "I drive New Mexico 44") to bounce over the almost invisible two-track dirt "roads" down which the informant guided us. His unerring sense of direction led us to the exact spot, at the base of a large rock. In that part of the country, however, "at the base of a large rock" is not a very useful descriptive landmark. Early winter snowfalls had almost disappeared, a mantle of hard-crusted snow tonsuring the north sides of rocks and trees.

His pointing finger dragging his handcuffed left hand with it then indicated that if we shifted a few dead branches and started digging, we would find our man, the missing Mr. Zilla. The designated spot was in sand, one of the few places not frozen solid at this 7,000-foot altitude. Using a modified archaeological technique, we skimmed an inch or so of sand off the surface of the ground at the base of the rock, then went down another inch, then another. Within a few minutes, a shovel tip caught a corner of a blanket. Bringing our efforts to bear on that part of the sand, we soon had most of the blanket uncovered, then a shoe. Within the shoe was a foot, and attached to the foot was our man.

Obsessed with the need for secrecy, Officer French left for town to put the informant behind bars for his own protection, while the rest of us continued the excavation. We dug down, freeing the jackknifed body and preparing it to be lifted out when the county deputy medical investigator arrived with his body bag and seals. With the exertion of digging soon completed, the cold began to creep in and time began to drag. We piled up some dead sagebrush, lit a match to it, and stood there absorbing heat and sagebrush smoke as the sun passed its zenith, low in the southern sky. However, the combined effects of the fire, the heat generated by stomping around, and the wan sun were not enough to keep the cold from gnawing at our fingers, toes, noses, and ears. As the minutes ticked slowly past, Officer Gunn, who had been left behind with the three of us, began to display a rising nervousness. Where was his partner? Had he and his charge been stopped on some back road by the other participants in the murder?

Was his comrade at that very moment lying somewhere with the last bit of life slowly trickling out of him? Were we stranded miles from just about anywhere, without wheels or any means of communication while a pack of ruthless killers stalked our isolated redoubt?

This sort of thoughts contributed little to one's peace of mind. With a flurry of activity, Officer Gunn began to move up the store of weapons left behind—pistols, rifles, shotguns—and to prop them up against a handy log, along with piles of ammunition. Within a few minutes, he had improvised a little log-and-brush Alamo and had all of his weapons loaded, cocked, and propped within easy reach. Then, suddenly, from far off in the distance came the sound of a vehicle. He eased himself down behind his fort and ran a hurried last-minute check of his firearms stash. The roar of the engine increased in volume, and as our blood pressure peaked a vehicle burst over a slight rise and through the thin screen of leafless vegetation. It was his partner, back from jail and bearing only vaguely warm but very welcome hamburgers to get us through the rest of the afternoon.

The deputy medical investigator pulled in after Officer French and without going through any of the typical ritual of feeling for a pulse or listening for a breath, officially pronounced the just-unburied and decomposed victim dead (Figs. 3.5, 3.6). That rite of passage completed, the body was bagged, sealed, and loaded in the back of the investigator's vehicle for the trip back into town. After extinguishing our smokey sagebrush fire, the rest of us followed, finally relaxed after a trying and occasionally suspenseful day.

"Oh, oh!" the still-nervous Gunn grunted from the front seat. "There's a car following us." In such a remote area, the probability of two cars being on the same "road" at the same time just by chance is low. Could it be that the feared killers of the late Mr. Zilla were behind us, intent on pulling us over and resolving the threat to themselves by adding four more notches to their revolvers? As English struggled against the forces generated by stout springs acting against the rough two-track road, Gunn snatched the radio microphone off the console and called for assistance from the patrolman stationed in this region. Alas, he was at the far end of his district and it would be at least a half-hour (at warp speed) before he could reach us. We were on our own. Once again, Gunn began to ready his arsenal, preparing to shoot out through the back window, conveniently located between the two forensic anthropologists. Slowly the car gained on our bucking four-wheel-drive vehicle. Then, improbable or not, the

Fig. 3.5. The buried body of Mr. Zilla, wrapped in a blanket.

car, which had nearly caught up to us after a couple of high-tension miles, abruptly veered off. I have often wondered what would have happened had the car continued to gain on us and had attempted to pass.

A FEW LAST WORDS ABOUT HANS

The case with which this chapter began bristles with instructive examples to be plucked like so many feathers from a chicken. For example, there is the matter of the unresolved manner of death. How can one tell who was holding the gun? Was it suicide or homicide? The answers to these kinds of questions certainly make a difference to the way a case is treated, so the determination of the manner of death is exceedingly important. However, even careful investigation may sometimes fail to produce answers. That is the reason for the "undetermined" category.

Bone reacts differently depending on the range at which a shot is fired. In the case of a head wound, if the gun is in contact with the head, there might be some damage to the bone as the barrel slams into it. Unburned powder and soot would be projected into the area around the entrance (Di Maio, 1985). In the Maxwell Collection is a skull with a self-inflicted

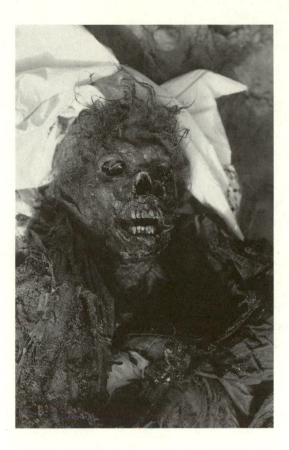

Fig. 3.6. Closeup of the head of the body shown in Fig. 3.5. The decomposition is consistent with that expected for a shallowly buried body at an elevation of 2,133 m (about 7,000 feet) for three years.

gunshot wound to the head. Even defleshing, simmering, and degreasing the skull could not erase the darkly discolored ring of unburned powder deposited around the entrance wound when the weapon discharged. The victim had drilled a nicely centered hole through the thickness of his frontal bone, right above the eyes, with the exit centered low on the back of his skull. He could not have done much better had he practiced. This is the sort of thing, however, that you usually only get one try at. Yet, there are documented examples of self-inflicted multiple gunshot wounds to the head. The Maxwell even has one: a skull in which there are two self-inflicted small-caliber entrance wounds in the right temple. (For additional information on gunshot wounds, see chapter 7).

Hans' skull showed no powder burns around the thin wall of bone at the entrance wound, though there was an area of fractured bone just below the entrance wound. It was in just the right position to have been caused by the bouncing of the barrel of the semiautomatic handgun that did the job. So it was a contact wound after all. But did he do it? The entrance and exit lined up in such a way that he could have held the gun in that position himself and pulled the trigger. But could a conscientious person conclude that it was therefore impossible that someone else did it? No. If asked on the witness stand, one could not testify that it would have been impossible for someone else to have pulled the trigger. The exact circumstances having been clouded by the passage of three years, the cause of death was left as a contact gunshot wound to the head, but the manner of death as undetermined. Could he have been murdered by his wife Gunny? It is, of course, possible, but the evidence from the skeleton is inconclusive, so we must be as well.

The Press

The ambiguous conclusion to the Hans Zopf case is the kind of result that is sometimes difficult for members of the fourth estate to fathom. Nonetheless, it is often necessary to explain to members of the media what was done in a specific case. Many press reports about the work at the OMI concentrate on identifying an unknown body, but most of them don't even acknowledge the OMI as the source of information about the skeleton. Sometimes, especially if it is a very interesting case (and a slow news day) the reporter will seek out more details, and the trail may eventually lead to the forensic anthropologist's telephone. Or the news media may be present at the scene of the discovery, and in such cases they may seek to interview the forensic anthropologist.

Just as with historians or mathematicians, some forensic anthropologists crave the spotlight more than others and make themselves readily available to the press. Some even court media attention, while others shy away from it. In New Mexico, the forensic anthropologist has always functioned as a member of the medical investigator's forensic pathology team. That typically means that findings and reports are given to the duty pathologist and investigator to use as they see fit. The police are the first to be contacted with this information. Most often they disseminate the findings through their regular channels, so a news item will usually read, "The Albuquerque Police Department has determined that . . . ." Inquiries and information are therefore funneled directly to them for action. In the rare circumstances when the media called me, I simply told them that OMI had all of the information and would provide it to them, giving the name of the investigator to contact. This allowed the OMI to reveal whatever information they felt it prudent to release. In some instances, this was not enough. For example, when the riot broke out in the New Mexico State Penitentiary, the local news media were quickly overshadowed by the presence of the voracious national media. The unpleasantness at the prison (more fully discussed in chapter 10), began on Saturday, February 2, 1980. Prisoners, buoyed up by a homemade hooch, overcame guards sent to quiet them down and erupted into the prison. Within a short time, it had fallen to the rampaging horde. With their newly won total access, prisoners began "cleansing" the penitentiary of undesirable inmates. Rumors of scores dead quickly circulated. However, by Sunday noon, enthusiasm for retribution had waned in the dark, cold prison where power and heat had been shut off. Authorities regained control of the prison by simply walking in and taking over.

OMI investigators and pathologists on the scene, consulting with authorities, decided that a forensic anthropological search for any remains still in the prison was in order. Our hastily assembled crew of experienced volunteers—students and former students—spent two days poking, raking, and investigating all of the troublesome areas. Authorities, catering to media requests, and ever mindful of the need for tight security in this hulk of a maximum-security facility, conducted several tours of journalists through the ransacked and gutted buildings. We would look up to see a battery of lenses aimed at us from the distant doorway as the guides herded them through. On some of these tours, they saw the lot of us on hands and knees, searching through debris on the gym floor. Late in the afternoon of the first day, I heard a voice call my name. Two young fellows standing at the door, reporters for the University of New Mexico *Daily Lobo*, had bested all of their national competitors, somehow talking their way, unescorted, under high-security provisions, through two sets of gates, past prison officials, guards, National Guardsmen, and police into the depths of the prison. It seemed to me that such diligence deserved a reward greater than satisfaction, so I agreed to a short interview.

We had been carefully combing the debris on the floor of the gym, recovering additional fragments of bone from the three burned bodies recovered by the investigators, putting them in three plastic garbage bags, one for each body. I explained what we were doing. Next day's *Lobo* featured the story, saying that we had found another three garbage bags of bone fragments—a *Lobo* scoop. In fact, three full garbage bags might hold a whole newsroom full of people if all that was left were bone fragments. The story was picked up by the other local media and by the national press as well. That night, the phone rang at home and I had to tell several disappointed national reporters that the bags weren't full: we had recovered enough bone fragments to fill, maybe, two or three cigar boxes. They didn't call again.

While one should strive to be helpful to the press in their role of providing information to the public, it is important to be as precise as possible and to say no more than is necessary. A careless remark can be lifted out of context to distort the entire meaning of an interview, and in the rush to meet a publication or broadcast deadline, a reporter will never call back to clarify or verify a statement. The ultimate contemporary media goal of a pithy little soundbite can never accurately portray the exacting practices and attention to detail employed in a medicolegal investigation.

The attention of the media can be both unnerving and exhilarating. It can divert one's attention from the task at hand. It can also appeal a little to the "ham" that must make up the character of each of us. Certainly we professors are not immune. In the happy focus of lenses and microphones, one can easily blurt out something that on reflection seems less than appropriate and academically dignified. Recovering an historic-era skeleton from an excavation for a satellite dish at a radio station, I was explaining the details of the situation to a news crew. In attempting to emphasize the fact that this region has been occupied by a succession of peoples for thousands of years, I observed, "Sometimes it seems as though you can hardly stick a shovel into the ground without finding somebody else on the other end of it." What got air time? The cogent explanation of the occupational sequence and why so many burials were to be found at this location? Of course not. They went for the pithy soundbite. Even worse than saying something that can be taken out of context is that one might be so carried away in that fleeting moment of Warholian fame to say more than one should, a cardinal "no-no" in forensic work.

Many years ago, I accompanied two forensic odontologists on an expedition to recover a body from a well in the northeast part of the country. The drifts of snow usually mantling the circum-Great Lakes region in a typical November had failed to materialize, but they were more than compensated for by a bone-chilling cold, accompanied by drizzly foggy weather. This was no place for someone from the sunny Southwest. Nevertheless, the inhospitable weather and spongy ground were not enough to keep the media from descending upon such a fascinating operation. In addition to the three outside experts (one definition of an expert being anyone from more than a hundred miles away), there were FBI agents, State Police in large numbers, and police and sheriff's officers from two counties. There were also, reminiscent of Arlo Guthrie's "Alice's Restaurant," scads of cop equipment, machinery, and support people.

Given the intense public interest, the district attorney realized that this was a golden public relations opportunity. After all, the public does have a right to know how its tax dollars are being spent. The district attorney played the media like a Stradivarius. As we gathered on the cold, saturated ground next to the well, he lined us up, ushered in the media, and explained who we were, why we were there, what we were going to do, and how we were going to do it. Then he politely shooed them away, and we began. Every couple of hours or so, he would bring the media back to the margin of our ever deepening and broadening hole to update them on progress.

In this way, he kept the reporters satisfied and interested, fed their egos within reason, and assured that coverage would be favorable. He also did his best to provide them with the most accurate, up-to-date information that he could so that the public would be informed. He seemed to do everything right. He kept in constant contact with developments, enlisted the assistance of others when necessary to explain some fine point of the work, but kept himself as the point of contact. It is important, when working in the public eye, that all information flow through a single conduit and that that person presents the information clearly and without bias or grandstanding.

The spokesperson should answer all questions forthrightly. He or she should never pretend to know the answer to a question, but rather promise to find out the correct information and pass it on at the next briefing. A bit of empathy for the reporters, who are only trying to do their job, helps to generate an atmosphere of mutual respect. Particularly in mass disasters, briefings must be frequent so as to reassure the public that the work is progressing with all due speed, given the care with which it must be conducted. Scenes of death and carnage, particularly multiple deaths, do not lend themselves to humor, so the spokesperson must be careful to conduct the briefings with all of the dignity and respect appropriate to those whose lives have been so abruptly terminated. It is not easy, but intercourse with the press is vital, and it must be accomplished in a manner suited to the solemnity of the situation.

Nonetheless, this should not be taken to mean that a briefing officer is obliged to offer free access to the scene. Nor should he or she disclose every bit of information uncovered, the exact condition of the bodies, or any other matter that would either hinder the investigation or appeal to the morbid curiosity of the general public. Media feeding frenzies come about because someone is, or many people are, dead. The person chosen to brief the media must therefore be knowledgeable, understanding, sensitive, and sensible. This is a tall assignment, requiring that the media go-between be selected with great care. The glare of public attention quickly fastens on scenes of death and it is important to keep the public informed. The public, after all, has a right to know, and it should be the duty of the briefing officer to carry out this most American of functions with grace, patience, and style. But one must also remember that the bodies that are the subjects of our investigations were living people not long ago: the delicate and very exposed feelings of their loved ones must be kept in mind at all times.

4

Listening to the Bones

Determination of Age, Sex, Stature, Race, and Other Things

Having successfully disposed of the basic question about whether a particular set of remains is human, the forensic anthropologist's next step is to begin the process of individualization. This is accomplished by ascertaining as much as possible about that individual skeleton through determining the "big four": its sex, age, stature, and race. In addition, the forensic anthropologist will try to isolate any other peculiar characteristics that may make the unidentified remains more recognizable and thus lead to an identification.

Sex

A good place to begin is with sex. In a sense, this is one of the easiest tasks, as there are only two choices—at least in New Mexico. Even if one chooses to wear clothing typical of the opposite sex, the skeleton does not lie. If the body is greatly decomposed, the organs upon which an evaluation of sex can reliably be based can be so far gone as to preclude a reliable conclusion, and occasionally investigators make a snap judgment of sex based on the attire found on a body. This is illustrated by the consternation manifested some years ago when an autopsy revealed a mixture of underwear on a badly decomposed body.

The body in question was received in an advanced state of decomposition, the circumstances suggesting that the person had left a western New Mexico bar after a somewhat longer than advisable stay. The individual's physical abilities being somewhat impaired by spirituous excess, the reveler must have stumbled into an arroyo and lapsed into a sleep that proved to be permanent. Another patron of the bar subsequently achieved an instantaneous semisobriety after stumbling in like manner—upon the now decomposed body, which had been lying exposed for more than one summer week.

At autopsy the sex was not immediately obvious, due to the decomposed state of the body. However, those in attendance took the very short hair, the flannel shirt, Levi's, and work boots as a reasonable indication that the body was male. Hence the consternation when, upon removing the shirt, the pathologists found a bra. This confusion was compounded by the jockey shorts that popped into view as the Levi's were stripped off. Under other circumstances, the forensic pathologist (or, indeed, the average person on the street) should have been able to look at those areas of soft tissue lurking beneath the bra and underpants to find those structures which would have made the sex immediately obvious. But the body was decomposed, remember? Along with the integrity of the internal organs, that of the external organs had also disappeared as a consequence of decomposition. Had one not already been on hand, this should have been the signal to call the forensic anthropologist.

The skull proved to be heavily built and thick, with a large brow ridge and showing prominent markings indicating the origin and insertion of large muscles. This is what one would expect to see on a male skull. Nevertheless, the pelvis was very clearly female. Anthropologists have contended that the probability of making the correct assessment of sex from the skull alone is only about 90 percent. The pelvis is generally less enigmatic and delivers its secret with less reluctance, rendering a correct reading about 95 percent of the time. With major portions of the skeleton, the accuracy rises to about 99 percent (Krogman and Iscan, 1986). There are many traits that betray the truth to the observant, but the tighter genetic control of the pelvis makes it more trustworthy than the skull for determination of sex. This initially puzzling decomposed body was female.

Dr. Clyde Snow, at the time in the employ of the Federal Aviation Administration in Oklahoma City and simultaneously the forensic anthropologist for the State of Oklahoma, once told of being brought a skeleton that was decked out in a fancy dress and matching toggery. As he began to look at the bones, though, he realized that the skeleton was not what it had initially seemed. The police were most reluctant to believe that this finely attired lady skeleton could be a gentleman skeleton instead, but Snow gave them chapter and verse, providing them with all of the details about sex, age, stature, race, and the other things he could. Eventually, as the wastebaskets in Snow's lab overflowed with uncollected papers, the police managed to locate some dental records of a man who answered the description that he had provided. Upon comparison, Snow was able to confirm that the skeleton belonged to the man whose dental records he held in his hand. He also realized that the reason his office and lab were starting to look a little unkempt was that this skeleton was in fact the building's custodian. When he contacted the victim's sister, Snow learned that she knew about her brother's penchant for clothes from the other side of the aisle. Not only did she know about this little quirk of raiment, she customarily tailored his newest selections to better accommodate his masculine frame. So, although you can fool most of the people most of the time, you cannot usually fool the forensic anthropologist.

The giveaway in this case was, once again, the pelvis. Not surprisingly, the pelvis, like all other human structures, has been molded by 3 or 4 million years of cumulative species experience with bipedality. The sometimes conflicting demands of locomotion and childbirth have shaped the pelves of males and females differently. Occasionally, however, people attempt to fool with mother nature, reshuffling the hand dealt at birth. Prolonged hormone treatment would seem to be capable of blurring the otherwise usually clear skeletal dichotomy between the sexes, though such cases rarely come to the attention of the forensic anthropologist.

For any species to succeed, it must be able to reproduce, or its impact on the terran fossil record will be negligible. In humans, the problems of childbirth are compounded by mother nature's exquisite little joke—the experiment with intelligent life. Shuffling through the fossil sequence leading to *Homo sapiens*, one is impressed most by the rapid growth in brain size. Along with whales and dolphins, we humans have the largest brains around, but unlike these large-brained aquatic mammalian cousins, we are terrestrial and have fallen into the unusual habit of walking about on our hind legs.

The rules of the evolution game specify that a species cannot simply pop into existence. It has to come from somewhere. That means that our anatomy has to be traced back to something that existed previously. Other than birds and a whole bevy of dinosaurs, we are the only habitually terrestrial bipeds. Birds are indeed "birdbrains" so do not have to contend with passing gigantic eggs. Dinosaurs were also egg-layers and do not give evidence of particularly lofty intelligence. We humans, on the other hand, being blessed (or cursed) with self-awareness and the ability to engage in rational thought (thus, if you are reading this, you must be human) are faced with the problem of giving birth before the foetus's head becomes too large to pass through the birth canal. Why not just enlarge the birth canal? This is the obstetrical dilemma. If the birth canal were enlarged enough to accommodate the very large head of a well-developed infant—one large enough to have the brain developed to the point where the infant could move about as many other mammals do at birth, the pelvic opening would be very wide. It would be so wide that the heads of the femora (the thighbones) would be so far apart that females of our species would not so much walk as waddle.

The compromise reached by the clever evolutionary process resulted in the pelvis being narrowed down from this hypothetical wash bucket to a soup tureen, narrow enough to make bipedal locomotion practical but wide enough to allow the head of the infant to pass through with (it says here) minimal discomfort and disruption to the mother. But the compromise also means that human infants are born earlier in their development that most other mammals and are thus dependent upon their parents for everything for a long time. Males, not being constrained by the requirements of childbirth, may have a pelvis that is narrower and thus, in locomotor terms, more efficient.

Hence, the female pelvis may be seen to differ from that of the male in just those ways that facilitate childbirth and essentially all of the differences that we see—wide subpubic angle, wide pubis, wide sciatic notch, elevated auricular surface, and a wide sacrum—are consistent with that function. This, in turn, suggests that there are some biomechanical functions more easily and economically achieved by males (on the average) than by females (on the average). Interestingly, although there had been for some years an undercurrent and some observations holding that adult criteria for determination of sex could be applied to infants, one of the first to actually test this was David Weaver (1980) (Fig. 4.1).

Sexual dimorphism (the bimodal distribution of characteristics according to a person's sex) is not confined to the pelvis, but is spread throughout the hard as well as the soft tissues of the body. Males are hormonally preadapted to hypertrophy of muscle masses. Consequently, even males who are not bodybuilders tend to have larger ridges and crests on their bones where the muscles attach. Not only that, all of their bones are heavier and thicker (including the skull) and articular surfaces (joints) are larger than those of females. These observable dimorphic traits are useful in distinguishing between males and females. Other traits may be measured—

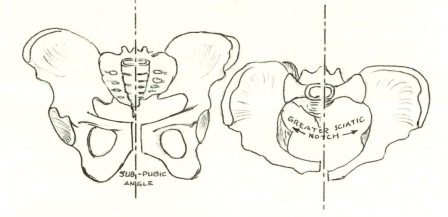

Fig. 4.1. The human pelvis, male on the left and female on the right.

the vertical diameter of the femoral and humeral heads, for example, can be used in those cases where the difference is great enough—but in many such measuring instances, the dimensions will fall into an overlap range, so that they cannot be used as a sexing criterion. Thus, even though sex is a straightforward matter with an outcome of either male or female, the skeleton is not always unambiguous. In some trying instances, the best we can do is simply not enough to resolve the question with assurance. There is one last thing to remember: males and females *do* have the same number of ribs (Fig. 4.2).

Age

Forensic odontologist Homer Campbell and I were once called in to assist in identifying the decomposed body of an "old codger" on whom the autopsy was winding up. The pathologist snapped the skull x-ray smartly into the viewer and stepped back. We advanced on the plate, and looked at it and then at each other. We both laughed. The pathologist looked puzzled. He was, we explained, not particularly old at all. "But," the pathologist said, "he must be old. His mouth doesn't contain a single tooth!" We pointed to the deep alveoli (the areas of the jaws that hold the teeth) and noted several other features of the skull that seemed inconsistent with great age.

Upon viewing the bones, that opinion was solidified. Their surfaces

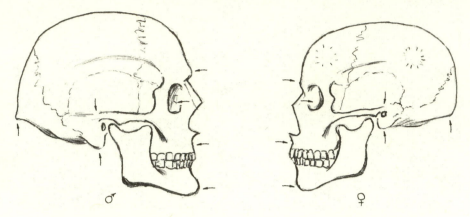

Fig. 4.2. The human skull, male on the left and female on the right. Arrows point to sexually dimorphic characteristics.

still retained the smooth ivorine texture typical of younger individuals. Viewing the skeleton of an elderly person, one would expect to see areas of patchy-looking transparent bone in the orbital walls of the skull, the scapulae (shoulder blade), or other areas of thin bone. None was present. The whole skeleton appeared to be in good condition, lacking the osteophytes (little spikes of bone) one might find on the vertebrae of an older individual. That is, there was no sign of the osteoarthritis that begins to show up on bone around the age of thirty (Stewart, 1958). In fact, he appeared not to be over the age of thirty. He was later positively identified as a 27-year-old. This was accomplished in part by comparing the x-ray of his clavicle (collarbone), which had been fractured and healed, with one taken as he was being treated for the fracture.

In our usual frame of reference, a person does not lose all of his teeth until considerably later in life. Llewelen Gumm probably had the bad luck of being born with a lousy set of choppers and opted for their complete extraction. Campbell could find no evidence that he had worn dentures and none were found with the body. His driver's license photo portrayed him with that sort of collapsed-mouth look that accompanies the extraction of all teeth. The obvious conclusion that Mr. Gumm had accumulated an impressive number of years prior to his demise was wrong. Things are not always as they seem. That is why it is a good idea to keep a forensic anthropologist around.

Age can be a very slippery topic. Here there is an entire range of possible answers, from well before birth to beyond the century mark, yet it is immediately evident if one is dealing with a maturing skeleton or a declining one. The aging process might be considered in terms of a roller coaster ride. There is a short, steep ascent up the growth curve, followed by a momentary leveling off. Then begins the descent, wherein one uses up the skeletal capital accumulated on the upward climb.

In recent years, research has shown that while one's skeletal peak may be said to be achieved at about the age of twenty-five to thirty and that it is all downhill after that, there are means that can brake the descent. Good nutrition, including adequate calcium, but even more importantly skeletal stress, will help to keep one in shape. Yes, that's right. Stress is healthy, but like all things it should be taken in moderation. It is the eternal tussle between the musculoskeletal apparatus and gravity that maintains one's skeleton in good condition. Astronauts living in the zero-gravity of near-earth space have demonstrated conclusively how the lack of skeletal stress in the absence of gravity leads to osteoporosis (the thinning of bone). Long confinement to bed can produce similar results, as can inactivity. The expression "bone idle" would seem to have a basis in fact. Osteoporosis enhances the possibility of fracture and is a significant factor in the production of "dowager's hump" and broken hips seen in the more delicate, less massive skeletons of postmenopausal women. All such features can, of course, be of use in helping to establish the identification of an unknown body.

Humans share with all of their mammalian cousins a nifty method of growing bones, epiphyseal. In the young, the bones are ossified not as a unit, but in pieces. Usually there is a single center of ossification at about the middle of the shaft of a long bone, from which transmutation from the cartilage of the early foetus to bone is accomplished. The ends are separate units with their own centers of ossification, the epiphyses, held to the shaft by plates of cartilage. The bone grows by adding a layer of cartilage at the epiphysis and turning the layer of cartilage closest to the shaft into bone, pushing the epiphyses farther from each other, thereby lengthening the bone (Fig. 4.3).

If a youngster dies, the cartilage soon disappears, leaving behind just these separate bits of bone. A child under the age of puberty could leave a pile of more than four hundred separate bony elements rather than the 206 bones found in an adult. Many authors gathering data on bone length

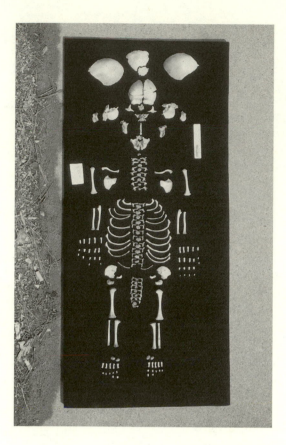

Fig. 4.3. The bones of a full-term human foetus laid out in the anatomical position. None of the skull bones or any of the others has fused. The bones of human infants are sometimes mistaken for nonhuman ones, or may not even be recognized as bones. (Photo courtesy of Luana Valdez Buelow.)

to test the expectation that kids get taller as they get older have shown that there is a clear relation between the length of the shaft itself (the diaphysis) and the age of the child. Tables have been devised for a number of different populations (Johnston, 1962, Ubelaker, 1989), since growth rates do vary depending upon numerous circumstances. Each of these epiphyses has its own particular time of appearance and union, and the appearance and fusion of these separate elements is therefore a reliable guide to one's age during the years of active bone growth (Fig. 4.4).

While all of this is going on, the child is developing, erupting, and then gradually losing its deciduous (baby) teeth. The first permanent tooth shows up in the mouth at about age six and others follow along until about the age of eighteen. Their secret development in the jaws prior to erup-

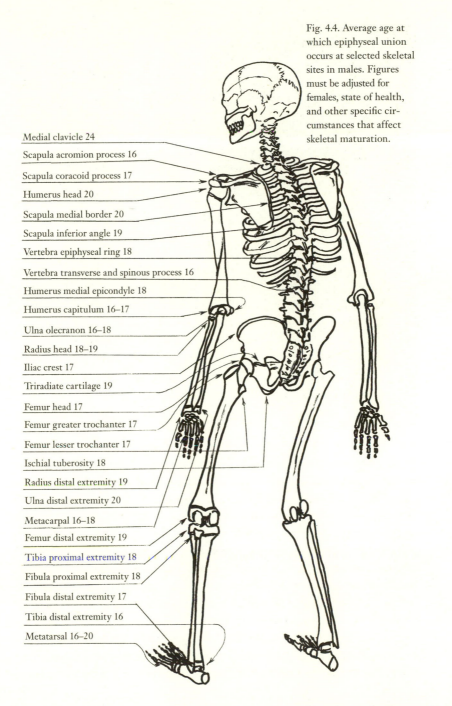

Fig. 4.4. Average age at which epiphyseal union occurs at selected skeletal sites in males. Figures must be adjusted for females, state of health, and other specific circumstances that affect skeletal maturation.

Medial clavicle 24

Scapula acromion process 16

Scapula coracoid process 17

Humerus head 20

Scapula medial border 20

Scapula inferior angle 19

Vertebra epiphyseal ring 18

Vertebra transverse and spinous process 16

Humerus medial epicondyle 18

Humerus capitulum 16–17

Ulna olecranon 16–18

Radius head 18–19

Iliac crest 17

Triradiate cartilage 19

Femur head 17

Femur greater trochanter 17

Femur lesser trochanter 17

Ischial tuberosity 18

Radius distal extremity 19

Ulna distal extremity 20

Metacarpal 16–18

Femur distal extremity 19

Tibia proximal extremity 18

Fibula proximal extremity 18

Fibula distal extremity 17

Tibia distal extremity 16

Metatarsal 16–20

tion can be disclosed by x-ray. Thus, for that period from about five to six lunar months of foetal age to around twenty-five years, there are events of appearance of ossification centers, bone growth, epiphyseal fusion, and dental development upon which to base an estimate of age. The spaces between these events, rather short in the very young, begin to lengthen as the child grows. Therefore, while one might expect to be able to estimate the age of an infant to within six months, the margin of error extends to as much as five years or perhaps even more when working with the remains of an individual who has completed his or her growth. The more incomplete the remains are, the more tentative the conclusions must be. In other words, the older one becomes, the more difficult it is to estimate age from the skeleton. Two good reviews of age determination from immature skeletons are those of forensic anthropologists Douglas Ubelaker (1987) and David Weaver (1986).

Of course, all of the bones are growing in addition to the limb bones. One of the most complete summaries of foetal aging was based on a Hungarian sample (Fazekas and Kosa, 1978). The measurement data cover not only the long bones, but those of irregular shape, such as the bones of the skull and pelvis. Their book derives from skeletal preparations that they have done, and though the sample is small, the work is an important one. For a variety of reasons, the older a child becomes, the more secure its grip on life becomes, so there is very little information about the skeletons of youngsters beyond the age of two or so.

Reaching full skeletal maturity in the mid-twenties, the skeleton then begins its long slow glidepath to senescence. Unfortunately, the markers along this declining path are less distinct. In general, what happens is this: the bone gradually becomes a little thinner, a little more porous, and lighter. The alveolus pulls back from the roots, teeth accumulate various defects and restorations (fillings) and some are lost. Joints begin to deteriorate and osteophytes proliferate. These are quite general markers and the times at which these events occur vary considerably with the individual and with the circumstances prevailing in that person's life. Yet, as Stewart has shown in his discussion of the development of arthritis in the vertebral column (1958), a certain regularity underlies the idiosyncracies of individual aging (Fig. 4.5).

At least as early as the 1920s, some anthropologists recognized that the bones of the pubis undergo clear and fairly regular change. Various methods of aging the *os pubis* have now been devised, but the one that seems to

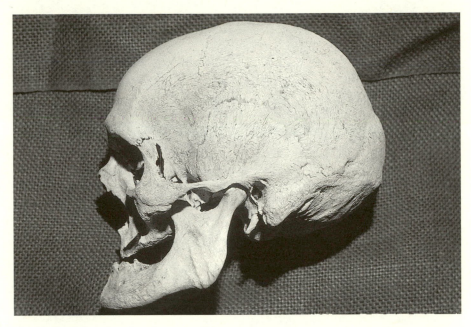

Fig. 4.5. Skull of an edentulous sixty-year-old man.

work best is a modification of the Todd method worked out by forensic anthropologists Judy Suchey and Sheilagh Brooks (Brooks and Suchey, 1990). This "Suchey-Brooks" method is built upon a superbly documented sample of over a thousand pairs of pubic bones collected, prepared, and analyzed by Suchey. It monitors and evaluates the changes taking place at the symphysis of the two pubic bones. Other events taking place at various locations in the skeleton make it possible for the forensic anthropologist to make an estimate of age that is most likely to fall within ten years of the actual age for middle-aged individuals but more for older ones, given fairly complete remains or critical portions thereof (Fig. 4.6).

It is also tempting to use the fusion of skull vault sutures as a means of estimating age. It is quite a straightforward procedure to observe the extent of suture closure. Unfortunately, ease of accomplishment is not enough, and Brooks' caution (1955) about using this marker as a basis for determining age remains good advice. However, forensic anthropologist Robert Mann and his colleagues have found the maxillary suture to be useful (Mann, Symes, and Bass, 1987).

All of the techniques discussed above are anthroposcopic and nonde-

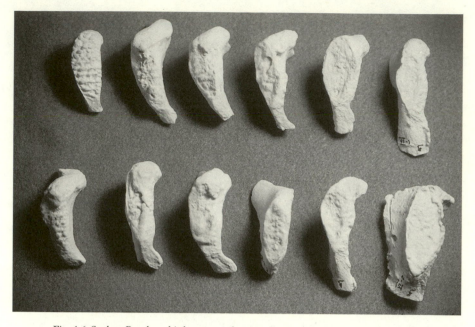

Fig. 4.6. Suchey-Brooks pubic bone casts showing changes in symphyseal faces with age. Casts by France Casting. (Photo courtesy of Susan B. Jimenez.)

structive. That is, they depend upon observation alone and do not alter the bone in any way. The same observations may be repeated year after year with no detrimental effect to the bone other than incidental damage from careless handling. Nondestructive analysis is the preferred method in anthropology and is particularly important in forensic anthropology. It is necessary to maintain an uninterrupted chain of custody in which the evidence can be demonstrated in court to have been passed from one analyst to another without alteration. Sometimes, however, destructive testing is necessary.

In those instances when the remains are fragmentary or incomplete, age may be estimated by an osteon count. Forensic anthropologist Ellis Kerley (1965) devised a method of bone aging based on this procedure. Without going into mind-numbing detail, the microscopic structure of bone includes cells known as osteons. In general, the longer one is alive, the more osteons one makes as a part of normal bone remodeling. Eventually osteons die and their places are taken by new cells, which begin to lay down their own concentric layers, looking rather like the wavelets spreading out bull's-eye fashion from a pebble dropped into still water. These lamellae encroach upon and erase old lamellae surrounding the dead osteon.

Microscope slides are prepared from several small cores that have been removed from the shafts of the leg bones and ground flat. By slipping the slides under a lens of the prescribed power, one can count the number of osteons in a defined field and, from that, calculate an age within about ten years of the actual age. Forensic anthropologist Sam Stout (1988), however, cautions that there are a number of factors besides the age of a person that can affect bone remodeling, which would in turn affect any age estimate based on this procedure.

Stature

In April of 1988, a foot in a tennis shoe washed ashore in Elephant Butte Reservoir. This is a huge body of water, pent up by Elephant Butte Dam, and named for an adjacent pachydermous prominence. The dam floods the channel of the Rio Grande, the *other* great river of the Southwest. Bisecting the state of New Mexico from north to south, the Rio Grande has provided water for drinking and the irrigation of crops from prehistoric times to the present. At the southern edge of "The Butte" lies the town of Truth or Consequences (known as Hot Springs until seduced by the offer of fame from radio and television game show host Ralph Edwards), a resort and home for snowbirds escaping dreary northern winters.

The Butte and the smaller Caballo Reservoir just to the south not only meter out their life-giving fluid to people and produce down to the gulf coast of Texas, but are startlingly blue oases in an otherwise hot and dusty land. As spring sprinkles the rocky reddish brown landscape with delicate flowers, the sandy shores of The Butte are visited by ever larger crowds of bass fishermen, jet-skiers, speedboaters, water sprites, and sun-worshipers.

By Memorial Day, a throng equal to a quarter of the population of Albuquerque settles down shoulder to shoulder in this dichotomous temporary city. The hot, dry, dusty desert lies at their backs, and the sparkling, cool, blue lake is spread before them. Occupying a whole range of accommodations, from expensive recreational vehicles to homemade pickup campers and tents, they devote the long weekend to splashing, reading, eating, buzzing around the lake, and drinking. Since nature has provided no shade, it is necessary to import whatever is desired. In the heat of the relentless sun, it is critical to maintain fluid levels in the body. Sometimes, however, people effect this replenishment of bodily fluids with a large proportion of alcohol. As a result, revelers occasionally fall out of boats or foggily venture too far from land. Perhaps that is what happened to the person to whom that foot belonged.

A foot is not much on which to base an identification. From its size, it was most likely male. Growth was complete, so it was adult. The bones, released from their adipocerous (adipocere is a crumbly soapy material, formed of soft tissue after long immersion in water) jacket betrayed no obvious anomalies or other clues to identity. The Nike shoe wasn't much help either. A standard procedure in osteology is the estimation of stature from long bones (those of the arms and legs), but this case consisted of only a foot. Reasoning that if stature could be estimated from long bones, it might also be estimated from the short bones, specifically either the metatarsals (bones of the ball of the foot) or metacarpals (bones of the palm of the hand), I decided to measure the length of the metatarsal bones. The corresponding bones of a number of males from the Maxwell Museum's documented skeletal collection were then measured and the ratio between their lengths and the stature of each of those individuals was calculated. Using those ratios, it was possible to predict the stature of the person that used to be on the other end of the foot that floated ashore. The effort, however, did little good, since the rest of the person has not been found, and the foot remains unidentified. Although this required a bit more work than would usually be lavished on a foot, it seemed worthwhile to make the effort. In fact, the Smithsonian's Doug Ubelaker ran a similar study when he was also faced with defeat in a foot case (Ubelaker and Scammell, 1992).

This Elephant Butte foot project aroused the interest of some graduate students, who asked, in effect, "Can you really do that?" They decided to follow it up, measuring everything they could in the Maxwell's documented collection and then arranging for a visit to the Smithsonian's Terry Collection in the quest for more data. Eventually, after several months of collecting data and analyzing it, they discovered that short bones can indeed be used to estimate stature and that the results are very nearly as good as those derived from the long bones (Byers, Curran, and Akoshima, 1989). Documented skeletal collections, such as the Smithsonian's large Terry Collection or the Maxwell's small documented collection discussed in the last chapter, are the only means to solve such problems, and having one close at hand is surely the fond wish of every foren-sic anthropologist.

Estimation of stature may be one of the most straightforward tech-niques of bone analysis. It is difficult to make a major mistake in the cal-culation of stature, though the pathologists' rough-and-ready rule that height is five times the length of the humerus (upper arm bone) is a little too rough to be of ready use. To estimate the living height of an individ-ual from that person's bones, you need only to place the long bone into an osteometric board and measure its length according to the proper stan-dards, drop the measurement into a formula (Trotter and Gleser, 1952), push the button on your calculator, and you have the stature. Of course, there is a trick or two. Before you can select a formula, you must not only know which bone you are measuring (not usually a problem), but also have determined the sex and the race of the person. Even incomplete bones can be used to estimate stature (Steele, 1970).

Each of the formulae is prone to a certain margin of error, however, so the final result—even if you have a complete bone and have measured it correctly—may be out by a few centimeters (by over an inch) in either di-rection. Forensic anthropologist Alison Galloway (1988) points out that age is also a factor in making an accurate stature estimate, since beyond age forty-five, people lose stature at the rate of about a millimeter and a half (a sixteenth of an inch or so) every year. The stature formulae were not designed to compensate for someone with unusually long or short limbs or odd proportions. Because of these and many other variables, forensic anthropologists feel it necessary to give a stature estimate as a range that covers 2–3 cm (an inch or so) on either side of the computed value. Police often take such estimates quite literally, so if the anthropologist, translat-ing out of the metric system, says "This person was about five feet seven inches tall," they may reject an otherwise good match who is five feet eight inches. For that reason, it is best to be a bit generous with stature ranges.

An alternative to estimation of stature from either long or short bones, with their inability to accommodate differing body proportions, is the Fully method (Lundy, 1988). However, the Fully method does take more time to accomplish and requires an essentially complete skeleton, so it can-not be used for the majority of cases seen by the forensic anthropologist.

A significant problem in any estimate of stature is that the anthropol-ogist does not know how accurate the given "known" stature is (Willey and Falsetti, 1991). Often these figures are taken from driver's licenses. In many states, the height and weight on driver's licenses are self-reported. While females tend to underestimate their weights, males tend to over-estimate their heights. To allow for this little quirk of human behavior, the forensic anthropologist may have to conclude that the best estimate for a male that was calculated at five feet six inches to five feet eight inches would be five feet seven inches to five feet ten inches.

Racial Attribution

In the late 1970s, an Iowa physician and his family were picnicking at the base of the Ship Rock in far western New Mexico. Twelve miles south-west of the town of Shiprock, which is the largest town of the Navajo Nation and a Navajo business and trade center, the 7,178-feet-high basaltic sailing vessel known as Ship Rock juts abruptly up from the rolling red desert landscape. This hard black volcanic plug, the neck of an extinct volcano, was left after the surrounding softer rock slowly eroded away and was carried by intermittent streams down to the San Juan River that runs through Shiprock town. Perhaps some of the suspended Ship Rock particles made their way over the dozen or so miles past Shiprock into Utah and even as far as the Grand Canyon.

Finishing their isolated midday repast, the physician and his family started off on a hike around the base of craggy Ship Rock. They had not gone far before they bumped into some bones lying in the sand amid scattered basaltic fragments from the towering landmark. They gathered up the bones—a human skull, part of a pelvis, and some leg bones—and took them to the San Juan County Sheriff. Most physicians are happy to offer opinions, and this one was no exception. With the skull present, most people would have felt competent to venture a guess that the bones were human, but he went on—so far as to say that they were Indian, and female. One problem in any sort of analysis is that observers may be moved by a logic that grows out of context. Out here, on the red desert steppes of the Navajo Reservation where green is an abstract concept, it is reasonable to assume that these skeletal remains were Indian.

But they were not. The facial skeleton exhibited the sharp features more likely to be found in the faces of most of the residents of nearby Farmington, an Anglo trade and tourist center, than in the Navajo town of Shiprock. In the latter population, the face is flatter and smoother featured. The features of this skull were so classically white that a first-year forensic anthropology student could have made the correct diagnosis. Moreover, the physician's guess about sex was also wrong. No measurements were required to see that the pelvis, the skull, and the other bones found were all obviously "textbook" male. But, after all, it is the job of the anthropologist rather than the physician to analyze bones. Despite now being headed in the right direction, the bones were never identified. Perhaps, like the vacationing physician, the Ship Rock skeleton had ventured far from home.

Though forensic anthropologists feel that population affinity is a proper subject for forensic work, the issue of race continues to be somewhat contentious among physical anthropologists. Nonforensic anthropologists do not deny the fact of human variability, but they dispute the notion that such variability can be compartmentalized into the traditional "races." The problem that forensic anthropologists have is particularly acute. They recognize that the word "race" is tainted by a long history of abuse and distortion, but the substitute term "ethnic group" suggested by Montagu (1964) and adopted by many anthropologists focuses on the sociocultural dimension and thus is not particularly useful to one who is studying the physical attributes of either soft or hard tissue. Obviously the physical or biological anthropologist is studying physical variability, *not* a cultural perception of that physical variability. Such variability is in evidence throughout the skeleton, even in the developmental differences seen in a study of rib aging by forensic anthropologists Yasar Iscan and colleagues (1987).

In our anthropological tradition of egalitarianism the minute genetic differences producing the morphological variability we apprehend neither "prove" nor necessarily even suggest that any one group is superior to any other—just different. As physical anthropologists, and as professors, we appreciate that both physical and mental abilities vary greatly within any population. The question not convincingly answered at this point is whether there are any systematic mental differences between populations. It is—let's face it—a legitimate question, but studies thus far invariably ask it in such a way that unbiased answers are not possible. This is probably because many of those asking such questions are not so much seeking truth as the promulgation of a point of view antithetical to human happiness and welfare. Interestingly, the bulk of experiential information suggests that the egalitarian position is not only tenable but, on the broad scale, correct.

As forensic anthropologists, we should rise above the sometimes acrimonious exchanges seen and continue our efforts to interpret osteological morphology, then place it in a context that will be understood by those who are not used to thinking in terms of human evolutionary history. Whether one "believes in" race is immaterial. The fact is that we can meaningfully assist law enforcement agencies and others in the difficult quest for the identification of unknown bodies by continuing to ferret out and interpret human variability and presenting our conclusions in a way that will be understood by the populace at large.

Nonacademics do not seem to have a problem recognizing that race exists and that it is a handy way (when not misused) to categorize people. Forensic anthropology is practically (results) oriented, and it certainly doesn't help to narrow down possibilities for an identification by constraining the forensic anthropologist in such a way that all he or she can say is that since a skeleton has been found, somebody is dead. You don't need to be a forensic anthropologist to work that much out. On the other hand, if the forensic anthropologist can tell the police that they should be looking for a white male, in his mid-twenties and about five feet eight inches to five feet ten inches tall, he or she has performed a valuable service by markedly decreasing the search parameters. To refuse to include race (whether one sugarcoats it by calling it "ancestry" or something else) is to deny that we can do something that we can, and to keep our knowledge from the authorities whom it could assist.

The fundamental problem facing forensic anthropologists is that they are assessing the physical variability that characterizes particular populations. They must then translate this skeletal variability into the biosocial context that is the arena within which is found the concept of race held by law enforcement and the public. Thus, in common with other physical anthropologists, the forensic anthropologist deals with attributes that appear most often in one population as opposed to another, but while others may concentrate on the various genetic markers of those populations, the forensic anthropologist is concerned with skeletal markers.

The attribution of "race" to a skeleton has traditionally been accomplished through the evaluation of a long series of nonmetric traits—those which are observed, but not measured. These nonmetric traits yield rather broad categories. It may not be feasible, given the present state of the art, always to make distinctions much finer than the traditional three "major geographic races" with nonmetrics alone. However, nonmetrics has also been used to produce smaller categories (Fig. 4.7).

The use of metric data offers an alternative approach and much hope for the future. For instance, discriminant functions were calculated from eight cranial measurements (Giles and Elliot, 1962). The formulae assign sex to a given skull and plot the scores to place the skull into black, white, or Indian categories. Though based on a limited sample, the Giles and Elliot method is greatly admired, and the technique is still widely used. Since their work, there has been an increased emphasis on measurement. W. W. Howells (1973) collected a series of measurements of 1,927 skulls of seventeen populations from around the world. Using his data, forensic anthropologist Alice Brues devised a computer program that will match an unknown skull to the best fit from the Howells populations. Similarly, forensic anthropologist George Gill and colleagues (1988) found that only six measurements of the midfacial skeleton were sufficient to separate skulls of Indians from those of whites, around 90 percent of the time. Even simple measurements of the cranial base are highly reliable in distinguishing populations (Holland, 1986). Clearly, the continued scrutinization of skeletal characters, along with careful measurement of bones, continues to be a useful approach (Gill and Rhine, 1990). Combined with the increasingly powerful personal computer, analysis of skull measurements has the potential for considerably sharpening our conclusions about the population from which a skeleton is likely to come.

The forensic anthropologist can then look at or measure (or better, both, since the one provides a cross-check for the other) the skull and other relevant structures to ascertain the greatest similarity to known populations. He or she can then translate that information into a form that will be readily understood by the general public. Say, for example, that the skull has the narrow nose, retreating cheekbones, and generally sharp-faced features typically associated (along with many other specific features) with people of European ancestry. It would probably not help the investigation too much for the forensic anthropologist to say, "This skeleton has a galaxy of attributes seen most frequently in individuals of European ancestry." It would be better to say something like "This skeleton is probably white." Of course, one could substitute "Anglo," or "Caucasoid," or whatever other term is most likely to be understood most clearly by the populace in that place. This piece of information will narrow the search for an identity, making the job of the authorities easier and faster. As a consequence, the entire description could read something like this: "The skeleton found yesterday on the west mesa is believed by the police

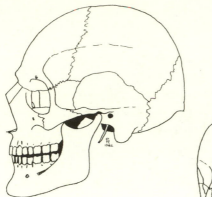

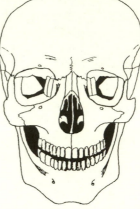

a

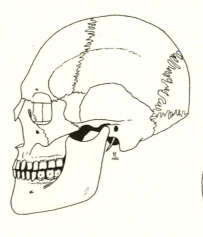

b

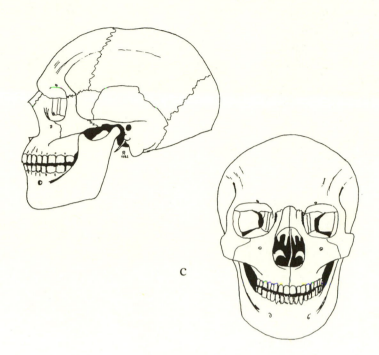

c

Fig. 4.7 Caucasoid (a), Mongoloid (b), and American
Black (c) skulls, illustrating the major differences
between them. (Source: Gill and Rhine, 1990.)

to be a white male in his thirties, close to six feet tall. The remains were found clad in a red and green flannel shirt and Levi's. He is believed to have been dead for between six months and a year. Anyone with information on the possible identity of this skeleton is requested to contact the police." This kind of description is, of course, much more informative than the not-very-helpful "A skeleton was found on the west mesa yesterday. Anyone with an idea who it might be is urged to contact the police."

Other Skeletal Findings

SIDING

In the context of forensic anthropology, the term "siding" has nothing to do with the exterior finish of a house, but is simply an incidental finding of the skeletal analysis: it is the determination of which side of the body the bone is from. While some bones, such as the vertebrae and some skull bones lie along the midline of the skeleton and are single symmetrical bones, the bilateral symmetry found among vertebrates necessitates that some bones, like those of the arms and legs, be paired. With a little practice, left can easily be distinguished from right. The real trick is making sure to say what you mean.

When we look at a skeleton, we generally view it face-on, so that its left is on the observer's right and vice versa. It is altogether surprising how easy it is to hold the bone up in one hand, oriented as it would be on a skeleton that one is facing, and call it as if it came from that opposite side. To the inevitability of death and taxes must be added the inevitability that at some point a forensic anthropologist will say right when he or she means left. It is also likely that this will happen at the most inopportune time. It is a very easy thing to do, but a very difficult thing to explain to a jury. One can imagine a cross-examining attorney, his voice dripping with venom, as he asks, "Now, Doctor, you have called this critical bone a *left* humerus in your report, yet Dr. Dridupp has identified it as a *right* humerus. Which is it?" You say, chastened, "A right." The attorney glances at the jury, the expression on his face revealing to them that he has just neatly caught you in a trap of your own making and is cocking his verbal sawed-off shotgun. "You say you are an expert in skeletal analysis," he croons, then indignantly fires, "and yet you cannot even tell left from right?" Such are the perils of forensic work.

South Carolina forensic anthropologist Ted Rathbun was trying to identify the skeletal remains of a young lady whose skull showed a healed fracture of the right zygomatic arch (the thin arch of bone that can be felt just in front of the ear). The body had been tentatively identified as Fayce Furst, a woman who had fractured her zygomatic arch in a bicycle accident a few years earlier. A number of circumstances made it most likely that the body was that of the young woman with the old fracture, except that all of the hospital records located the fracture on the left side. If the bicyclist really had fractured her left arch, this body with the fractured and healed right arch could not be Ms. Furst.

Not willing to give up so easily, Rathbun sought out x-rays, and much to his delight and relief he found that they showed that it was the *right* arch that had been fractured after all. The identification was made. However, a little carelessness on the part of the physician at the time of treatment or an x-ray technician mislabeling the radiographs nearly sunk an otherwise convincing (and correct) identification.

BONE FRACTURES

In addition to these "big four" of skeletal analysis, summarized in tabular form for easy reference by Bennett (1992), there are several other kinds of information about the individual whose remains are being examined that might come to light during the forensic anthropological investigation. One of the most obvious is broken bones. It is very important to determine whether a bone was broken antemortem, perimortem, or postmortem. In the usual usage, an antemortem fracture is defined as one that the subject survived. The amount of healing that has taken place will depend upon the length of time between the fracture and the person's death. If many months or years have passed, the healing will be complete, but a callus of bone will betray the presence of an old fracture.

In 1977 an elderly man disappeared from Albuquerque with a pocketful of money he intended to use to buy a new Cadillac. The family put out a reward poster, but weeks passed until, on September 11, two men looking for recyclables found a decomposed human body partially buried under weeds, clothing, and other items. The Valencia County Sheriff and OMI investigators went to the scene, south of Belen. In the weeks since death, the body had begun to skeletonize. Excavated and brought to the OMI, the skeleton was quickly cleaned and laid out for examination. The few teeth left promised the possibility of an identification, but no dental records could be found. Though circumstances suggested that this was indeed the long-sought Verdad Tafoya, the OMI was reluctant to release the body until a positive identification could be made. In cases such as this, it is likely that the identification is as alleged, yet some extra effort is required to make sure that no mistake has been made. This demanding verification process is sometimes difficult to explain to next of kin who are suffering with an unredeemed sense of loss.

Fortunately for the investigation, the left seventh and eighth ribs and the right seventh rib had been fractured a couple of inches from the vertebral column. This incident had taken place many years before and the ribs had healed, leaving moderately large bone calluses (lumps) at the fracture sites. Since his name was assumed to be known, the investigators visited the hospital suggested by the relatives to see if some x-rays of a person with that name could be found.

They were rewarded with x-rays of a Mr. Tafoya. In fact, they uncovered several sets of x-rays of several Verdad Tafoyas. One was only three years of age; one had some rib fractures, but not in the same places. All were quickly ruled out. After a couple more days of searching, they finally found some x-rays of an elderly Mr. Tafoya, taken several years previously. Those old x-rays showed the left seventh and eighth and the right seventh ribs recently fractured just a couple of inches from the vertebral column. The skeleton now laid out before us showed those same fractures in exactly the same places, fully healed. That evidence, combined with all of the circumstances, confirmed the identification (Fig. 4.8).

Incidentally, Mr. Tafoya's death was engineered by his young wife, who, with her boyfriend, intended to use her considerable inheritance to support them both in style. She had overlooked an important detail, however, since Tafoya had changed his will the previous month to leave the bulk of his estate to his grandsons. At trial, the prosecution anticipated that the boyfriend would implicate Mrs. Tafoya in return for a reduced sentence. He apparently preferred to have her on the outside if he was on the inside and refused to do so. She was observed leaving town shortly thereafter, presumably for greener pastures—which, in New Mexico, means most anywhere else.

Perimortem fractures, having taken place around the time of death show no healing. However, "perimortem" means only that the injury occurred in the same time frame as the death and not that it is necessarily directly connected with the death. Still, these fractures must be carefully inves-

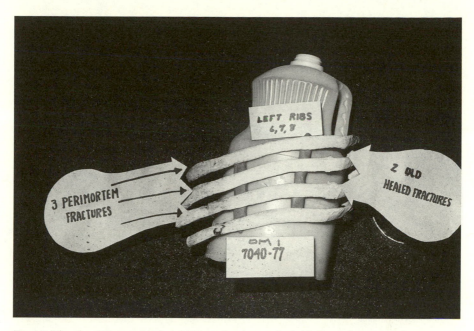

Fig. 4.8. The ribs of 74-year-old Verdad Tafoya, showing two healed fractures (antemortem) on the right, and three perimortem fractures on the left.

tigated since they can offer important clues about the events surrounding the death.

An example illustrating how perimortem fractures may be useful is a case involving an eighteen-year-old female, whose decomposed body was found in the northern part of the state some years ago. At autopsy, the forensic pathologist assumed that the massive injuries to the skull were due to blunt injury and were thus the cause of death, but the extent and nature of these injuries was unclear because of all of the remaining soft tissue. The skull was removed and the soft tissue cleaned away. This is slow, delicate, messy work that nobody really cares to talk about very much. One wishes neither to nauseate the general public nor to make things more difficult for the family at a difficult time by discussing the details of preparation. However, when the nature of a wound is obscured by a mass of sagging, disorganized, decomposing soft tissue, the only way to see what happened is to clean the skull thoroughly and put the pieces back together (Fig. 4.9).

When that had been done for Ernestine Vallejo, it was evident that

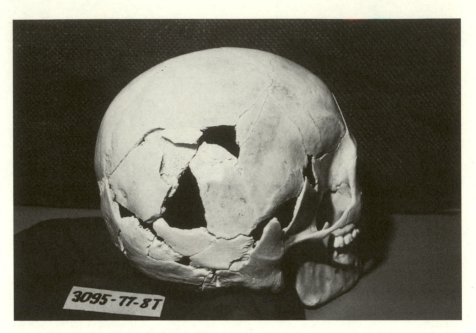

Fig. 4.9. The skull of eighteen-year-old Ernestine Vallejo showing blunt force fractures. The semi-circular defect (indicated by the arrow) shows the curve of the crowbar or claw hammer used in the murder.

two major blows had been struck on her head. A narrow fracture ran almost horizontally across the frontal bone, not far over the eyes. About in the center was a little "divot," about a half-inch long. It was clear that this was a focal point of the impact of a rather sharply edged and moderately heavy weapon. On the lower right rear part of the skull, there was a complex of interconnected fractures. Visible in this seemingly random fracture complex on the reconstructed skull was a smoothly curved fracture line. The flatside curve of the claw of a claw hammer in the lab tool drawer matched the curve exactly. The claw also matched the little divot in the frontal. Did this mean that someone with access to the lab had borrowed that hammer, journeyed over a hundred miles to the north, bashed Ms. Vallejo over the head, and returned the hammer to the drawer? No. A whole range of claw hammers and crowbars could have matching curves and claws. These are "class characteristics," shared by any number of potential weapons. If there had been some imperfection in the weapon that had left a unique mark on the skull, that "individual characteristic" would have been an important factor in linking a particular weapon to a victim.

Just after noon on September 28, 1976, someone stumbled across what appeared to be a shallow burial. Investigators accompanied the Luna County Sheriff to the scene, about thirty miles north of Deming, not far from New Mexico's very productive chile belt. Animals had greatly disturbed the burial, leaving the skull and other bones scattered on the ground. An upper dental plate was with the skull. A "mother's ring" with two stones was still in place on the mostly skeletonized hand, and a button was found nearby. While the body was being transported the 220 miles to Albuquerque for autopsy, the sheriff returned to his office to review his missing persons records. His eyes soon fell on the report for Mrs. Joslyn O'Conner, who had been reported missing by her brother on Mother's Day of 1975. Accompanying her husband from Silver City to his new job in El Paso, Texas, an argument led, according to the husband, to his dropping Joslyn off in Deming and continuing on to El Paso alone.

The forensic anthropology analysis showed the remains to be a white female, in her forties. On the left side of the skull was a small, rounded defect: a depressed fracture of the outer bone table. The outer layer of bone had been hinged downward, compressing the spongy bone beneath it and causing a small linear fracture to appear in the inner bone table opposite the outer fracture. This was a square-edged, well-defined impact, about the size of the heel of a high-heeled shoe or a geologist's hammer. On the rear of the skull was a series of interconnected fractures, which lacked the sort of focal damage seen on the previously described fracture. It seemed that these had been caused by a larger, blunter instrument—a rock, perhaps. Several large rocks were found around the body. It is possible that the fractures were caused by those rocks.

According to the forensic dentist, the remodeling of her toothless upper jaw was what might be expected after more than five years of wearing her upper plate. Dr. Campbell compared records received from Mrs. O'Conner's dentist with the denture found with her. He found that the molds used to make the teeth for the upper plate and the colors used in the teeth were an exact match with those used by the company that manufactured the teeth. Given this, and the fact that the lower teeth matched those in the dental chart, he concluded that there was no doubt that the remains were those of the 45-year-old Joslyn O'Conner.

The dental and anthropological analysis thus confirmed what the sheriff had suspected. The remains found in that shallow grave belonged to Mrs. O'Conner. The fact that the body had been disposed of by burying and the existence of the unhealed fractures in the skull provided ample grounds for some intense questioning of Mr. O'Conner.

These fractures just mentioned are perimortem fractures since they were all distinct and no healing had taken place. Since there were no other major injuries elsewhere on the bodies, it is likely that the defects described were connected to the deaths of both Ms. Vallejo and Mrs. O'Conner. Such analysis takes time to do properly, and using both forensic odontology and anthropology independently gives an extra assurance that the correct identification has been made.

Mrs. O'Conner's skull only needed to be cleaned to expose the defects. Ms. Vallejo's also had to be reconstructed. Having done so, it became possible to show how she had been murdered. The most likely scenario would seem to be that someone struck her first on the forehead with the claw and then smashed the rear of her skull with one or more blows of the flat side of something like a claw hammer or a crowbar. One thing we do know is that whoever did this is still out there.

Then there is the case of Ms. Tilton, a twenty-year-old convenience store clerk abducted at knifepoint, whose body was not found until police were led to the junkyard scene by her murderer. She had been gagged and bound at the wrists and ankles. Thus immobilized, she must have stared in disbelief and horror as he raised a washing machine tub over his head and brought it down on her face—twice. Due to the tremendous force involved and the delicacy of her bones, we could never completely reconstruct the bones of her face.

Twenty-eight-year-old Mrs. DuFrees's burned car was found alongside a road near Santa Fe. No bone fragments were recovered, so investigators tentatively concluded that she had burned up completely in the conflagration. Within a few days, however, a hiker chanced across what appeared to be a human hand protruding from the ground. This sort of thing is not normal, even in Santa Fe, so the police were called and the OMI investigator carefully recovered the decomposing body from its (need I say it) shallow grave.

It is curious, by the way, how many of those attempting to dispose of a body by burying it in a "shallow grave" seem to think that a foot of digging will be sufficient to hide their grisly deed (the word "grisly" being mandatory in writing on this topic). It seems that either some body part is left exposed, or the body is buried so shallowly that dogs or coyotes quickly dig it up. In one case excavated by forensic anthropologist Susan Jimenez on the west side of Albuquerque, a body was buried about a hundred feet from Central Avenue. "Buried" should perhaps read "partly buried," since the entire bloated and decomposing right arm was left exposed. Even attempting to hide the deed by disposing of the body far from town will not prevent its discovery. Most people who dispose of bodies leave them quite close to roads. Many of these roads are so heavily traveled that it would seem well-nigh impossible to bury a body without being seen in the act. (Fig. 4.10)

The badly decomposing body of Mrs. DuFrees was autopsied. The entire middle portion of the left side of the skull appeared to be missing. Upon completion of the formal autopsy, the skull was removed, many of the "missing" pieces having fallen inside, and fully cleaned. It was then reconstructed. When that was finished, there were several defects clearly visible. Above the eyes was a slightly curved defect. There was another, just about centered at the top of her head. Another, on the left side, cut through the zygomatic arch, fractured the skull vault beneath it, and snapped off the rear of the mandible. Three more long defects penetrated the left side of the skull, shattering it and reaching well into the brain. She had been struck at least six separate blows with an instrument with a slightly curved blade. It is likely that the instrument used was a garden shovel, later employed to dig her grave. Taking the extra time needed to clean and reconstruct the skull, it was possible to see exactly what the defects were and from those to deduce the events which had led to her death (Fig. 4.11).

The list could go on, but these should suffice to illustrate the importance of analyzing skeletal defects and how that can best be accomplished by forensic anthropological cleaning and reconstruction. It is by this means that the forensic anthropologist is able to open new doors to the understanding of crime.

Subsequent to death, an individual could sustain postmortem injuries to bone. In general, these are not of medicolegal significance, but it is important to verify their existence so that the unwary or overly enthusiastic will not take them to be important in determination of the cause and manner of death. This kind of defect is seen most often where bones have remained buried long enough to have taken on some staining from the

Fig. 4.10. Susan Jimenez recovering a decomposed "shallow burial" in Albuquerque.

soil and are somewhat weakened by soil acids and the leaching of organic matter from the bone. An unexperienced excavator will often attempt to wrest such bones from the grip of the soil before they are fully uncovered. This careless and uninformed excavation technique can snap and fragment even bones that are in good condition.

In addition to the antemortem fractures described earlier, Mr. Tafoya's skeleton had been so inexpertly excavated that three more ribs and the right femur had been fractured in the process. While ribs are delicate, the femur is such a heavy bone that considerable force would be required to break it. In all of these bones, the fractures were jagged and undoubtedly fresh, so that there was no possibility of confusing them with perimortem ones that might have had a bearing on his death.

The forensic anthropologist's simple solution to reducing postmortem breakage to a minimum is "Let us recover the bones," a request not always honored because of distance or time constraints. To recover old bones in delicate condition, a great deal of time and effort are required. We always like to think that such jobs are best done by those trained in recovery rather than in investigation. Removing such bones from their soil

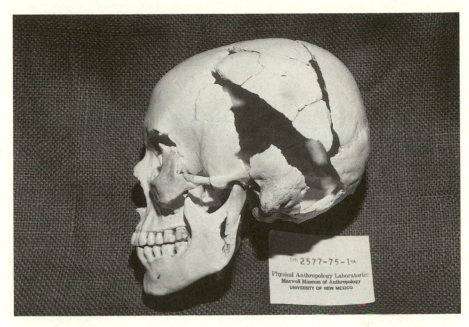

Fig. 4.11. Multiple defects to the skull of 28-year-old Mrs. DuFrees, probably caused by a shovel. At least five separate blows can be seen in this view.

matrix requires cleaning around each bone with a trowel, brushes, and dental picks until it can be lifted free without damage.

Like perimortem fractures, those produced postmortem show no healing. They also have a different pattern of fracturing, since live responsive bone behaves differently from bone that has lost its flexibility. A live bone shows a more active response in developing more radiating fractures from the point of impact than does a dead bone. There is also a color contrast evident in bones that have been fractured postmortem. As the outer layers of bone will have begun to absorb some of the color of their surroundings, and the inside will not, there is usually a dramatic color change from a darker outside to a lighter inside.

The analysis of a skeleton in the medicolegal context is the essence of forensic anthropology. Determination of the specific demographic parameters of that skeleton is the first step toward an identification. Having discussed the principles of skeletal analysis, we can now move to identification.

5

The End of the World

Decomposed Bodies, Autopsies, and Case Reports

A short distance west of the high-plains town of Santa Rosa, a rancher went out to feed his cattle one July morning. Close to a mile above sea level and receiving less than fourteen inches of precipitation a year, this area, cut with arroyos, intermittent streams, and widely scattered postage-stamp ponds and stock tanks, would be regarded by some as the end of the world. Carpeted with short grasses and studded with chollas, this land borders on the old Anton Chico Spanish Land Grant. You don't have to venture far from the road to be impressed by the immensity of the place. Under the endless blue sky, the vestiges of civilization quickly disappear, along with the interstate highway, behind a little dip in the rolling plains. The breezes carry off the sounds of traffic, lending a particularly timeless quality to the grand panorama.

On the way to provision his cattle, the rancher recognized a not very welcome smell, the odor of rotting flesh. Homeward bound, he detoured to locate the source of the smell. He thought perhaps one of his cows had taken sick and died, or maybe it was one of the strange cattle mutilation cases (usually blamed on those pesky extraterrestrials that seem to favor New Mexico) that crops up every once in a while. Coming over a slight rise, a strange sight caught his wary eyes: two lumpy blankets lying on the ground. From those blankets, one green and one pink, arose the odor that had attracted his attention earlier. First came relief, as none of his stock was dead, but then dread: those rope-tied blankets were about the right size to harbor human bodies. He hightailed it back to the ranchhouse and called the Guadalupe County Sheriff, who alerted the local deputy medical investigator. They were both met at the scene by the rancher.

There was no telling how long the bodies had been there, but it must not have been long. The hard yellowish ground betrayed no clue as to how they had arrived, but one thing was sure—they had not walked in. There was no evidence that the murders had taken place at that spot. In fact, other than the blankets and the bodies, there was no evidence to recover. But this made the situation all the more puzzling. With no leads at all, how would it be possible to identify these bodies and find out what had happened to them?

A Windy City Story

A couple in the Chicago suburb of Skokie, like so many parents, did not fully approve of their adopted daughter's companion. A part of their disapproval might have stemmed from the fact that one time when the daughter had promised something to her boyfriend and forgot to bring it, he went to the house to get it for himself. Finding no one home, he let himself in and removed the object.

This would not have been such an issue had the boyfriend possessed a key to the house. When Bernie and Melba Toste returned home to find that their house had been broken into, they summoned the police, but as the investigation continued it emerged that this had, after all, been a "friendly" break-in, so no charges were leveled. Nevertheless, the incident seemed to gel feelings of resentment and unhappiness on the part of the parents.

Apparently the daughter, Francie, also harbored some reciprocal unhappiness with her parents, since before long she and her companion, who we might just call Bill, began to discuss the attractions of moving to Mexico where they could afford to live in high style. They could afford it, that is, if they were able to generate a sizeable number of U.S. dollars to exchange for an even larger number of Mexican pesos. They decided that an easy way to do this would be to sell her parents' house. The only thing standing in the way of executing the plan was Mr. and Mrs. Toste, who had not been consulted.

Francie and her friend Bill decided to solve that nagging little problem by rubbing out her parents. Bill farmed the job out (for a miserly sum) to a friend. That penurious pal, unable to afford any of the expensive high-tech means of despatching unwanted people, selected a hammer as his instrument of annihilation.

Executing the Plan . . . and the Parents

One bright July day in 1982, when Mr. Toste was out of town on business, the Mexican retirement plan was set into action. The murderer was let into the house, and with several well-placed blows to the top of her head, he ended Mrs. Toste's life. The process was rather messy, however, disrupting the superficial blood vessels of the scalp and spattering the kitchen with blood, so while the loving daughter headed to the airport to pick up her father, her companion and his friend set about wiping the kitchen clean.

When he returned home, the unsuspecting victim was set upon by the assassin, who successfully repeated his earlier attack strategy. Mr. Toste put up a bit more resistance but eventually also succumbed. This time, there was even more mess to clean up, but warmed by their success the joyous crew fell to and scrubbed everything down, removing every last drop of blood they could find and tidying the place up. The bodies were wrapped in blankets (green for father and pink for mother) and tied with rope.

Things were going smoothly. The happy couple decided to celebrate their new plutocratic status by visiting some friends and thought that they might simultaneously get rid of the bodies. But a problem surfaced. How could they slip the bodies from the house into the car? The garage was attached but not connected by a doorway. They could simply have carried the bodies out through the frontyard and into the garage, but there was always the danger that a nosey neighbor might become suspicious of these very large and very late green and pink Christmas presents being hustled out of the house. The hammer had been their answer to the first problem and proved to be the answer to the second as well. They smashed a hole in the wall, passed the bodies through it into the garage, and settled them into the trunk of the car.

Hitting the Road

Leaving the hurley-burley of bustling Chicago behind them, Francie and Bill headed south, with saguaro-studded Phoenix as their goal. As they headed south and then west, trees gave way to sagebrush, and the problem of body disposal loomed ever larger. Week-old bodies in the trunk of a car in the middle of summer have a way of reminding one of their presence. There comes a time when just driving a little faster doesn't help.

Nor would it be good manners for houseguests to arrive at their destination with two over-ripe bodies still in the trunk. Turning west on Interstate 40 in Oklahoma, they were struck by the increasingly desolate aridity of the Texas Panhandle. Texas Panhandlers, though (what else could you call them?), think of their little corner of the Lone Star State as about as close as you can get to heaven and still have your feet on the ground. New Mexicans, however, have always been a little leery of their outsized neighbor to the east. In a sentiment still echoed today, a New Mexico territorial governor in the 1830s sadly observed, "Poor New Mexico. So far from heaven; so close to Texas."

Finally, as the last furtive traces of green were shoved aside by towering red buttes and the intensely blazing sun of New Mexico marking the western border of the llano estacado, they came to somewhere quite close to the end of the world. They may have thought, "If this ain't the end of the world, you can see it from here." Passing by phantom Los Esteros Lake and through the narrow oasis of the Pecos River bottoms, they left the town of Santa Rosa five miles behind. Halting at the side of Interstate 40, they opened the trunk, hauled the bodies out, and unceremoniously dumped them a short distance from the road, certain that such remote environs would be unlikely to be visited by *Homo sapiens* in this century. With this weight lifted from their trunk and their minds, they happily sailed on to Phoenix.

MEANWHILE, BACK IN SKOKIE . . .

Unfortunately for the vacationers enjoying the Phoenix sun, the Tostes were well known and well liked. One neighbor, having seen nothing of them for a number of days, was concerned that her phone calls and raps on the door went unanswered. In frustration, she called the police, requesting that they check to make sure everything was all right. You might expect that such calls are unlikely to receive high priority by a large metropolitan police force, which has an ample assortment of injuries, robberies, rapes, murders, and other unpleasantries to concern itself with. As luck would have it though, the call came in as a detective standing near the phone was closing out his shift. The address sounded familiar to him. It was. He was the one who had investigated the earlier break-in at the Toste house. He volunteered to stop and check it out on his way home.

Though there was no answer to his knock on the door, everything seemed to be in order. The accumulation of mail and papers, however, did suggest that nobody had been around for a few days. Being a thorough sort, he walked around the house, making sure that everything was all right, even peering in through the windows. Moving to the edge of the front window, his eyes darted over to the margin of what appeared to be a large, messy, irregular hole in the wall that the house shared with the garage.

Images of supper fading from his head, he placed a few calls and was rewarded with a search warrant. Accompanied by investigators, he returned to the house to ascertain that there was indeed a very large hole battered in the wall and that the car was missing from the garage. Some very thorough investigation turned up tiny spots of dried blood on the undersurfaces of the kitchen chairs, table, and cabinets. It was clear that some dastardly deed had taken place in that very room. Given the circumstances, the investigators quickly hypothesized that one or both of the parents had been murdered and that the body (or bodies) had been spirited away in the family car.

In reviewing his notes from the previous visit to the house, the detective discovered that the daughter Francie had mentioned someone in Phoenix by name during the interview. He got on the phone and gave the Phoenix Police the particulars of the situation, including the name of the acquaintance in Phoenix and the license plate number of the missing car. It was the only lead they had.

Meanwhile, Back in Phoenix . . .

The next morning one of the people residing in the house that the Phoenix Police had surrounded stepped out for a stretch and a breath of morning air. Rubbing the sleep from his eyes, he found that he was staring down the barrel of one of the Phoenix SWAT team's rifles. Those remaining in the house were advised to come forth quickly with their hands in the air. Among them were the daughter Francie and her companion Bill, surprised at having been found but secure in the belief that they were out of reach.

Questioned intently about the disappearance and presumed murder of Bernie and Melba Toste, Bill chuckled, saying that, sure, maybe he and Francie had killed the old folks, but their bodies would never be found. They had been dumped somewhere so remote (after all, what could be more remote than the end of the world?) that the cops could look till the cows came home, but the search would prove fruitless. Without a body, he thought, there was no evidence of murder. He soon discovered that the arm of the law is longer than he had anticipated.

This information was phoned back to the Skokie detective, who got out a map and sat down to see if he could figure out where the end of the world was. Following any of the likely routes to the south would have put Francie and Bill in Oklahoma, where they would logically have taken Interstate 40 west into Arizona. So where was the end of the world? Was it the Sooner State of Oklahoma? No, probably not: there were oil wells, Indians, and cowboys, and not much else there, but it didn't seem quite remote enough to qualify as the end of the world. It would do if there was nothing else, but there might be better prospects. The panhandle of Texas seemed more likely, but those Texans ("Don't mess with Texas" warn the roadside signs) probably wouldn't allow bodies from outside the state to be dumped next to their highways. His circling finger quickly lit on the state of New Mexico. That had to be it. If people think of New Mexico at all, they probably think of it as foreign in some sense, populated with Indians (do they still attack vacationers from the effete East with arrows or do they use rifles?) and Mexicans, harmless enough aside from their penchant for fiery food. Some people east of the Mississippi even think that New Mexico isn't a part of the United States and call to find the currency exchange rate. One New Mexico sports enthusiast hankering for a seat at the 1996 Atlanta Olympics was frustrated by his inability to convince ticket sellers over the phone that New Mexico was a part of the United States. A supervisor was not much more enlightened: "New Mexico, Old Mexico, it doesn't matter. I understand it's a territory, but you still have to go through your nation's Olympic Committee" (Belshaw, 1996).

Once again grabbing the phone, the detective called the New Mexico State Police and asked, "Do you people have coroners, or what?" The New Mexico contact responded more or less, "Oh, no, we have a statewide medicolegal investigation system." This disclosure elicited a huge sigh of relief from the detective, because this meant he would not have to call every one of the thirty-three counties in the state alerting them to be on the lookout for a couple of unidentified bodies dumped somewhere out on the vastness of the desert where they would never be found. He only had to call one number, that of the OMI situated in Albuquerque.

Once in touch with the duty investigator, we can imagine that the conversation went something like this: "You haven't by chance come up with a pair of unidentified bodies dumped by the side of the road in some God-forsaken desert, have you?"

"Let me see now . . . oh, yes, just this afternoon we had a couple of bodies wrapped in blankets come in from alongside the interstate near Santa Rosa. We'll be doing the autopsies tomorrow morning."

"Really? What can you tell me about them?"

"It's an older man and woman, one wrapped in a green blanket and the other in pink, and tied with rope." With some further exchange of information, the detective concluded that those two bodies probably were the missing Bernie and Melba Toste. He advised the OMI investigator that he and a colleague would be in Albuquerque the next morning with all of the medical and dental records of Mr. and Mrs. Toste. If the bodies were indeed the Tostes, those records should be all that would be required for a positive identification. The seemingly insoluble mystery of the blanket-wrapped bodies was about to be tied up as tightly as the bodies themselves had been.

The next morning, they were met at the airport and brought to the OMI, where the autopsy was about to begin. In addition to the forensic pathologist and the usual support staff, this autopsy also brought in the forensic odontologist and the forensic anthropologist. The identification was quickly made on dental grounds, with anthropological findings in agreement. The victims had been dead for nearly two weeks, and though the weather had been somewhat cooler than normal it had still been hot enough to produce a considerable amount of decomposition. This meant that the analysis of the soft tissue, which is the specialty of the pathologist, would provide less information than would otherwise be the case.

Decomposition and Time Since Death

A body begins to decompose as soon as life is lost. A great deal of research has disclosed that the process of decomposition is regular enough that its progress can be used as a means of determining how much time has elapsed in the early stages since death. This is an important—and sometimes critical—matter in establishing the circumstances of death (Stevens and McFeeley, 1987; Micozzi, 1991).

Forensic anthropologists William Rodriguez and William Bass (1983) have found that flies quickly home in on dead bodies. They may even begin laying eggs in the corners of eyes or the mouth of someone who is still alive but unmoving. Given a warm environment these eggs can hatch in a matter of hours. The newly hatched maggots eat their fill, fall off, and pupate. The next generation of flies repeats the process, and within a couple of days in a favorable environment the writhing mass of maggots can almost obscure a body.

Within the first few hours after death, a series of changes begins in the body (Henssge et al., 1995). It will start to cool immediately. This cooling starts slowly, accelerates, then levels off as the temperature of the surroundings is approached. As a general rule, this cooling occurs at the rate of about one and a half degrees Fahrenheit per hour. Although it seems as if there is something particularly heat-draining about touching a dead body, almost as if it were attempting to suck in warmth to compensate for its lack of internal heat, a body cannot get any cooler than its surroundings. The rate of cooling can be affected by the conditions—whether it is lying in sun or shade, and so on. Furthermore, the calculation of time since death can be thrown off if the body was warmer than the normal 37 degrees C (98.6 degrees) in life, due to the presence of a fever or because the deceased had been exercising. Contrarily, if the person's temperature was lowered in life, for example from having been trapped in a walk-in freezer or locked out of the house by an angry spouse on a cold winter night, the core temperature will be lower than expected for the time since death. In short, body core temperature offers only an approximation of the time since death.

While the body's temperature is dropping, another process is at work. This is putrefaction, in which the tissues of the body break down. One of the first stages in that process is rigor mortis, in which the muscles stiffen. Rigor first affects the small muscles of the hands, feet, and face. From there it moves to larger muscles. At the height of rigor, a body may be stiffly suspended by a block under the head and another under the feet. Reaching its maximum development around twelve hours after death, rigor generally passes off after twenty-four. Another change, going on at the same time, is livor mortis. With the heart no longer pumping, blood, under the influence of gravity, settles into the dependent (lowest) parts of the body causing a bluish purple discoloration there. Where the body touches a surface the vessels are compressed, forcing blood out so that any such areas are blanched or lighter than the surrounding tissue. Livor becomes perceptible after about two hours and takes about twelve hours to become fixed. Before that time, moving a body into a different position will cause secondary livor to form. Consequently, an investigator can see whether a body has been shifted from its original position in the first half-day or so by someone trying to cover up a crime. It does happen.

These are the very earliest stages of decomposition. Since most bodies are discovered within the first twenty-four hours after death, the process has not usually progressed much further. However, in a few cases, a person dies alone of natural causes or of an accident or suicide in a house, or when away from habitations. In one case the remains of an elderly Albuquerque man were not found for over a month. An area a few miles from town that the family felt he would have visited was intensively searched. His decomposed body was eventually discovered there, but it was tucked into a little recess in a small arroyo in an area so irregularly contoured and scrub-covered that, as one searcher commented, the body might not have been seen even from ten feet away. Sometimes, a person is murdered and the killer conceals the body so well that it is not found until decomposition is well advanced.

The rate of decomposition and skeletonization is affected by numerous factors: the temperature, access to the body by insects, the burial of a body (even its depth), the activity of carnivores and rodents, trauma, the amount of moisture, the size and weight of the body, embalming, clothing, and soil conditions to name a few (Mann, Bass, and Meadows, 1990). The process may be accelerated by an increase in temperature. This can be produced by exercise just prior to death, infection and fever, exposure to direct sunlight, warm surroundings, heavy clothing, or obesity. On the contrary, decomposition may be decelerated by tight clothing, placing the body in a cool location or on a surface that drains heat from it, or by burial. An increase in altitude will also act to reduce the body's temperature, slowing the process.

Estimates of time since death by forensic anthropologists are mostly based on the appearance and condition of bone and the remaining soft tissue. Elevation, temperature, precipitation, vegetational cover, exposure to the sun, time of year of deposition of the body, the extent of disruption of the body by predators (Haglund, Reay, and Swindler, 1989), and other factors all affect the rate at which the body decomposes and skeletonizes. This means that standards worked out for one area of the country are not always directly applicable in other regions. At the University of Tennessee, Dr. William Bass created a unique research facility that has been the primary source of much of the information on the rates of decomposition and skeletonization used by forensic scientists (Rodriguez and Bass, 1985). (The Tennessee facility is featured with some artistic license in the fiction work of author Patricia Cornwell [1994].) The Tennessee data can probably reasonably be applied to the warmer and wetter regions of the country. For the cooler and wetter regions of the northwest, the study conducted by forensic anthropologist William Haglund and colleagues (1989) in the Seattle area should prove useful. For the desert Southwest, Galloway and colleagues (1989) have done a retrospective study of skeletonization around the Tucson, Arizona, area, which can be applied generally throughout the hotter and drier regions of the country.

Determination of time since death based solely on the condition of the soft and hard tissues is thus difficult and dependent upon the accumulation of a great deal of experience in the area in which one is based. Moreover, as time since death increases, the accuracy of the estimate decreases. Fortunately, there are several parallel analyses that can also shed some light on the time since death. Artifacts accompanying the body and any clothing covering it can both suggest time frames within which the person might have died (Morse, Duncan, and Stoutamire, 1983; Bass, 1984b). Coins, for example, may mark an upper limit, since it is unlikely that the murderer will return to the scene some years later with freshly minted coins to throw off potential later discoverers. The growth of perennial plant roots (Willey and Heilman, 1987) may be used in cases in which more than a year has elapsed.

Forensic entomologists have been able to achieve great accuracy by analyzing the larvae and pupae as well as the insects that are found on the body. Such a determination of time lapse results from a knowledge of the life cycle of the insects involved, as well as the succession of insect types that visit the body as it ages (Rodriguez and Lord, 1993). Using the developmental stages of three species of arthropods found in a Hawaiian case, the time since death could be fixed at between thirty-four and thirty-six days (Goff and Flynn, 1991). In one instance, so many years had passed since death that although entomologist Neil Haskell could not fix the number of years , he could determine the season in which the victim had died.

What This Case Tells Us

In this case, from the end of the world, it becomes clear that the type of medicolegal system in operation in any given region will have a significant impact on the smooth-running and perhaps even the success of the process of identifying remains. There is much to be learned using this case as an example. The oldest organized system of death investigation is the coroner.

Established in 1194, the office of the coroner descends to us from the British system in which the coroner, already a man of substance and importance, was appointed by the crown (hence the original term "crowner") as the king's counterbalance to the powerful sheriff. The coroner's function was to make sure that deaths were investigated and that, perhaps most importantly, the crown received its due from the estate of the deceased. In conducting his office, like the sheriff, the coroner became very wealthy, as some of the money that was on its way to the crown's coffers inevitably managed to stick to his fingers.

The office lost much of its power and prestige on its trans-Atlantic voyage, becoming elective in many states. No longer was the coroner a pillar of society but in some places a postman, or a filling station operator. Some (the ultimate vertical merger of interests) were morticians. As the population increased, the rural countryside was transformed into urban agglomerations, and greater demands were placed upon the office. In the interest of better coming to grips with understanding both the cause and manner of death, municipalities began to insist that their coroners also be physicians. As the personal options for producing death in others continued to proliferate, larger cities began to adopt medical examiner systems, in which the investigation of death was overseen by a board-certified forensic pathologist, one who specialized in the determination of cause and manner of death. Beginning with Maryland in 1939, states across the country slowly began to adopt such systems.

In the case of Mr. and Mrs. Toste, the Chicago detective was relieved when he made his phone call because he learned not only that he would not have to alert every county in the state but also that he was also virtually guaranteed a properly handled death investigation since he would be dealing with a sophisticated medical examiner system headed by a board-certified forensic pathologist. Amateur elected coroners in small thinly populated counties may have hearts of gold, but they rarely also have the medicolegal expertise to make trustworthy judgments on the cause and manner of death. In many cases, they recognize their limitations and arrange with outside agencies to conduct any autopsies.

Cause and Manner of Death

What do the terms "cause" and "manner" of death really mean? There is an important medicolegal distinction between the two. A *cause* of death is an incident that precipitates a series of biological events culminating in death. Take, for example, a man who has been shot in the head. The cause of death here is the gunshot wound. Technically, the *cause* of death would be that gunshot wound, the mechanism being exsanguination (bleeding to death). As you might guess, the causes of death are legion, ranging from the mundane to the truly bizarre. A medical examiner sees them all. A forensic anthropologist sees but a selection, but that selection necessarily includes some pretty strange ones as well.

Is there anything else we need to know about this hypothetical fellow who has been shot in the head? One very important question remains unanswered. That is, as it would be phrased in the vernacular, "Who dunnit?" The *manner* of death is the agency responsible for his death. It may have been the person himself, or someone or something else. Someone may be dead of a gunshot wound suffered as the result of cleaning a weapon he or she thought was unloaded. Here the manner of death might be considered to be insufficient attention to detail but instead is most likely officially to be considered as "an accident." If an individual shoots him- or herself intentionally, the manner is "suicide." If someone else shot the individual, the manner is "homicide," the severity of the crime to be tempered by a determination of intent. Even the matter of intent may sometimes be illuminated by the autopsy. If the most searching examination fails to reveal what or who set the mechanism of death in motion, the manner may be signed out as "undetermined." Only one—and the most common—manner of death is left: "natural." Natural deaths comprise the largest category, making up nearly 66 percent of the total. Most of these do not typically involve the medical examiner to any great degree, since no investigation is warranted. It was only in the raucous days of the Old West—and maybe just the fictional one at that—where death resulting from a gunshot wound was considered natural.

This Windy City story also points up a matter of importance in identification. Although it is always done on television, the visual identification of a decedent by friends or relatives is not relied upon in the most demanding of systems. It is not trustworthy. What you see on television is the nervous identifier being conducted into a large, presumably cold, sterile room. On one wall is a bank of three-feet-square stainless steel doors, seeming to extend up into the ionosphere. Not even bothering to read the name on the end of the crypt, the coroner or medical examiner reaches out, opens a door—invariably one at a convenient viewing height—and rolls out a stainless-steel tray containing a lumpy sheet-covered body. With a deft flip, he throws back the sheet to reveal the face of the victim. The woman (isn't it always the girlfriend?) draws close, stares for a moment, and then breaks into a sob: "Yes, that's John!"

In real life, even the prospect of such a confrontation between the living and the just recently dead fills the potential viewer with dread at what might or might not be there. Many have not seen a dead body before and would prefer not to start now, or at least not under these circumstances. Fear that their loving companion is dead (or, in some instances, desperate hope that he or she is) can distort and attenuate a person's observational powers. There is a somber legion of misidentifications by visual means, and a misidentification is more dangerous than none at all since it shuts off inquiry. It also means that John's body is still out there. When it is eventually discovered, people begin to ask, rather as Groucho Marx used to, "Who's buried in John's tomb?" They also wonder how the authorities could so stupidly get the identification wrong. This creates bad feelings that can be avoided by having the identification of a body done not by relatives or friends stealing a quick glance but by experts following established scientific procedures. The information leading to an identification is typically produced by a forensic autopsy.

The Autopsy

The principal evidence in investigations, such as that of the Tostes' murder, is the body itself and the means for investigation of death is the forensic autopsy. The purpose of the forensic autopsy is to ascertain both the cause and manner of death. An autopsy is a demanding procedure best accomplished in an organized manner to assure that no important steps are left out (Baker, 1967). The forensic autopsy is even more demanding (Knight, 1983; Gantner and Graham, 1990; Spitz, 1993). The standard protocol of the New Mexico OMI specifies the sequence of steps to be taken but allows for alteration according to the specific demands imposed by a particular case. The protocol defines the structure of the procedure, while affording the autopsy team the necessary freedom to capture all of the nuances, the tiny details peculiar to each individual death.

The body is received unaltered from the scene, its integrity assured by the body having been directly transported to the autopsy facility in a body bag sealed at the scene by an investigator who marks the seal with his initials, the date, and time. The seal is broken to start the autopsy, the data on the seal becoming a part of the written record of the process. The bag is unzipped, and the pathologist dictates his or her observations on its condition and appearance of the bag and everything inside. The contents of the pockets are inventoried, listed, read into the record and bagged as evidence. The clothing is removed item by item, with each piece described as fully as possible. The pathologist notes any defects in either the clothing or the body (be they gunshot holes, knife marks, or whatever) and reads labels into the record. The body is then described again, including all scars, indications of surgery, blood smears, and defects. It is turned over so that all surfaces can be clearly seen and described. Photographs and x-rays are taken as appropriate. Trace evidence (fingernail clippings, swabs, and the like) is taken. Then the body is washed and its surface inspected again to find additional information that may have been hidden by blood, dirt, and so forth. In gunshot wounds or stabbing deaths, the defect may be probed before internal organs are removed, to reveal more information about its depth and path. In a complex case involving multiple trauma this external component of the autopsy may literally consume hours before a scalpel even touches the skin.

Then, a Y-shaped incision is made, starting at both shoulders and running slightly downwards to the sternum (breastbone), continuing straight down from there to the pelvis. The skin and muscle are peeled back, and the chest plate (sternum and part of the cartilage binding it to the ribs) is removed. Next, according to various procedures, the organs are removed, one by one or as a complete block, leaving the thoracic cavern empty but for the occasional tiny connective tissue stalactite and a pool of blood around the vertebral stalagmites running through it. Each organ is inspected, weighed, and sectioned, and a sample removed for later histological (microscopic) examination. All of this information is incorporated into the case record. Samples of the vitreous humor (the fluid of the eye), blood, urine, and other fluids are taken for toxicological evaluation.

As the autopsy progresses, the pathologist makes an incision in the scalp, which is pulled back from the skull. An oscillating saw is used to remove the top of the skull, and the brain is removed, weighed, described, sectioned, and sampled. Any defect introduced at or near the time of death having an influence on the course of death is carefully examined, and all preexisting conditions that may have contributed to that person's death are also noted.

It may be that a death resulted from a person having fallen asleep at the wheel of his or her car and smashing into a bridge abutment, but he or she may have driven into it intentionally or have been the victim of a heart attack. An autopsy is necessary to find out which of these scenarios is the real one, since the manner of death in such a case would have been, in order, accident, suicide and natural.

After all the organs have been examined, if there are no other special procedures to follow, the organs are replaced in the body cavity, the skull-cap is replaced, and all incisions are sewn up. Making the incisions in the manner described makes it possible for an open-casket funeral to be conducted without any of the observers being aware that an autopsy has taken place. By slightly altering the Y-shaped incision, even a family's desire to clothe the deceased in a low-cut gown can be accommodated.

As described, this is a more or less standard autopsy, this portion of it revolving around the forensic pathologist. If the body is unidentified or there are other matters at issue, the services of other forensic specialists may also be required. If the body is decomposed, burned, or skeletonized, the organs and organ systems that the pathologist is trained to evaluate are compromised or missing, and a forensic anthropologist may be (should be!) consulted. Depending upon the circumstances of the death, a phalanx of other experts might also be involved, but most of them, such as the forensic engineer, crash analyst, psychiatrist, and others are less concerned with the details of the autopsy than the circumstances the person was in at the time of death.

While acknowledging the roles of the many people with specialized knowledge that can contribute to the resolution of a case, this book concentrates on the work of one of those experts—the forensic anthropologist, whose job it is to look at the skeleton, or its image, on x-ray film. Since the forensic autopsy is so rigorous, the input of numerous experts may be required to resolve a case. Other members of the forensic team include the forensic odontologist, who looks at the details of tooth shapes and the dental repairs done during the deceased's lifetime. Those dental restorations and replacements, when charted and compared to antemortem dental records (made by the victim's dentist), will often lead to a positive identification. The forensic pathologist may also call on the services of a fingerprint specialist for a comparison with available records. Another expert who is usually brought in is the forensic toxicologist, who assesses the "poisons" or foreign chemicals present in a body at death. Depending on the requirements of the case, other experts will be summoned as necessary.

In complex, difficult, or vexing cases, an expert may have to revisit the remains, checking on specifics, necessitating much lab time and visits to the library to confirm details and make comparisons with other, similar cases. This is not to suggest that an autopsy should routinely be redone. Indeed, like an archaeological excavation, an autopsy necessarily destroys some of the evidence and its context. The best result is achieved by performing an autopsy correctly so that it does not have to be redone. Not to do so is to create new questions. For that reason each one is demanding and time-consuming, but an autopsy properly done *is* done.

Of course, on occasion, new information surfaces after the autopsy has been performed and the body buried, or there may be allegations that the autopsy was inadequate or improper. In those cases, it may be necessary to exhume the remains in order to collect further information or to confirm that an observation was made correctly. Since a pathologist has already autopsied the body, the organs will have been sectioned and sampled, leaving much less information to be pried from the body the second time around. However, a second autopsy can, at the very least, reveal whether the original one was executed properly and thoroughly.

The classic example of this is the autopsy of President John F. Kennedy, assassinated in November 1963. It was not performed by forensic pathologists. Lacking experience in forensic autopsies, even the most well-meaning physician can make serious errors, especially if being pushed to hurry the job or to take shortcuts. To be honest though, it is probably difficult for those performing an autopsy to retain their serenity and attention to detail when the autopsy suite is awash with armed and nervous FBI and Secret Service agents pacing about and looking at their watches. Having been denied a searching, time-independent autopsy of Kennedy's body, questions linger unanswered, and the best evidence—the remains of the dead president—is not available for reanalysis.

Inevitably, some questions cannot be fully answered by reference to autopsy notes, photographs, and sketches, particularly where those data are incomplete. That is why the legacy of the Kennedy autopsy is confusion. Had the autopsy been done properly by trained forensic pathologists and other forensic specialists, many of the matters still at issue would probably have been settled. Subsequent reexamination of notes and photographs made at the time of autopsy, both by the physicians performing the work and by an independent group of forensic experts, has done little to dissipate this muddled legacy. A member of that team of experts allowed access to autopsy records in the National Archives, Smithsonian forensic anthropologist J. Lawrence Angel, did his best to clarify damage to the skull caused by the bullet. Even this was not sufficient to resolve the matter, since he, too, was denied access to the primary autopsy evidence, the body itself. In short, the questions will remain unanswered unless the body is exhumed for a searching probe by trained and experienced forensic experts. Indeed, even exhumation may not now shed any light on the case because of the nature of the original autopsy and the passage of time. Fortunately, the government has taken steps to assure that this sort of mistake will not be repeated. There is now a standby forensic team, ready to perform a proper autopsy should the need ever arise again.

The Discovery of Bodies

Yet another matter raised by this Skokie story is the discovery of bodies. In this instance, the slayers were certain that they had disposed of the bodies in a place so remote that no one would find them, and that even if found they could never be identified. Of course, people do disappear, and decades can pass without their remains being found, but in this case the Phoenix-bound couple was seemingly so convinced that New Mexico was a totally uninhabited wasteland that they didn't bother to put more than a couple of hundred feet between the blanket-wrapped bodies and an interstate highway. But even "wastelands" are not immune to the touch of a human foot. The rancher with whom this chapter opened was engaged in a routine task, the provisioning of his cattle, when he discovered Mr. and Mrs. Toste. Within only twelve days of their murder, their bodies were found and the analysis begun. "Forever" may not always be very long.

On the other hand, only about forty miles farther west, near the same interstate highway where these bodies were found, another body would be slid under a tree one wintry evening six years later. That body would not be found until a year and a half had passed, and then only due to the help provided by an informant. In the Green River serial homicide case near Seattle, thirty-six bodies were found over a four-year period, starting in 1982. Bodies were discovered between three days and thirty-two months after their disappearance. Identification required as little as a day and as much as twenty-six months (Haglund, Reay, and Snow, 1987).

Of course, some bodies never will be found. The victim will fall to the depredations of coyotes and dogs and, in some regions, the drying and flaking of bone induced by the merciless sun and harsh soil conditions. But more often than not, bodies are discovered—eventually—and, even after many years, the combined talents of a forensic anthropologist and an odontologist are likely to produce an identification.

The Case Report

The penultimate step in forensic work is the case report. Most medical examiners have a standard autopsy protocol, a procedure that establishes what will be done and the precise order in which the steps are performed. Forensic anthropologists are also under an obligation to report their findings in a timely fashion to the agency that has requested their aid. In the Panglossian best of all possible worlds, this would mean that the forensic anthropologist would wheel from the lab bench to the keyboard to complete the report immediately after the analysis. However, since most forensic anthropologists are also university people, other obligations may intervene. Inasmuch as the report is of importance to the agency's people, however, no effort should be spared put it into their hands as soon as possible.

There is a considerable amount of discussion among forensic anthropologists about just what the report should include. Since the skeletal analysis is part of the evidence pertaining to a case, it should represent accepted standards of language and offer clear and unambiguous conclusions. Some forensic anthropologists advocate a terse, crisp, almost telegraphic style for the official report—a very concise statement of what was found and the conclusions. Language is very important. Since the report is the only means we have for conveying our observations and thoughts to others, that communication should be crisp, precise, accurate, and grammatical. In reading over the reports of others, many find themselves put off by poor language and misspelled words. Such writing leaves one with a residual feeling that the writer was so hurried or uncaring as not even to bother to reread the document. One of my favorite examples of fractured writing is an investigator's report from the early days of the OMI.

This case concerned a severely decomposed body found in the mountains east of Albuquerque. A detective with the Albuquerque Police Department had some rather specific ideas about who this body might be. The investigator summarized those as follows:

> the body could be one of a possible five persons known to be missing in that approx. area, they are as follows:
>
> 1. One of three Mexican-Americans that an individual from California who was passing thru Albu. and stopped to camp killed approx. 8 months prior. He stated that he had shot three men who were down the road from him breaking horses who attempted to assault him. He states that he shot the three men with a .44 mag. pistol and dumped in another place in the mountains. He was unsure as to the exact place dumped.
>
> 2. The body of a male who approx. 8 mo. ago shot his girlfriend, a companion of the girl, and another man in Albu. who drove on the back road of Crest and whose auto was found pushed off road due west of the place the body was found over the next ridge.
>
> 3. A possible Ralph Camper, 20/M/Cauc. who was wearing a blue denim jacket, blue denim pants, and midcalf brown work boots with crepe soles (white) who disappeared on 12–2–74. When APD [Albuquerque Police Department] officers investigated his trailer house they discovered it to have been completely ransacked with blood stains and spatteres all over the front room. His auto was found by the Mexican Federal Police in Juarez, Mexico approx. 4 months ago being used as a taxi.; there was evidence that it had been in an accident.

While bad writing may be difficult to define, one can say of it as the Supreme Court observed of pornography, you can recognize it when you see it. Indeed, any comment on this writing sample would be akin to gilding the lily; it speaks for itself. With the long description of clothing for Mr. Camper, the investigator clearly thinks he has a live possibility for the identification. Indeed, the clothing described for Mr. Camper matches exactly that found on the body, as described on the first page of his report. Incidentally, only fragments of the skull were found. It had apparently been shattered by massive blunt trauma and most of it washed downstream from the body as it fell apart during decomposition. There were no teeth, but an identification was eventually made by comparing the features of the pelvis, including a spina bifida occulta (an unusual narrow opening on the back of the vertebra) to those seen on an antemortem x-ray of Mr. Camper.

While dwelling on bad examples, we have probably all read investigators' reports asserting that an arm was "decapitated." Also somewhat puzzling is the speculation of one investigator that a body found wedged into a culvert had "been pushed or pulled in."

Coming from an academic background, forensic anthropologists are always tempted to include citations and a bibliography as one would for any formal paper, but most agree that, for a variety of reasons, this is not appropriate or even desirable in a forensic report. Of more pressing concern is the audience for which the report is written. If the recipient is another forensic scientist, the use of proper anatomical terms without explanation is reasonable. If, on the other hand, the report will be read by sheriffs or law enforcement people, it is best to eschew the fancy stuff. The purpose of the report is to convey information, and that purpose is not met if the findings are served up in such a highfalutin form as to be opaque to the reader.

For the sake of the record, however, a proper, unbiased, objective scientific report should be prepared for every case, with all of the precise anatomical details needed for reference, should it come to trial, an event that might not occur until years later. Even the best of memories can fail in critical small details with the passage of time and the continued onslaught of cases. If the recipient of the report is without an anatomical background, a summary report can be distilled from this complete scientific report. It is crucial that the forensic anthropologist adhere to accepted standards of analysis, with age and stature (for example) estimated within realistic and justifiable ranges. Spurious accuracy is likely to lead to uncomfortable confrontations in the courtroom.

At the very least, any report should contain a statement setting forth the chain of evidence. Next should come an inventory of the material received and its condition. Then, say some, there should be a series of terse statements setting forth the conclusions about age, sex, race, stature, time since death, ante-, peri-, and postmortem trauma, and any other matters addressed in the analysis. If one follows this less-than-one-page practice of report writing, it should conclude with a statement confirming that notes and full details of the analysis are on file, so that if questions arise people will know where to look.

A report so brief as to give neither a summary of what was done and what its conclusions are based on may be taken as evidence that not very much was done. An example of this kind of brevity is a report by a forensic anthropologist who is infrequently consulted. His report, on a badly burned body, runs fewer than a hundred words. It offers no details of what features were observed and how they were evaluated. What did he see? Did he properly judge the significance of those observations? It is impossible to say.

The opposite point of view is that the forensic anthropologist's report should contain every detail of the analysis, what was looked at or measured, the results, and the interpretation of those results. The logic here is that since the report constitutes part of the case file, it may be reviewed by lawyers, pathologists, and perhaps other forensic anthropologists in preparation for the trial. The report should thus contain sufficient information to allow any other forensic anthropologist to understand exactly what was done, how it was done, and how the conclusions have been reached. Such a reviewer is unlikely to be able to see what the original investigator observed since the evidence will probably have been buried by that time. If called to testify, he or she can verify that the examination was conducted according to accepted practices and that the results are correct. Unless that is not so.

Any case can come to trial. Even if the forensic anthropologist who worked on a case is not required to appear in court, the substance of his or her report will be entered into evidence. Consequently, prudent forensic anthropologists behave as if they will have to testify about every case. In essence, they operate under a fear that anything they say may come back to haunt them on the stand—and it may. This also means that they must always be careful never to push any data beyond its natural breaking point. It is true in forensics just as in real life that nobody is listening until you make a mistake.

Does this mean that speculation of any sort is forbidden? Again, there is room for disagreement. Some feel that speculation about any matter should never be engaged in, as this will surely provide grounds for misunderstandings if not attack in court. Others feel that speculation is acceptable as long as it is clearly labeled as such. In general, however, the safest course is to confine speculation to oral communications between the forensic anthropologist and the agency he or she is working for. There is sometimes a wish to make one's predictions a part of the record, but it is probably best to avoid the thin ends of limbs.

6
Forensic Anthropology

A Short History

Several books have been written for the general audience about the larger world of forensic medicine. A couple of now classic books were written by British forensic pathologists: Sir Sydney Smith's *Mostly Murder* (1959) and Keith Simpson's *Forty Years of Murder* (1978). Simpson, whose judgment has been said never to have been proven wrong in a murder case, has often been described as a modern Sherlock Holmes. America's "Coroner to the Stars" Thomas T. Noguchi, with Joseph D. DiMona, penned *Coroner at Large* (1985), which discusses a number of famous Hollywood deaths. Noguchi also has an entry in the popular world of the fiction murder mystery. One reason for the flood of books is intense reader interest in stories of untimely demise and mayhem, which seem to appeal even to those of gentle dispositions. Many such readers probably have fond recollections of the television show *Quincy*, in which the hero, a forensic pathologist, was a real Renaissance man, doing much of the investigation, the autopsy, the lab work, and anything else needed to solve the case—which he always did. The real world of forensic medicine is much more compartmentalized and specialized, and not every case is solved. A standard reference written for the professional, and providing the gritty details of death investigation, is *Spitz and Fisher's Medicolegal Investigation of Death* (Spitz, 1993).

Forensic anthropology is a part of the world of legal medicine, and though the number of its practitioners is growing rapidly, it is still a small field, with just over two hundred in North America, including advanced students. Despite this, several popular books have been published on the subject—Joyce and Stover (1991), Ubelaker and Scammell (1992), and Maples and Browning (1994)—perhaps because forensic anthropologists have a way of getting involved in interesting cases. There are also two edited volumes written by and for forensic anthropologists: Ted A. Rathbun and Jane Buikstra's *Human Identification* (1984) and Kathleen J. Reichs' *Forensic Osteology* (1986). Numerous fictional works have flowed from the pen of anthropologist Aaron Elkins, whose fictional hero Gideon Oliver ("America's skeleton Detective"), is a forensic anthropologist. Elkins has created a lively and realistic view of forensic anthropology at work, with information gleaned from practicing forensic anthropologists. However, Gideon's escapades and constant flirtation with death are not typical of the day-to-day activities of forensic anthropologists, who lead much less hair-raising lives. Identifying aircraft crash victims, bodies found in burned buildings or cars, bloated green corpses discovered in remote areas, or piles of bones that the authorities aren't sure are even human are cases typical of forensic anthropology. In fact, the forensic anthropologist is sometimes not brought in until all of the other, "more common," avenues of investigation have been fruitlessly explored.

But wait a minute. We are getting ahead of ourselves. What has this focus on recent deaths to do with anthropology? It may be useful to remind ourselves that American anthropology consists of four rather disparate fields of study welded together like one of those fanciful junkyard extravaganzas seen in frontyards in artsy neighborhoods. In most of the rest of the world, these four are regarded as separate fields of study. They are ethnology, the study of the behavior of living peoples; linguistics, the study of the evolution and function of language; archaeology, the study of peoples no longer living by excavation of their architecture and artifacts; and physical (or biological) anthropology, the study of human anatomy, variability, and evolution.

Most physical anthropologists begin their studies with a focus on the human skeleton. Some apply that knowledge to understanding the ways in which populations of our immediate ancestors vary from one another, the sorts of diseases they had, and how those diseases affected their lives. Others branch off from human anatomy to work on the anatomy and behavior of apes and monkeys. Still others use their knowledge of the human skeleton as a stepping stone to understanding the skeletons of our most ancient fossil ancestors and the emergence of *Homo sapiens* from those primitive forbears.

Forensic anthropologists have simply bent the study of skeletons in the opposite direction: they use what they have learned about bones to identify and analyze contemporary skeletons whose identity and circumstances of death are unknown or are questionable in some way. That means that individuals whose bodies were not discovered until they had begun to decompose, or who were burned "beyond recognition," or who had become mummified or skeletonized become the object of attention for the forensic anthropologist. Forensic anthropologists may also work with "fresh" remains where important information can be gleaned from a study of their bones—either the bones themselves or their images as seen radiographically. In each of these cases (and others as well), the principal source of information about the individual is the skeleton; the soft tissues usually analyzed by forensic pathologists have lost most of their fact-yielding potential due to the effects of time, environment, or fire.

But this branch of anthropology is more than just the study of bones in a forensic context. It may, and often does, involve the search of an area for remains, followed by their recovery. A given case may call on the taphonomic experience of a forensic anthropologist to ascertain how bones have been scattered and partly consumed by carnivores, birds, rodents, or humans, or by the action of water. It might also require the reconstruction of complete bones from their shattered fragments. In addition, the forensic anthropologist may be thrown into contact with a grieving family. Finally, every case handled has the potential for drawing the forensic anthropologist into court as an expert witness. In short, forensic anthropology is much more than applied osteology.

In 1980, the New Mexico State Penitentiary suffered a disturbance in which large sections of the buildings were severely damaged by inmate-set fires and thirty-three prisoners died—although in the immediate aftermath that number was unknown. There were stories of bodies being "stacked like cordwood" on the stage of the burned-out gymnasium. Other areas had also been torched. To ascertain whether any of the rumors were true, and to discover whether there were other bodies hidden under the drifts of ash, forensic anthropologists were called to the scene. Who better to look for bones blackened and fragmented by fire than those who know bone best? When news of this excursion became general, one critic huffed, "Anthropologists? Why anthropologists?" But you already know the answer: forensic anthropologists were there because they are the ones who study bones and know what effect fire has on bodies.

In effect, forensic anthropologists are called when the more commonplace analyses can provide but little information. Given the passage of time or the impact of fire on bodies, the muscles, the organs, and all of the other structures will have become so degraded that they provide almost no information, even to skillful and highly trained experts trained in other specialties.

Nobody can be an expert in everything, an important fact to remember in medicolegal investigation. This is because the final arrow in the medicolegal quiver is courtroom testimony. The reason why allied fields are lumped together as "forensic medicine" is that they include an obligation to impart and interpret one's findings to a jury when called to do so. The job of the expert witness is neither to convict nor free a suspect. The jury must balance all that it has heard in order to render a verdict. One is thus advised to draw the boundaries of one's expertise precisely and accurately so as to avoid misleading the jury and imperiling an otherwise pleasant visit to the witness stand.

Many people seem to be fascinated by the work that forensic anthropologists do. To the uninitiated, the extraction of information regarding someone's age, sex, and so on from the skeleton seems akin to magic. Yet, curiously, as Rodney Dangerfield would complain, they "don't get no respect" from their colleagues. Their anthropological peers shrug off forensic anthropology as "mere applied skeletal biology" that anyone who knows bones can do. Worse, being practical and applied, some anthropologists argue, it is not theoretical; and anthropology without theory is like morning without coffee. Lacking a theoretical component, they say, forensic anthropology is not a serious field—it is not really academic at all. While it is true that theoretical osteology is not the number one issue for forensic anthropologists, they are constantly concerned about the significance of the skeletal traits they observe and they do try to place their findings within the wider context of human evolution. Yet, their main concern must always be the application of their knowledge to human remains in a medicolegal context.

Nor do forensic anthropologists receive much admiration from their medical colleagues. The latter, being physicians, have taken anatomy in medical school, and even though they do not normally encounter clean dry bones, they certainly know them when they see them. To think that a physician, with all of that medical training, could not also analyze a skeleton is ludicrous, and the medical community seems to feel that if you were to give a forensic pathologist a copy of the seminal reference book in forensic anthropology, Krogman and Iscan (1986), he or she would be able to do his or her own forensic anthropology. This notwithstanding, there is something to be said for experience. Even the most highly educated and motivated forensic pathologist probably sees no more than a few dozen skeletonized cases in his or her professional lifetime, and those are not examined in the detail or from the perspective that forensic anthropology demands. The average forensic anthropologist will have studied several dozen skeletons as an undergraduate—and hundreds, perhaps thousands, more since. Having examined that many skeletons, the forensic anthropologist sees things that the untrained eye neither perceives nor is capable of evaluating.

Though a new discipline, forensic anthropology has carved a niche for itself, one disturbingly misunderstood by those anthropological and medical practitioners on its opposite borders. In the interest of spreading some enlightenment and perhaps some appreciation, it may be valuable to cast an eye back down the trail to see something of its origin.

A Short History

What follows here is not intended as a definitive and comprehensive history of forensic anthropology. It is, at best, a brief, abbreviated chronology. A full history would certainly be possible, particularly since the origins of the field are so recent, but that recounting will be left for someone else. Forensic anthropology has been largely an American enterprise, though it is beginning to spread more widely. Excellent summary articles have been written on the topic by Kerley (1977, 1978), Snow (1982), and Iscan (1988). As Ubelaker has observed (Ubelaker and Scammell, 1992), the history of forensic anthropology lends itself to division into three stages. The first of those covers the formative years, starting in the early nineteenth century and ending in 1939.

People seem to delight in tracing the origins of a field of study into the dimmest reaches of recorded history. One forensic anthropologist, tongue planted firmly in cheek, has suggested that the origins of forensic anthropology can be found in biblical times. A more common origin myth among forensic anthropologists is that the field began with the Parkman case in 1849. The story of the demise of George Parkman at the hands of fellow Harvardite, John White Webster (who owed the well-to-do Harvard benefactor Parkman a considerable sum of money) has been told to death, yet a quick summary may be useful. To put the matter in context, a bevy of expert witnesses gave testimony, including Oliver Wendell Holmes, anatomist, dean of the Harvard Medical School and father of the Supreme

Court justice who bore the same name. Another star witness was Harvard professor of anatomy, Jeffries Wyman, who became the first curator of the Peabody Museum of American Archaeology and Ethnology in 1866. Wyman and Holmes concluded that the dismembered remains found in Webster's privy, tea chest, and stove were Parkman's. The evidence was presented in a sensational trial in Boston in March 1850, at which the jury found Webster guilty. Before he gained further fame by becoming the first Harvard professor to be hanged, he confessed to the deed.

Others trace the origins of forensic anthropology to the semiscientific work of Cesare Lombroso in the last quarter of the nineteenth century. While Lombroso employed anthropometry (measurement) as a means for identifying criminals, his work was imbued with a host of presumptions about criminality. He was also guilty of the very nonscientific practice of fitting his data to his conclusions, a practice viewed with little sympathy today in scientific circles.

Smithsonian emeritus anthropologist T. Dale Stewart placed the beginnings of the field with the sound, scientific work of bald, bearded Thomas Dwight, an anatomy professor at Harvard in the late nineteenth century (Stewart, 1979). Unlike Wyman, Dwight was an anthropologist, who focused on human skeletal anatomy and concerned himself with many of the same osteological problems that remain matters of forensic anthropological attention: the accurate evaluation of age, sex, and stature from the skeleton. He conducted some of the earliest quality research on those topics, and this focus on skeletal variability is part of what shifted human skeletal analysis away from anatomy and into anthropology. Dwight also participated in some medicolegal investigations, solidly pointing the way ahead for forensic anthropology.

Stewart sees George Dorsey, a Harvard alumnus and curator at the Columbian Field Museum in Chicago, as Dwight's direct intellectual spawn. Dorsey's fame rests principally in his landmark testimony at the Leutgert trial in 1897. He identified tiny bits of bone found in a vat as the parts of Mrs. Leutgert which had not been turned into soap by her husband Adolph Leutgert, a sausage manufacturer (Snow, 1982). (It is strange that Leutgert was so intent on making his late missus dissolve into mush that he overlooked a golden opportunity to make the evidence disappear by incorporating bits of her into other Chicagoans' bratwurst.) After this stunning debut as a witness, Dorsey turned his attention elsewhere. Not only was he the first "forensic anthropologist" to testify in court, he was also the first to suffer the slings and arrows of his colleagues for stepping so visibly out of the cloistered academic world. Joyce and Stover (1991) offer an excellent review of this formative period in forensic anthropology.

Upon close reading, neither the Parkman nor the Leutgert case would stand up to the scrutiny that such cases would receive in a court these days. Neither of the expert testimonies meets contemporary standards for a positive identification. This is reassuring in a sense, since much has been learned about the fine details of human skeletal anatomy in the past 150 years. The standards of evidence have also become much more demanding, which should be of some comfort to those innocents who are tried on faulty or mishandled evidence.

At this point in the history of forensic anthropology, the trail suddenly grows cold. There are occasional little flares of interest, such as H. H. Wilder and Bert Wentworth's *Personal Identification* (1918) and some minor publications by Paul Stevenson from the 1920s through the 1950s. T. Wingate Todd was also gathering and publishing data on skeletal variability in this time period. He amassed important information on pubic symphyseal aging and, with Lyon in 1924, aging by suture closure. However, his interest was directed toward prehistoric Indian skeletons rather than modern ones. In fact, the major figures in physical anthropology in the first five decades of the twentieth century had neither an interest in nor anything to say on the subject of skeletal identification, as what is now called forensic anthropology was then usually called. Nevertheless, nearly all were involved to some extent.

Ubelaker and Scammell (1992) note that Earnest Hooton, an important figure in the development of American physical anthropology, examined some dozen cases over a thirty-year span, but never published on any of them. They also recognize the work of Ales Hrdlicka, the first physical anthropologist hired by the Smithsonian in 1903. He did casework for the FBI, but, like Hooton, never published anything about that work. As Kerley (1978) succinctly put it, "The list of physical anthropologists who have been engaged in medicolegal activities is a long and impressive one that includes most of the major physical anthropologists of the first half of the twentieth century." For all of them, it was a very minor matter, however. Maybe every couple of years, a sheriff would arrive with a beer carton full of bones to look at, but none of these anthropologists actively pursued forensic work. There was not enough of this activity to conceive of it as a specialty focus in the first half of the twentieth century.

One person who did finally focus on this type of work was Wilton M. Krogman. In 1939, he produced his short "Guide to the Identification of Human Skeletal Material." Its publication is now regarded as the watershed event that brought to a close the formative years of forensic anthropology and ushered in an era of consolidation. In just under thirty pages, he alerted both the FBI and other readers of the *FBI Law Enforcement Bulletin* to the potential for human identification from the skeleton. As Stewart recalls (1979), there really was nothing else in print on the topic of human skeletal identification in those early years besides Krogman's brief but critically important paper. It was about that time, says Snow (1982), the FBI discovered a "nest" of anthropologists conveniently located right across the street at the Smithsonian. Before long, puzzling boxes of bones received from around the country by the FBI in Washington began to be shuttled across the street. The Smithsonian's physical anthropologist, Ales Hrdlicka, gamely shouldered this burden until his death in 1942. His curatorial replacement was his student T. Dale Stewart, who continued the FBI work. When J. Lawrence Angel arrived in 1962, the forensic work shifted to him and finally to Douglas Ubelaker in 1977.

With the outbreak of World War II, anthropologists of all sorts were pulled out of the ivied towers and into war-related research. Among the contributions made by physical anthropologists was the design both of uniforms and equipment. These efforts continue to this day at Wright-Patterson Air Force Base in Ohio and the U.S. Army Natick Research, Development, and Engineering Center in Natick, Massachusetts.

A more relevant focus was on the identification of the skeletonized remains of war dead. While this work was carried out by Europeans in their military theater, it was performed by an odd-sounding combination of morticians and academics in the Pacific theater. The U.S. Army set up a lab in Japan, moved it to Thailand, and finally settled in Hawaii. Establishing the Central Identification Laboratory near Honolulu (CILHI) in 1947 brought anthropologist Charles E. Snow into the employ of the U.S. Army, beginning a long and fruitful association between the military and forensic anthropologists. He took on the work of military identification for physical anthropologists (Snow, 1948). When his leave of absence from the University of Kentucky expired in 1949, he was replaced by Mildred Trotter. Her hard-won battle to convince the army that research was necessary in order to accomplish the identification with which she was charged resulted in the publication of data for the determination of stature. This large sample produced tables and formulae that are still being used for that purpose today (Trotter and Gleser, 1952).

With the end of the Korean War in 1953 the army went to Stewart, asking what needed to be done in the way of further research on war dead. Stewart recommended that research into the determination of age from the skeleton be undertaken. The following year, he was brought to the new Identification Laboratory in Kokura, Japan, for six months, to collect the necessary data. Assisted by anthropologists Ellis R. Kerley and Charles P. Warren and a small staff, he collected detailed observations on 450 skeletons. Data analysis was turned over to Thomas W. McKern. Published by the U.S. Army (McKern and Stewart, 1957), this study set new standards for understanding the details of skeletal maturation. It also supported a revision and extension of Trotter's earlier work on stature estimation (Trotter and Gleser, 1958).

The end of World War II saw the bulk of anthropologists returning to the halls of academe, largely abandoning the practical for the academically sanctioned theoretical, but many of those who had had a taste of the real world of identification were not content to vegetate in the rarefied world of theory. As we have seen, they formed one nucleus around which the field of forensic anthropology began to coalesce. The other nucleus was academic.

In addition to those who have or who will be mentioned, others who were teaching osteology and contributing in other ways to what would become forensic anthropology included Frederick S. Hulse at the University of Arizona, Theodore D. McCown at the University of California at Berkeley, Georg K. Neumann at the University of Indiana, Daris Swindler at the University of Washington, and James E. Anderson at the University of Toronto. Although these names may not come immediately to mind when one thinks of forensic anthropology, each of these skeletal biologists had some influence on the development of the field. Their influence was primarily through the production of students who were attuned to the delicate nuances of skeletal analysis and who went on to practice the arcane science of forensic anthropology. But with no formal training—and not even a real identity—forensic anthropology developed at a slow pace through the middle of the twentieth century.

In 1940, Alice M. Brues completed her Ph.D. at Radcliffe. Like many other anthropologists, she devoted her talents to aiding the war effort. She worked as an assistant statistician at Wright Field in Ohio, where her duties centered on the development of anthropometric data to establish standard dimensions for cockpits and other military equipment. During this period, she authored a number of in-house reports. In 1945, Brues returned to the East Coast as a "genuine Wright Field Expert" to join an anthropology group working on problems in the sizing and fitting of gas masks at the Chemical Warfare Service Development Laboratory.

FORENSIC ANTHROPOLOGY MOVES WEST

Until after World War II, forensic anthropology had been pretty much an East Coast enterprise. Then, in 1946, Brues moved back into the academic arena, going to the University of Oklahoma to teach anatomy at its medical school. In 1950, she was approached with a skeletal identification problem by the Oklahoma Bureau of Identification. Soon she was a regular consultant, averaging around three cases a year—a phenomenal rate for the time. She brought her experience to bear in a paper on skeletal identification, which, appearing in the *Journal of Criminal Law, Criminology and Police Science* (1958), was reprinted widely. As she continued to ponder bones in her lab, William M. Bass completed his studies under Krogman in 1961. Moving from the University of Pennsylvania to the University of Kansas, he began to teach skeletal identification as an integral part of his osteology classes. Soon he, too, began receiving bones from law enforcement agencies.

This part of the era of consolidation was the beginning of what might be seen, in retrospect, as the "golden age" of forensic anthropology. Krogman updated and expanded his 1939 paper into a book, *The Human Skeleton in Forensic Medicine* in 1962, which quickly became the accepted standard reference. Alice Brues, tiring of the anthropologically unrewarding demands of teaching anatomy to medical students, moved to the University of Colorado in 1965. Casework eluded her there, but she imparted to her students an enthusiasm not only for physical anthropology but forensic anthropology too. A number of them went on in forensic anthropology, doing casework and teaching students of their own to partake in the rapid growth of the field in the early to middle 1970s.

But William Bass and his colleagues at Kansas became the real powerhouse of forensic anthropology. Teaching osteology and the usual courses in physical anthropology in the early 1960s, forensic anthropology began to creep insidiously into his courses. Bass was soon joined by Ellis Kerley, who had earned his Ph.D. in 1962 and had just finished an internship at the Armed Forces Institute of Pathology. The faculty at the University of Kansas apparently embarked upon making their institution the leader in physical anthropology in the West, and they soon added Thomas McKern, who had earned his Ph.D. in 1955, to the faculty. However, by the end of the 1960s this bastion of forensic anthropology began to become unglued.

In 1971, Bass left to take up a chairmanship at the University of Tennessee, pushing at least five new Ph.Ds. out ahead of his departure from Kansas. By the next year, Kerley had gone to the University of Maryland, and McKern to Simon Fraser University in Vancouver, where he died in the late 1970s. Kerley remained involved and influential in medicolegal anthropology, but the largest educational impact was made by Bass, who created a second beehive of forensic activity in Tennessee. He accounted for over twenty practitioners of forensic anthropology by the time of his 1994 retirement—more than any other person. His program is now being continued by one of his former students, Murray Marks. Thus, the pervasive Bassian influence permeates forensic anthropology, since each of his students went on to influence his or her own students in turn, and now the students of students have students in a multiplication scheme that would elicit the envy of a Ponzi.

The many students of William Bass have greatly impacted the field of forensic anthropology with their teaching and research, and their work at the army's Central Identification Laboratory, the Armed Forces Institute of Pathology, and other medicolegal venues. The Bass student with the greatest educational impact is his first student at the University of Kansas, Walter Birkby, who arrived at the University of Arizona in 1963 and immediately set about organizing the Arizona State Museum's skeletal collection with fellow graduate student Kenneth Bennett. Birkby was soon appointed its curator and began teaching in the Department of Anthropology. He began his forensic anthropology casework for the state of Arizona in 1965, having handled over 1,500 cases as this is written. Following the deeply worn path of his Kansas mentor, Birkby began teaching forensic anthropology and had a program in place by 1983. By the time of his retirement in 1996, he was vying with his Arizona advisor, Frederick Hulse (Giles, 1996), for the second-highest output of forensic anthropologists in the nation. In a curious show of gratitude for all he had done, his program and his laboratory were eliminated by the university upon his retirement.

When J. Lawrence Angel arrived at the Smithsonian in 1962, he took over most of the caseload from Stewart. During his twenty-four years of forensic work, according to Ubelaker and Scammell, Angel analyzed a total of 565 cases, which is an impressive accomplishment, especially so early in the game. An appreciation of the work of Larry Angel and a concise history of Smithsonian involvement can be gleaned from Ubelaker and Scammell's book *Bones* (1992). Although it was the one institution that the FBI could count on for anthropological analysis, the increasing number of forensic anthropologists elsewhere in the nation began to siphon off a bit of that work. The FBI caseload at the Smithsonian typically amounted to thirty-five or forty cases a year.

Stewart also continued to be active in identification work, organizing a symposium on skeletal identification, which was presented in 1968. Many of the hallowed faculty of this three-day symposium are still active in forensic anthropology, and the list of attendees is a stellar agglomeration of those important and influential throughout contemporary forensic medicine (Stewart, 1970). This may be seen as a critical step not only in establishing an identity for forensic anthropology, but in demonstrating that the subfield had much to offer forensic medicine.

By the early 1970s, Angel was offering a week-long forensic anthropology course at the Smithsonian. Ubelaker has continued that tradition. Though this course has typically been attended mostly by forensic pathologists and military graves registration people, it has also attracted the occasional anthropologist. Somewhat ironically, this first formal course in forensic anthropology was aimed principally at an audience outside of anthropology, but in that aim it followed Stewart's 1968 symposium.

It was also in the early 1970s that a clear identity began to form. Clyde Snow (1982) has written an engaging account of the founding of the Physical Anthropology Section of the American Academy of Forensic Sciences, but to summarize briefly, Ellis Kerley was determined to establish a physical anthropology section of the Academy in 1971. He and Snow emerged from a marathon telephone campaign in which they persuaded all of those who they knew had an interest in skeletal identification (as it was then usually called) to join the Academy, finishing the day with the names of enough committed people needed to form a section.

The following year, 1972, the section met officially for the first time, marking the beginning of the modern period in forensic anthropology. It grew quickly, trebling in size every ten years. By 1975, the membership had grown from the original fourteen to twenty-two; by 1980, it had climbed to forty; in 1985, it was eighty; and by 1990 it was 130. The official figure for 1995 was 197. Incidentally, in keeping with the academic tradition of "getting them while they are young," sixty-five (33 percent!) of the 1995 membership were student members. Because of its academic base, forensic anthropology has always been very student oriented.

The field has also attracted more females than most other scientific specialties. Three of the fourteen founding members of the physical anthropology section of the American Academy of Forensic Sciences were female; ten years later 21 percent of the membership still possessed two X chromosomes; by 1990 that percentage had almost doubled to 40 percent. A hint of the future may be seen midway through this last decade of the twentieth century, when females comprise 46 percent of the total membership of the section and 64 percent of the student membership. It won't be long until the males are outnumbered and the "old boy" network of forensic anthropology is fully transformed into an "old girl" one. None of those with whom I have discussed this phenomenon has posited a completely satisfactory explanation for this appeal of the seemingly macabre to the fairer sex.

The 1950s saw only five people who generally would be recognized as significant figures in forensic anthropology earning their doctorates. In the 1960s, twenty-three were graduated, and in the 1970s, forty-one more were thrust out into the world. The pace slowed somewhat in the 1980s with thirty-two joining the ranks, but the 1990s promise to be the most productive decade ever, with twenty new forensic anthropologists cranked out in only the first three years.

As the "Section" (as forensic anthropologists call it) was founded, the students of the forensic anthropology "pioneers" were also beginning to follow the trail into medicolegal skeletal analysis and would shovel some of their experiences with this fascinating work into their osteology courses. Finally, by the late 1970s, formal university courses in forensic anthropology were beginning to materialize. The typical forensic anthropologists in this period were people who had been trained in osteology by one of the pioneers who had eagerly made themselves available for the occasional forensic case. With that example before them, they became professors in anthropology departments or museum curators (or both), joined the Academy to find like-minded folks, and slid farther down the ladder of academic respectability as they concentrated more and more of their energy on forensic casework and forensic teaching.

With the cooperation and support of the Academy, the American Board of Forensic Anthropology was organized in 1978. Its purpose was to establish standards for the recognition of competence to practice, and to facilitate the recognition of forensic anthropologists' expertise by courts and other forensic scientists. In a perfect example of lifting oneself by the bootstraps, the Board, consisting of the brightest names in the forensic anthropological firmament, met to anoint itself as officially certified. Its members then reviewed the submissions of about fifteen others and certified them as well. After all the big names and a few small ones who wanted in were in, the door was slammed shut, thereafter to be pried open only by those passing a comprehensive and exhausting eight-hour written and practical examination.

With certification, forensic anthropology took on a new legitimacy. From its sound academic base, forensic anthropology slowly expanded, turning out the first Ph.Ds. with specialized formal training in the subject in the early 1980s. With the primary pathway into forensic anthropology now being academic training rather than on-the-job experience, the thirty-two new Ph.Ds. awarded in the 1980s were to anthropologists specifically trained in the perspectives of medicolegal anthropology and seeking work in that area.

It was not until well into the 1980s that a forensic anthropologist succeeded in finding full-time employment beyond the ivy-covered walls of a university or museum. By the mid-1990s, about two dozen had found employment outside of academia. Some of these positions combined forensic anthropology with investigation or pathology for medical examiner systems, mostly in the southeastern United States, while others were with the federal government. While three are presently employed by the Armed Forces Institute of Pathology in Washington, D.C., a dozen or so are currently engaged in the recovery and anthropological identification on the remains of armed services personnel from Vietnam, Cambodia, Korea, and World War II for the army's Central Identification Laboratory in Hawaii.

While this extra-academic expansion was going on, the rapidly increasing number of forensic anthropologists was also getting busier. In the late

1960s, the half-dozen anthropologists engaged in forensic work were each handling about three cases a year. By the mid-1970s the average caseload had risen to six a year. By 1980 it was about nine, and in 1989 it was sixteen (Wienker and Rhine, 1989). It continues to rise. By 1990, I estimated, we were seeing a total of over 2,200 cases annually in the nation—a huge increase from the two dozen or so only two decades earlier.

In the beginning, the mandate of forensic anthropology was to identify unknown persons who, through no fault of their own, had become skeletonized. This typically involved the forensic anthropologist analyzing a skeleton and reporting its sex, age, race, stature, any peculiarities (such as broken and healed bones), and other information that would be useful in making an identification to the medical examiner or law enforcement official from whom the case had been received. One of the first attempts to survey the field was a small volume, Mahmoud El-Najjar and K. Richard McWilliams' *Forensic Anthropology* (1978).

As they gained experience, forensic anthropologists realized that analysis of the skeleton could also be helpful in establishing identity where a body was decomposed, had been burned or mummified, or where more than a single set of skeletons or mangled remains had become jumbled together (commingled). Other forensic anthropological foci also began to develop: the rebuilding in clay of faces on skulls to provide leads in identification, photographic superimposition of skulls and victim photographs, other photographic analysis, bone histochemical analysis, and so on. Some also began to make identifications directly from x-rays and to consult on "fresh" remains.

In 1979, Clyde Snow took early retirement from the Federal Aviation Administration where he had been working as a research physical anthropologist while accepting forensic cases from Oklahoma and elsewhere. Interrupting an increasing flow of forensic cases from around the nation, he acceded to a request for his assistance in Argentina in 1984 (Joyce and Stover, 1991). There he trained a group of Argentinean students in the recovery and analysis of the *desaparecidos*, those unfortunates who had been whisked off from their families by their own government—usually in Ford Falcons in the middle of the night—never to be seen again, or at least not until Snow and his team carefully excavated their buried remains to demonstrate their violent deaths and to identify them.

With this move, Snow upped the ante of forensic anthropology, from splashing in the placid pool of individual murder to immersion in the dan-

Fig. 6.1. Excavation of a mass grave in Bosnia. William Haglund in foreground. (Photo courtesy of Gilles Peress/Magnum Photos)

gerous waters of state-sanctioned murder. As forensic odontologist Lowell Levine remarked when receiving the T. Dale Stewart Award of the American Academy of Forensic Science for Snow (then off on another mission), "Clyde Snow has put himself in harm's way" with his recovery and identification of bodies of people murdered by the state. Since then, this indefatigable investigator has undertaken further such projects in Bolivia, Guatemala, Chile, the Philippines, Sri Lanka, and Croatia. He has recently been joined in this important work by other forensic anthropologists, including Karen Burns and William Haglund (Fig. 6.1).

The urgency of this work recently led to Haglund's resignation as chief investigator for King County (Seattle), Washington. As this is written, he works under the auspices of the United Nations, which has him shuttling back and forth between Bosnia, Rwanda, and other trouble spots.

In the recovery of hundreds of bodies from mass graves (of which, there seems to be an abundance), he shares the fervent hope of many that the cycle of violence can be broken by gathering evidence that will help bring the perpetrators of mass murder to account for their crimes. His Bosnian efforts led, in the summer of 1996, both to field recovery of bodies from mass graves to rotating a number of advanced students in forensic anthropology and other forensic specialists through a makeshift morgue located in a bombed-out factory. They found it a moving and worthwhile experience (see also Owsley, et al., 1996). Attempts to design a permanent world court to judge such matters are once again before the United Nations. However, for now it would seem that the future holds considerable and expanding potential for the further involvement of forensic anthropologists in the recovery and identification of the bodies of people so casually killed and buried by rogue governments.

A Regional Perspective

The national forensic meetings have never taken on the "meat market" atmosphere of other national meetings attended by anthropologists. Those conclaves are invariably attended by vast crowds of newly minted Ph.Ds. searching for employment. With few jobs in forensic anthropology, the forensic meetings have more of an academic-social feeling. Attendees gather to listen to papers, to discuss their findings later with presenters, and to catch up on news and interesting cases from the past year.

The anthropology sessions are usually so well attended and the pace so unrelenting that many hoped-for discussions never materialize. Other debates seem to spring up unexpectedly to take their place. One is frequently frustrated by not being able to follow up a question on a particular line of research or inquiry because of the shifting discussional parameters within the groups that gather outside the meeting room. Invariably someone would grumble that we should have a summer regional meeting to discuss matters of interest in more depth than was allowed by the hectic pace of the national one.

At one of the national meetings, I asked why we didn't just organize a regional group. Nobody objected, but nobody seemed ready to do it either. A month or so later, the thought resurfaced, and since no one else seemed about to get the ball rolling, I wrote Dr. Rodger Heglar, one of the "old hands," then teaching at San Francisco State University, suggesting that we get organized. Announcements were duly sent out to the ten forensic anthropologists then living west of the 20-inch isohyet, inviting them and their students to a summer meeting for an informal discussion of the means used to assess race from the skeleton. In July 1981, seven of us gathered at the College Cabin of the Southern Utah State College, just outside of Cedar City, Utah.

The 2½-day July session, which concentrated on the characters we each used for racial attribution, was so successful that we decided to repeat it the following year. Attendance increased and we were launched on a path that brought us to the present day, though we changed our location to the shores of Lake Mead, outside Boulder City, Nevada. Our Mountain Desert and Coastal Forensic Anthropologists is an organization in name only, with no officers, no dues, and only one unofficial committee. We have become so successful that we have all but taken over the Lake Mead Lodge for the three days of the meeting. Intended for trans-Mississippian forensic anthropologists, we have nonetheless drawn attendees from as far away as Hawaii, Alaska, New York, and Canada. Everything is very informal at these meetings, with a loosely defined program of volunteered (or cajoled) presentations, some workshop sessions on a variety of topics, and lots of time for in-depth discussions in the late afternoons and evenings. These meetings have resulted in many papers and a seminar presented at the Academy meetings, the publication of one book, another in press, and a newsletter—not a bad record for an organization that doesn't officially exist.

Within a few years, our example was followed in the Southeast by the Mountain Swamp and Beach Forensic Anthropologists, in the Northeast by the North East Forensic Anthropology Association, and finally in the Midwest by the Midwest Bioarchaeology and Forensic Anthropology Association. Each of these regional meetings has its own flavor and its own way of eliciting participation.

Who is a "Forensic Anthropologist"?

One of the perennial problems of the discipline of forensic anthropology is fixing on a definition. This may sound like a trivial problem, but it is not. Even some of our other anthropological colleagues have strange ideas of what forensic anthropology is. Some seem to feel that if you work on skeletons that are not ancient Indian skeletons, you are a forensic anthropologist. They think that an identification made on a body that is wearing tailored clothing or that can be recognized from cemetery records is forensic anthropology. This is not so, or not necessarily so. A person is a forensic anthropologist if his or her focus of attention is in large measure on skeletons of medicolegal interest. Such a person will, of course, have taken specialized coursework, participated in ongoing casework, field exercises, and workshops.

One measure of whether a skeleton can be said to be of medicolegal interest is if the person analyzing it may have to go to court to testify on his or her findings. It roughly comes down to this: if a person has been dead for such a period of time that anyone who might have had a role in his or her death could still be alive, the case is of medicolegal significance— in round numbers, say about fifty years. Of course, even those long dead of natural causes or accident, or whose deaths occurred under suspicious circumstances, still fall under the medical examiner's jurisdiction, but if a person can be shown to have been dead for more than fifty years, the case is probably without medicolegal significance. The remains, the circumstances, or the individual might be interesting, in its own right, but such an analysis is not really forensic. Nor does the fact that a forensic anthropologist has worked on a case make it forensic.

That latter point may be illustrated by a tasty little bite of Colorado folklore. In eastern Utah in 1874, a recent Pennsylvania transplant by the name of Alferd Packer was hired by some even greener-horns to be led over into Colorado's Gunnison country. Late fall was not a good time to be heading off by foot into the not fully charted and almost unpopulated high mountains of Colorado Territory in the early 1870s. With "more guts than sense," Packer led the way into the Colorado high country, where 13,000- and 14,000-foot-high peaks thrust up to wring moisture from every passing cloud. Exceptionally fierce early snowstorms descended upon western Colorado, and nothing more was heard until Packer emerged in the small San Luis Valley town of Saguache two months later.

He turned aside inquiries about his party in various ways but claimed in one widely accepted version that, trapped without food by a fearful onslaught of snow, his companions perished one by one. He and the remaining members of the party ate the bodies of those who had succumbed. And then there was one—Alferd survived the longest, to be rewarded with a break in the weather allowing his escape to Saguache.

When the weather moderated in the spring, a search party was sent out to what is now known as "Cannibal Plateau," up above Lake City, Colorado, the county seat of one of the least populous counties in the United

States, Hinsdale. Accompanied by a sketch artist from *Harper's Weekly*, the party discovered the still-articulated skeletons of Packer's five companions lying on the ground. They were hustled off to Lake City for burial in a common grave, and Packer was hustled off to jail. Although accounts of the trial vary, they agree that Packer was condemned to death for multiple acts of homicide. Transferred to a jail on Colorado's eastern slope, he was finally released to live out his last days in Englewood, just outside of Denver.

Coloradans have always wondered if he really murdered all of his companions. Forensic professor and lawyer James Starrs decided he'd try to find out, and he engaged the assistance of a number of forensic experts from around the country. To do the anthropology he enlisted the aid of Dr. Walter Birkby of the Arizona State Museum at the University of Arizona in Tucson. In turn, Birkby called on two of his many forensic anthropology students. Fuzzy images that might be skeletons showed up on the screen of their ground-penetrating radar over what was marked as the common grave of the five victims. Careful forensic excavation by the Arizona anthropologists revealed five skeletons in the same positions as those shown in the sketches published in *Harper's Weekly* in the 1870s. They were transported to Birkby's lab at the museum in Tucson for analysis (Fig. 6.2).

Birkby and his crew went over the skeletons with the forensic anthropological equivalent of a fine-tooth comb. They turned up and documented abundant evidence—in the form of cut marks and other bone injuries—that the five men had been killed and that meat had been removed from their bones by a person or persons unacquainted with the fine points of anatomy, or butchering. Birkby carefully concluded that they had been killed and defleshed (and might have been eaten), but that it was impossible to say just who had killed whom and in what order the men had died.

The identity of the victims has been established, and the cause and manner of their deaths have been pretty well cleared up in good forensic style, but the identity of the perpetrator(s) is still unknown and cannot be directly illuminated by the skeletal evidence. This leaves the matter of Packer's guilt or innocence right where it has been for the last 120 years. He may have been guilty of the practice of "survival cannibalism," having never lifted a finger against another person, or he may have killed them all in a dispute and engaged in cannibalism as an afterthought. We'll just never know.

The question of Packer's guilt has not kept students at the University

Fig. 6.2. Bruce Anderson, Dr. Walter Birkby and Todd Fenton (left to right) take a break from excavating the skeleton of one of the presumed victims of Colorado cannibal Alferd Packer. The Lake City, Colorado multiple grave was dug in late July 1989. (Photo courtesy of Bruce Anderson)

of Colorado in Boulder from celebrating "Alferd Packer Look-alike Day" or from wolfing down "Packerburgers" in the Packer Grill in the students' union. Nor has it prevented the businessmen of Lake City from reaping their annual harvest from curious and titillated tourists. But it is not forensic.

In short, we have here an excellent example of how a number of forensic experts have become involved in a case of great historic and popular interest; but however fascinating it may be to Coloradans, Packer is dead and cannot be brought to trial. Therefore, despite the typically forensic focus on identification and the cause and manner of death, this case is devoid of medicolegal significance. It is undeniably of considerable historic interest, but it is not forensic.

In the same way, the cases that are discussed by various authors—the identification of Josef Mengele and the skeletons of soldiers buried on the Little Big Horn (Joyce and Stover, 1991), the Lizzie Borden and Carl Weiss cases (Ubelaker and Scammell, 1992), the Tsar and his family, and the remains of Pizarro and of former President Zachary Taylor (Maples and Browning, 1994), and of Jesse James (Finnegan and Kysar, 1996)—were all investigated by a team of forensic experts, and the remains themselves were analyzed by forensic anthropologists, but that does not change the fact that they are of historic, not forensic, import. This is not to say that we, as forensic anthropologists, are not interested in hearing about, participating in, and discussing such cases, or that we may not learn things that can be applied in a forensic context from them. Nor is it meant in any way to belittle or downplay the efforts of the numerous forensic people that went into the analysis of cases of undoubted historic interest and significance. It is simply to say that even though forensic expertise and personnel were involved, the cases themselves were not of medicolegal significance.

Thus, the involvement of a forensic anthropologist in a case does not make that case an example of forensic anthropology. Furthermore, a physical anthropologist who is called in to consult for police on a forensic case does not instantly thereby become a forensic anthropologist. In the same sense that one swallow does not make a spring, handling a case or even a few does not make one a forensic anthropologist. In order to achieve that status, one has not only to do casework, but to accumulate a record of research, teaching, and other activities that are forensic (medicolegal) in their orientation and nature. It is not so much the activity per se, but the orientation to the world of forensic science that makes one a forensic anthropologist.

To be a forensic anthropologist one must first be an osteologist, but the reverse is not also true. If one is an osteologist, one is *not* also automatically a forensic anthropologist. Forensic anthropology is, after all, more than the analysis of human skeletons: it is the discovery, recovery, and analysis of human remains in a medicolegal context. It is knowing that one's pronouncements may have an effect on a family, its members' resolution of the loss of a loved one, their ability to change the course of their lives because of that loss, and their plans for the future being dashed by that loss. It is also the knowledge that there may be further legal implications, including court testimony, and the potential of having a role in determining whether a defendant loses his or her freedom or life as a result of that testimony. This seems clear enough, but somehow escapes the comprehension of some anthropologists.

One might expect that a person devoting so much energy to legal medicine would seek contact with others so disposed and would pursue membership in the American Academy of Forensic Sciences and other forensic organizations. There one's work can be brought into perspective through discussions with others, and the presentation of and attendance at papers. Eventually, such a person might seek to be certified by the American Board of Forensic Anthropology, the credentialing agency established in 1978. Obviously, one does not need such certification to engage in the practice of forensic anthropology, and there are many good practitioners who have not yet—and may never—apply for the testing to be certified. But one could certainly question the interest, commitment, and integrity of one who called him- or herself a "forensic anthropologist" and never bothered to join organizations that support the field or to seek out those who do. The factor prized most highly in the academic tradition is the sharing of information and learning from others. People who believe they do the best possible work by isolating themselves from contact with others doing the same sort of work delude themselves and demonstrate a clear anti-intellectual bias, which is antithetical to the free exchange of information that characterizes the world of academe.

7

To Mexico . . . The Long Way

The Intricacies of Identification

The Escape

Since this case has been settled, all the names and dates as you see them here are as they appear in the official records, except for the names of the victims. On July 30, 1978, three brothers entered the Arizona State Prison at Florence for a picnic lunch with dear old Dad. They brought a grand lunch with them into the prison, consisting of ham sandwiches, a six-pack of pop . . . and three guns. At about 9:20 A.M. Ricky, Raymond, and Donald Tison strolled back past the guards and out of the prison. With them was their father Gary Tison and his cell mate Randy Greenawalt, both convicted murderers. Ten minutes later, the guards and visitors locked in a closet by the escapees battered their way out and sounded the alarm. Roadblocks were set up to halt their green Ford (which the Tisons had already exchanged for a Lincoln) at the beginning of their long trip to Mexico.

THE FIRST FOUR VICTIMS

It was one of those bright, brassy, hot southern Arizona summer days as the prison escapees and their rescuers headed off to Mexico, the closest border crossing being at Nogales, about a hundred miles almost due south from Florence. For some reason, however, they headed west along Interstate 8 about two hundred miles until a flat tire halted their progress just east of Yuma. They repaired it and turned north from Yuma just inside the California border, traveling though the dry, hot, dusty Chocolate Mountains, where a second flat tire stranded them twenty-five miles south of the tiny town of Quartzite. A passing motorist, Marine Sgt. Ray Deeuss and his family, bound for a Las Vegas vacation, stopped to assist. They were bundled into the Lincoln and driven off the road into the desert, where all four of them were shot. The Tison gang then commandeered the Deeuss's 1977 orange Mazda, complete with a full set of tires, and continued north past the transplanted London Bridge at Lake Havasu City, turning east toward Flagstaff, two hundred miles farther north of Mexico than where they had started.

While on the road, the resourceful gang visited a hardware store where they purchased several cans of silver spray paint, which they used to alter the appearance of the highly visible orange Mazda. On August 2, after a leisurely three-day drive of almost six hundred miles, the gang arrived in Flagstaff. A woman there who had become friendly with Greenawalt while visiting her son in prison provided them with a pickup, guns, and ammunition.

The police were doing their best but were several leaps behind the Tisons. They were still looking for the green Ford. Acting on information provided by the penitentiary, the police assumed that the gang would probably visit the woman in Flagstaff, and with the help of the Phoenix SWAT team they staked out the house and set up roadblocks. Unfortunately, by the time they discovered that they had the name of the woman slightly wrong and shifted their attention to the correct house, the gang was gone. Only an hour before the police arrived, the Tison gang finished *burying* the Mazda (with its fresh coat of silver paint) in the woods near Flagstaff and headed off to Mexico. One can only imagine the thought processes of a gang of ruthless killers, who, trying to escape from the police, repaint a car with spray cans then bury it in the woods having driven more than five times the distance they needed to in order to reach their presumed destination, Mexico. Their interment strategy did, however, buy them more time, since by this time the police had found the bodies of the Deeuss family near Quartzite and were now looking for their orange Mazda.

On to Mexico (Or, Perhaps, New Mexico)

Leaving cool, forested, 7,000-foot-high Flagstaff, the gang resumed its drive toward Mexico through the Coconino National Forest and down into the parched high desert of northeast Arizona. After 150 miles of this eastbound travel, they crossed into New Mexico, farther than ever from Old Mexico (as they say in New Mexico). By August 7, the gang had covered the 376 miles necessary to arrive at the eastern edge of New Mexico, where they had arranged for a chartered plane to fly them from Clovis,

New Mexico, to Mexico. Arizona authorities had discovered the plan and notified the New Mexico State Police, who set their own trap. However, word leaked to the news media, and the gang arrived to find the small Clovis airport, a stone's throw from the Texas border, swarming with uniformed police and television crews. Having come so close to getting to Mexico, they didn't bother to cancel their flight plans but prudently departed to search for an alternate route to Mexico, which lay ever farther to the south from their position. Having gone west, north, then east, they decided to try north again. Could it be that they were not sure where Mexico was?

THE LAST TWO VICTIMS

By August 9, the gang had driven north into southern Colorado (nearly four hundred miles north of the Mexican border), where they encountered a newly married Texas couple, John and Marla Courtney. The honeymooning Courtneys were on their way to an exhibition football game in Denver the next day. Feeling the need of a fresh vehicle, the Tison gang killed the couple, buried their bodies in a shallow grave not far from Chimney Rock near the southern Colorado border, commandeered their van, and turned back towards Arizona. Two days later, on August 11, the gang was again headed for Mexico on the lightly traveled back roads near Casa Grande, Arizona.

In the meantime, sixty miles to the west, the Border Patrol station at Gila Bend had been broken into. The report of a silver sports car nearby alerted the Border Patrol who concluded that the Tisons had broken in, attempting to find guns and ammunition. Law enforcement officials immediately set up roadblocks to stop *northbound* traffic at every road junction between Gila Bend and Casa Grande. But it was not the Tisons who had made the unauthorized after-hours entry at the Border Patrol station, and by this time they were two vehicles beyond the orange-transmuted-to-silver Mazda, so the alert was based on dated information and wholly incorrect assumptions.

THE CAPTURE

As luck would have it, however, the gang chose the very same road, blocked by authorities, to continue their peregrination to Mexico. Imagine the sleepy gang being abruptly jerked into wakefulness when at about 2:45 A.M., its *southbound* progress was interrupted by the first *northbound* roadblock. The Tisons ran the block, but were immediately chased by police. At 2:58 A.M., with police in hot pursuit, they ran the second road-block at 90 miles per hour. The police manning this roadblock were ready. They fired fifty-two rounds into the general vicinity of the rapidly approaching van, and nine rounds connected. One shot hit driver Donald Tison in the forehead and killed him instantly. The vehicle ran off the road and into a ditch. Gary Tison, his two surviving sons, and Greenawalt ran off into the desert. Sons Ricky and Raymond Tison and Randy Greenawalt were quickly captured by the light of a circling Department of Public Safety helicopter, but Gary Tison eluded capture.

As a cloudless dawn broke over the desert the Tisons' journey was over—after thirteen days, six murders in two states, and more than two thousand miles of travel through three states in five vehicles—only about forty-four miles from where they began, all the time presumably headed for Mexico, a mere hundred miles away (Fig. 7.1).

A new search was mounted for Gary Tison. Up to twenty "sightings" a day were reported from Arizona, California, Colorado, and Utah. A Tucson man who resembled the elder Tison was arrested while vacationing with his family in Disneyland. Finally, eleven days later, on August 22, Tison's bloated and decomposing body was found about a mile from the capture scene. He had been injured in the crash of the van, and the relentless Arizona sun became his executioner.

The surviving Tison brothers and Greenawalt were tried and convicted. They appealed, were retried, and reconvicted. The conviction was upheld by the Supreme Court, which concluded that even though neither of the younger Tisons pulled a trigger, they were guilty of the "intent to kill."

DISCOVERY OF THE BODIES

Two unidentified and decomposed bodies were found in shallow graves near Chimney Rock in southern Colorado on November 15, 1978. They were presumed to be the bodies of the young Texas couple sought since their disappearance thirteen weeks earlier.

The sheriff sent the bodies to the OMI in Albuquerque, New Mexico, for autopsy. Buried three months, the bodies were in an advanced state of decomposition, which precluded the normal dissection and collection of tissue samples. During the autopsy, skulls, femora, and other structures were removed to facilitate analysis. The application of standard anthropological techniques resulted in the following findings. One individual

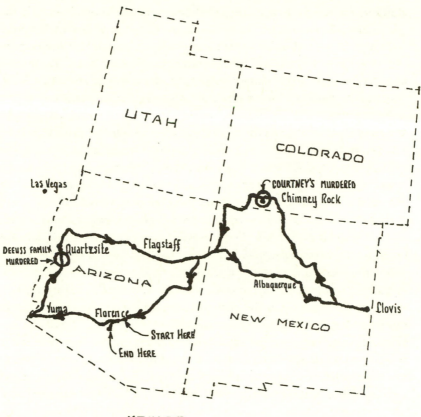

Fig. 7.1. The odyssey of the Tison gang.

was male, one was female. Both were in their mid-twenties and Caucasoid. Both had been shot once in the head, "execution style." Neither wound was typical, however.

Gunshot Wounds

In the classic execution murder, the victim is on his or her knees, head bent down, and a single shot is fired into the center of the occipital (the back of the skull). The skull vault is made up of three separate layers of bone: the ectocranial (exterior) and endocranial (interior) surfaces are thin layers of hard, dense "compact" bone; sandwiched between them is a layer of spongy or "cancellous" bone, looking rather like a thin layer of sponge.

Gunshot entrance wounds are generally round and uniform on the ectocranial surface where the bullet has entered, whereas the endocranial surface shows a "cratering" or "beveling" where the bullet has peeled the endocranial bone table away as it moved through. The beveling, not unlike that seen on a pane of glass impacted by a projectile, thus reveals the direction in which the bullet traveled (Adelson, 1974; Di Maio, 1985).

In most cases, a small-caliber, low-velocity handgun is preferred, so in some instances the projectile does not have enough power to punch its way out of the other side of the skull. When the round is large enough to generate the force necessary to exit, an exit wound typically appears somewhere on the frontal bone or the face. The exit wound is, according to the conventions of wound analysis, larger than the entrance, and its beveling is on the ectocranial surface where it exits from the skull.

The two bodies found in Colorado that had been shot in the head were both atypical in that the wounds of entrance were much lower than usual. The bullet had entered high on the female's neck and passed above the first cervical vertebra, entering the base of the skull, creating a small crescent-shaped defect at the posterior margin of the foramen magnum, the large hole on the skull base where the spinal cord enters the skull (Fig. 7.2). The bullet angled upward to exit high on the right part of the frontal, a classic exit wound with the expected external beveling (Fig. 7.3). Had the bullet entered the neck just slightly lower, it would have passed directly through the foramen magnum. This would have left the skull with an exit wound but no entrance. This is, of course, a physical impossibility: An estimation of the trajectory from the location and shape of the exit wound would quickly reveal what had happened, as would associated damage to the cervical vertebrae and the edge of the foramen magnum.

The skull of the male was intact and undamaged, (Fig. 7.4) not what you would expect where there had been a gunshot wound to the head. Nor were there radiopaque objects visible in the x-rayed thorax. As the body was moved during autopsy, a bullet fell from the oral cavity, and a small greenish stain could be observed on the palate. This stain also survived the preparation process. Looking below the intact skull, the transverse process of the first cervical vertebra (the little protuberance on the side of the first vertebra of the neck) was seen to have been shattered. It then became clear that the bullet had entered the posterior neck, passed through the lateral mass of the first cervical vertebra, plowed through the front of the neck and lodged in the mouth (Fig. 7.5). The particulars of

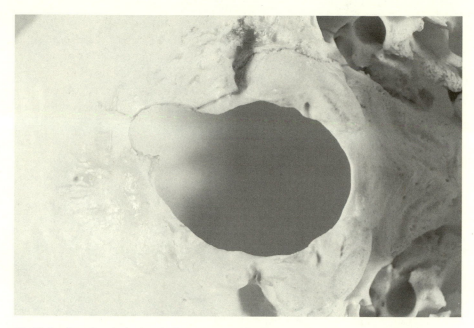

Fig. 7.2. Looking directly down at the foramen magnum on the base of Mrs. Courtney's skull. The asymmetrical elongation was caused by the entrance of a bullet. (Photo courtesy of the Office of the Medical Investigator, Albuquerque, New Mexico)

the findings were relayed to Colorado, then to Texas, and a match was quickly made to the honeymooning Courtneys.

Both of these cases featured a single gunshot wound of the skull, but sometimes a single gunshot wound will not satisfy an assailant, who empties his weapon into the hapless victim. Vexed by such multiple gunshot wounds, pathologists have to determine how many there are and how each affected the victim. This requires that each defect in the body be determined to be either an entrance or an exit and the trajectories traced. Pumping several rounds into someone's head compromises the skull's integrity, often leaving little shards of bone floating around in the gaping wound. If the discovery of the body has taken so long as to allow decomposition to progress well, pieces may not be quite where they should, or may even have fallen out. Some of them might not have been recovered at the scene, or may have been lost during transport if the body was not properly handled. Some might have been taken from the scene in the stomachs of carnivores. If a forensic anthropologist cleans and reassembles the skull, the

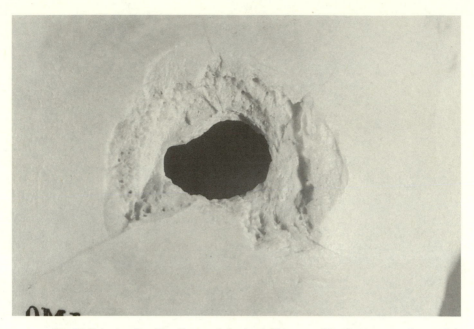

Fig. 7.3. Exit wound on Mrs. Courtney's forehead. The external beveling seen on exit wounds is clearly visible. (Photo courtesy of the Office of the Medical Investigator, Albuquerque, New Mexico)

nature of the wounds will become much clearer. This arduous and demanding assembly of a three-dimensional jigsaw puzzle may provide the only means really to be sure that one understands what has happened. Merely looking at the skull without taking the time to clean it can lead one to the wrong conclusion. Quality forensic work demands that the time be taken, and that the extra effort be expended.

Having established which defects are entrances and which are exits, one can move on to the next step, the sequencing of the defects. As a projectile strikes a head, it delivers energy to the point of impact. If the force is great enough, the elastic limit of the skull bone is exceeded, the projectile punches through, and fractures spread out from the impact site (Smith, Berryman, and, Lahren, 1987). The fracture lines extend from the point of impact for whatever distance is necessary to dissipate the energy locked up in the projectile. As with glass, however, a fracture line from a second impact site will typically not pass over an existing fracture but will dissipate its force in that first defect. Sutures, the squiggly lines

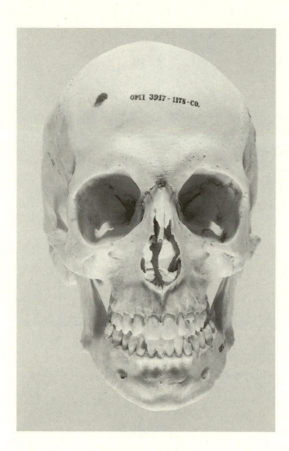

Fig. 7.4. The skull of 25-year-old Mr. Courtney. There are no defects in the skull from what was presumably an "execution-style" gunshot wound. (Photo courtesy of the Office of the Medical Investigator, Albuquerque, New Mexico)

that mark the junctions of skull bones, also usually stop a fracture, unless they are at least partly fused.

Therefore, all one has to do is look to see which fracture is stopped and follow it back to its source. The source is the impact site that has come after the one whose fracture was continuous. Through a combination of analysis both of entrance and exit wounds and the fractures that propagate from them, one can thus determine which wound came first—elementary, as Sherlock would have rightly observed.

The Presumptive Identification

Harking back to the dead honeymooners, their bodies were delivered to the OMI with a presumptive identification, but a positive one had still

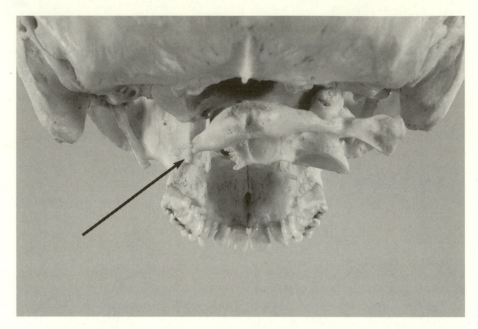

Fig. 7.5. The base of the skull seen in Fig. 7.4, viewed from behind. The arrow indicates the missing left transverse process of the first cervical vertebra, fractured by the passage of a bullet that lodged in his mouth. (Photo courtesy of the Office of the Medical Investigator, Albuquerque, New Mexico)

to be made. In fact, most forensic anthropologists prefer not to be told anything about a case and want to do their analysis free of any bias. This allows the skeleton to speak directly about itself. In many instances, though, anthropologists are presented with cases involving presumptive identifications; that is, cases in which the identity is assumed to be known. These present a particular difficulty, as the anthropologist must maintain a scientific openness that is possible really only when expectations about the case are not transmitted to him or her before the work begins. In a perfect world, the investigators and the police should refrain from providing any advance information about a case.

If "tipped off" to a belief that the remains are those of a 24-year-old female and a 25-year-old male missing since August, there is a danger that the anthropologist's perceptions will be clouded, and that he or she will unconsciously search for verification of that presumption rather than engaging in an open-minded search for the truth. If, on the other hand, the anthropologist works without any preconceived notion of what is expected, the results will be free of any possible taint of tailoring the conclusions to fit the expectations. Such a result is inherently more trustworthy. As author Aaron Elkins (1987), observed, "Forensic anthropology's like anything else. You tend to find what you are looking for."

The best that a forensic anthropologist can do in a situation where hunches have been passed on is either to rule out that presumptive identification or to rule it in as a possibility. In the case of the Colorado honeymooners, the agreement of the skeletal findings with the presumptive identification thus paved the way for and speeded up the positive identification that was later made on dental evidence. But speed is not the most important factor here. The subjects of the investigation are, after all, dead, and they will not get any deader if a final positive identification takes an additional few hours or days. The watchword is accuracy, and mistaking an identification is injurious to both family and friends as well as to the agency responsible. Insurance and death benefits may also be due to the next of kin. The identification, therefore, has to be done properly the first time, even if it takes a little longer. Of course, one cannot help but feel some pressure to accomplish the task with the greatest speed commensurate with the demand for accuracy. Nevertheless, once authorities explain the need for caution, families are generally gratified that such care is being taken and accept the delay.

The Positive Identification

The goal in any identification process is to make a positive identification—one that is secure. A positive identification results only when there are antemortem records (records made during life) to compare with a body. Most often, they are dental records. These x-rays or written records of treatment made by the dentist can be compared with the dental work seen on the remains. In most instances, such comparisons are made by a forensic odontologist, a dentist specializing in forensic work. In some locations, where there are no forensic dentists available, the forensic anthropologist may make a dental identification.

Other means of making positive identifications also depend upon locating good antemortem records. These could be hospital records of treatment, or x-rays made at the time of a skeletal injury or at various times in the healing process. In 1977, a body was found in a shallow grave near Hobbs in the oil- and gas-producing region of southeastern New Mexico.

The body was immediately assumed to be Mrs. Sue Churr, who had been missing for several months. As is typical, suspicion immediately fastened upon the husband—wholly justified, as it later turned out. The remains had decomposed to the point that the soft tissue had lost most of the integrity that would have harbored its information. Moreover, there were no dental records immediately available. The identification would have to come from the skeleton alone. This is always a challenge, since antemortem records (other than dental ones) are usually not sufficiently complete as to make an identification possible from the skeleton only.

The skeleton was analyzed by a forensic anthropologist who had no knowledge of its presumed identity. That analysis showed the body to be female, between twenty and twenty-five, Caucasoid, and about five feet four inches to five feet six inches tall. The missing Mrs. Churr was a 21-year-old Caucasoid female, about five feet five inches tall. The particulars all matched, but this kind of match does not make a positive identification. There are always many missing white females in their early twenties, approximately five feet five inches tall, and the body in this case could, in theory, have been any of them—or even someone else who had not yet been reported missing. As is often the case, luck was on our side: there was a very clear 25-degree A/P angulation in the proximal third of the left femoral shaft. In plain English, that means that about a third of the way down from the top of the left thighbone, there was a sudden marked backwards angle (Fig. 7.6). There was also a considerable asymmetry in the pelvis, a response to this injury.

This meant that this young woman had at some point in her life been in a serious accident that had fractured her left thigh. Since the shaft of the bone was so smooth, we knew that this well-healed fracture was many years old. The fracture must therefore have occurred while she was still a child. Moreover, such a serious fracture would have necessitated extended hospital treatment, leaving records somewhere. Investigators immediately contacted her family in the search for the necessary hospital treatment records.

Bone Fractures

When a bone is fractured, the trauma also slices blood vessels, which bleed into the wound. Eventually, this mass of blood and shattered bone turns a bit gooey. One can even hear a slurping sound as one moves around on a broken bone. In short order, as the natural remodeling processes break

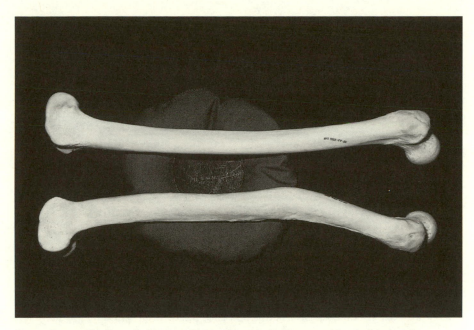

Fig. 7.6. Femora (thighbones) of 21-year-old Sue Churr, who had been struck by a bus at age eight. The impact fractured her left leg. The left (lower) femur shows a small callus and the angulation caused by the fracture.

down the old bone, other processes begin to lay down masses of woven bone (the most primitive sort), eventually producing the huge lump of a callus that bridges the fracture site. This primitive natural splint holds the broken ends in place until healing can take place inside. Given long enough, a good job of setting the bone in proper alignment, and a fracture that occurs when the person is young enough to be actively building and remodeling the skeleton, a bone can be restored to its former shape.

The exact duration of this process will depend somewhat upon age, younger bones healing more quickly and remodeling more fully than older ones. Obviously, knowing how long fractures take to heal can be very helpful in tracing records and in making an identification within a forensic context. Every skeletal collection contains a few examples of fractured bones, but in most instances we do not know exactly how much time has elapsed between the injury and the person's death. One interesting insight into this process is presented by the National Museum of Health and Medicine's Armed Forces Institute of Pathology in Washington, D.C.

(AFIP). The AFIP has been collecting bones from varied sources since before the Civil War.

With poorly controlled surgical conditions (Civil War surgeons not even cleansing their hands and instruments before sawing off yet another shattered leg) and without antibiotics, the survival rate for battlefield surgery was low in this clash between the North and South. After losing patients, some of the battlefield surgeons sawed off partially healed stumps of bone and sent them off to the AFIP. Included with the specimens was information about how much time had passed since the original amputation. These specimens and their records have been carefully curated to the present day and provide one useful source of information about how long bones take to heal. Some of these specimens have been expertly cast by forensic anthropologist Dr. Diane France of France Casting for sale to those curious about bone healing.

The San Diego Museum of Man boasts a similar collection, acquired from Stanford University. The medical school had been amassing bits and pieces of skeletons removed during surgery for many years, but—feeling that the modern computer age had no need of such specimens—surgeons allowed the collection to languish largely unused for some time. Finally they decided to dispose of it and contacted the San Diego Museum of Man. Curator Rose Tyson speedily organized a multivan rescue mission. Now those once unloved specimens have a happy new home, keeping company with another notable skeletal collection, the Hrdlicka Paleopathology Collection, a long parade of skeletal infirmities collected by anthropologist Ales Hrdlicka (Merbs, 1980).

Another, lesser-known osteopathology collection, like the Hrdlicka Collection, consisting of undocumented specimens, is the "Buffalo Collection," brought by Dr. James E. Anderson to the University of Toronto. Such collections are slow and difficult to accumulate, and because they are so uncommon, they are invaluable. Physical anthropologists and others are delighted with the opportunity to study them for the insights that they offer into bone remodeling, which can be gained in no other way.

Only two days after the autopsy and initial investigation of Mrs. Churr's decomposed body, dental records arrived. The OMI's forensic odontologist Dr. Homer Campbell made a comparison and established her identity on dental grounds. The day after, hospital records arrived from Las Vegas, Nevada. In 1964, Sue Churr was Sue Emahl, a lawyer's eight-year-old daughter, who had been struck by a vehicle on May 10 of that year.

The impact produced a clean fracture of the upper shaft of her femur. The strong muscles of her thigh contracted under the shock, producing an overriding fracture of the femur of 4 cm (about one and a half inches) with a posterior angulation of 30 degrees. According to additional records, by May 15, and with little Sue still in traction, the override had been reduced to about 1.5 cm (five-eighths of an inch) and the angulation to about 25 degrees. By July 24, her physician was able to report to her insurance company that the bone was knitting well.

The fractured and healed left femur of these skeletal remains was in the location noted by the physician, and the final angle of 25 degrees agreed precisely with what could be seen on the skeleton. Since she was eight at the time of the injury, she would have had thirteen years in the period of most rapid bone growth and remodeling for the femur to heal and re-contour. This matched all of the expectations generated by the original analysis of the bone. Hence, a reasonable conclusion was that these remains were indeed those of Sue Emahl (née Churr). Even if there had been no dental records, this match between antemortem records and the bone would have been sufficient to establish her identity. Regardless, confirming an identity on multiple grounds is always a comfort.

There are still further types of identifications. One is exclusion. In some cases investigated by the army's Central Identification Laboratory in Hawaii, military aircraft were brought down by hostile fire during the Vietnam conflict, but the remains were not recovered until many years later. In at least one instance, the remains of one of the crew could be positively identified by dental and other medical records. Unfortunately, the remains of the other crewman were very incomplete and missing critical elements needed to make a positive identification. Nevertheless, a second person was clearly represented by those extra body parts.

Of course, the flight records did show who was meant to be aboard that aircraft, and given that the second person who had been assigned to the downed aircraft had not resurfaced elsewhere in the intervening years and that the plane had been lost, the logical conclusion was that the remains were his. Analysis of the skeleton could not disprove that hypothesis. Even the "fog of war" cannot obscure the sense of such an identification. Is it possible that he survived the crash, was taken prisoner, and is still being held? Of course it is possible, but that explanation would also require that another, similar body was substituted for his at the crash scene—an unlikely scenario. Still, the identification, seemingly secure, cannot be regarded as positive, as it was arrived at only by the exclusion of other possibilities.

A slightly less adequate sort of identification is one based on circumstantial evidence. Consider the following example: there is an automobile crash in which the body is so badly burned as to prohibit an identification by the usual means; no dental records can be found; the owner of the incinerated automobile is missing; there are no suspicious circumstances that suggest there was anything other than an unfortunate accident; an anthropological analysis of the charred skeletal remains identifies characters that are consistent with those of the missing person. What you have here is a set of circumstances that consistently point to the conclusion that the burned body is the missing owner of the car. Moreover, there are no data that point in the opposite direction. Thus, a circumstantial identification can be made. Most investigators would, of course, try to push on, searching for x-rays or other records that would transform this into a positive identification, but if none can be found the identification would have to remain circumstantial. Such cases might lead to court, where matters of property or culpability need to be settled. The best that one can do, if called to court, is to testify that the remains are consistent with the presumed identity, for not even clicking one's heels three times and crossing one's fingers behind one's back will turn this into anything other than what it is—a circumstantial identification.

FACIAL REPRODUCTION

Sometimes even the best efforts of everyone involved with a case cannot produce an identification. Skeletal findings, disseminated via the news media, fail to produce a lead. After the body has been held for a specified length of time (which varies with the jurisdiction), it may be buried as a John or Jane Doe. The case, however, remains active, and the conscientious investigator does like Terry Coker, a former New Mexico OMI deputy medical investigator who kept all of the Doe files in his office and plugged away at them as time allowed. His diligence was often rewarded with a successful identification—in one instance, six years after the case came in. Such intractable cases might also be treated to a facial reproduction.

The story is told that remains presumed to be those of Johann Sebastian Bach were excavated during the nineteenth century. Before reburying them in a fashion befitting his stature as one of the greatest of composers, those in charge of the exercise wanted to make sure that the remains really belonged to Bach. Hearing a scratching sound from inside the coffin, the curious excavators pried the lid open to reveal an almost completely skeletonized body. Clutched in one bony hand was a handwritten sheet of music; in the other was an eraser. The scratching was being produced by the eraser being drawn back and forth across the music. Thunderstruck, one of the crowd gasped, "Herr Bach, what are you doing?" Fixing an empty eye socket on the questioner, the apparition replied, "Dummkopf! I'm decomposing!"

Some of my colleagues question the veracity of this version of history, but, in fact, Bach's bones were dug up, and in the interest of demonstrating that they were in fact the esteemed J. S. himself, W. His built a face on the skull. That face nicely matched a portrait and bust of the great man. He reported on his efforts in 1895, following the work of Welcker, who, in 1883 and 1888, built faces on the skulls of Schiller and Kant. To provide data for the building of these faces, Welcker had collected data on the thickness of facial tissues at nine points in the midline of the face from thirteen males. His also took thicknesses on these midline dimensions and added a further six lateral thicknesses on twenty-four more males and four females. Using averages of these thicknesses, he produced a remarkable likeness of Bach.

Their work was followed by Kollmann and Buchly (1898), who collected data on thicknesses of facial tissues at ten points in the middle of the face and at eight locations laterally. Several other researchers added to the data pool, but the work of Kollmann and Buchly remained the standard for decades. Using their data, one could take the skull of an unknown person, read the tissue thickness at each location, place markers corresponding to those thicknesses on the skull, and fill in the spaces with clay. This became a sort of "scientific parlor trick" that was used for many years to get some idea of what persons no longer living might have looked like. For example, in 1912, H. H. Wilder put faces on the skulls of prehistoric Indians from southern New England. For the first time, it was possible to gain some reasonable idea of what people from an ancient time might have looked like. Or was it?

Were these fabricated faces a reasonably accurate reproduction of the people alive at that time and place, or was this process just fun and games masquerading as science? And if the technique was genuine, could it be used as a means of identifying people who were otherwise unidentifiable? In 1964, Ilan reported a favorable forensic outcome in an Israeli case, where an individual had been identified with the help of a facial reproduction.

In a series of papers and presentations, Clyde Snow and his colleagues (1970) reported good results in a forensic test of this German average tissue thickness method. M. M. Gerasimov (1971) described a more anatomically sophisticated technique that reconstructed facial muscles and other tissues rather than using average tissue thicknesses. He demonstrated his talents on skulls ranging from ancestral human to recent Russian historical figures.

Facial reproduction was widely known (if not always accepted) in the rarefied atmosphere of academia. Indeed, most anthropologists would present the technique to their classes in the same lighthearted manner as geologists were prone to present the 1912 drifting continent hypothesis of Alfred Wegener. But just as Wegener would be vindicated by the discovery of plate tectonics, facial reproduction would become generally accepted among forensic anthropologists. The work of Snow and his colleagues opened the floodgates to further experimentation with the average tissue thickness method and its eventual acceptance as a technique of limited usefulness in forensic anthropology.

A case usually develops in the following manner. A skeleton cannot be identified despite the best efforts of investigators. The skull lands on the desk of the forensic anthropologist, who gets clay and tables out of the cupboard and begins the task (Fig. 7.7). Upon completion, the face is photographed, and the image disseminated via newspapers and television. Someone sees the face, calls the police, and says, "I think that is my friend from school, Corrie Ograffy." Then the usual investigative machinery kicks into gear. The family is contacted, hospital or dental records are found and compared to the skeleton, and voilà! The identification is made. An identification is never made on the basis of the clay face itself. The face only provides a spur to dislodge records that could not otherwise be found, which in turn allows the identification to be made in the usual accepted way. Many identifications have been made in this manner, thereby decreasing the backlog of John and Jane Does and returning missing persons to their families (Fig. 7.8).

Our first attempt to reproduce a face on a skull was in 1975. The results were so encouraging that I began to wonder if the technique hadn't been rapped a bit harder than was merited. We decided to do some testing of the method by reproducing faces both on unknown skulls and on ones for which photos of the decedent were available. One of these tests was on a skull that was found with a few other bones and some clothing

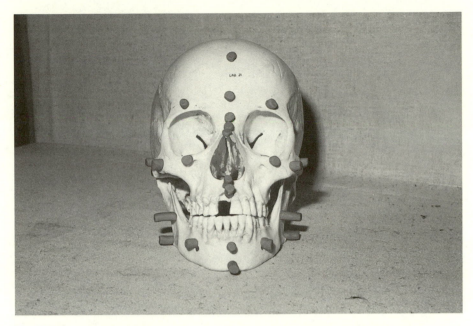

Fig. 7.7. Skull with tissue-depth markers applied in preparation for a facial reproduction.

about one and a quarter miles south of a Navajo chapter house, not far from Gallup on the Navajo Reservation in far western New Mexico.

The anthropological analysis showed that the skull was that of a female in her (probably) early twenties. Skull traits suggested mixed Indian and white ancestry. A driver's license in the pocket of the shirt found near the skull provided a putative identification. The license belonged to a 22-year-old Indian woman. The agreement between the analysis and the presumed identity, however, was not enough to make a positive identification, and we decided to build a face on her skull. After it was finished, a visit to the OMI turned up both a photograph of the deceased and her dental records. The dental records led to a positive identification, and the face in the photograph resembled our face, though she wore glasses. She was considerably heavier than we had assumed, with longer hair than the wig we had used, but we had reproduced an average face, which is what one must do if there are no reasons to do otherwise.

After one has reproduced a few faces, a powerful urge to do something a little out of the ordinary begins to manifest itself. A prominent dueling scar across one cheek, or maybe a raffish hooked nose, or perhaps even a

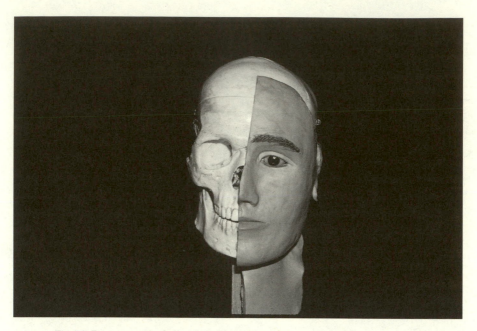

Fig. 7.8. Demonstration skull with facial reproduction on one side.

pair of Lyndon Johnson ears would have lent a wonderful air to the otherwise bland visage of Ms. May Happ, whose face we had reproduced in clay. Unfortunately, such delightfully idiosyncratic touches, while unleashing a little pent up artistic frustration, do not help in the identification process. The facial reproductionist must attempt to make the face as neutral as possible. The goal is to produce a rather standard set of ears and eyes and a nose that conforms to what the skull tells us it should look like, and to avoid any little touches that are not dictated by the shape of the skull itself. Unfortunately, what this also usually means is that, in seeking only the most neutral morphological territory, consecutive faces made by one person begin to resemble each other sharing the same eyes, ears, and noses instead of being true reflections of the skulls that lie beneath them. Motor habits and the desire to remain neutral tend to warp all faces reproduced by one person into the same mold, resulting in a series of faces that look like brothers and sisters.

Having seen Ms. Happ's picture, I could no longer touch the reproduction. The face thus revised would have become a product of an unwitting but still-real desire to make it look like her. Instead, I asked Marilyn London, then a graduate student in forensic anthropology who had done some work on the face, to imagine that Ms. Happ was considerably heavier than we had thought. London set about plumping up the face with gusto. When she was finished, we borrowed her glasses, replaced the short-haired wig we had used with a long-haired one, and were quite astounded at how closely the finished face now resembled that of Ms. Happ. It was also a dramatic example of how much hairstyle and a pair of glasses can alter someone's appearance.

Following the example of decades of researchers before us, we began to collect facial tissue thicknesses on individuals passing through the OMI. By using a fine needle to reach down through the facial tissues to the bone beneath it, the procedure left no marks for morticians to puzzle over. Eventually, another student, C. Elliott Moore, swung into serious collection of data, which resulted in his dissertation on facial tissue thickness. His data are widely used for this work today.

The reproduction of faces on skulls by this means is a slow, exacting process, which benefits from some artistic skill. Numerous people have brought their talents to the process, the best known being Betty Pat Gatliff. Gatliff, an accomplished artist and one of Snow's collaborators, went on to considerable fame with her finely rendered faces. A regular presence at forensic meetings, Gatliff enthusiastically taught scores of would-be facial reproducers the fine points of her unique ability to meld art and science effectively.

Because it takes many hours to build a face and because facial reproduction requires either a blend of anthropological and artistic abilities or close collaboration between an artist and an anthropologist, relatively few persist in this specialized work. There are also very few cases each year that merit facial reproductions. Not surprisingly, there has been a great deal of interest in devising computer programs capable of accomplishing the same goal much more expeditiously. Although some progress has been made, this is one area where the computer has not yet fully replaced a human. However, Robert George (1987) presents an alternative, which yields a profile sketch derived from lateral x-rays of the skull. J. Lawrence Angel used a similar approach earlier (Krogman, 1962).

If you are lucky enough to have a photograph of the presumed victim, another technique, facial superimposition, can be employed. In a method used by the late Tadao Furue (formerly of the army's Central Identification Laboratory), and a similar one developed by Walter Birkby (formerly with the Arizona State Museum), and others, the victim's skull and the photograph are mounted in a device. By carefully adjusting the position of each and reflecting their images off mirrors, images of skull and photograph can be merged. A fancier method, used by William Maples of the C. A. Pound Laboratory at the University of Florida in Gainesville and some others, employs video equipment to achieve the merging.

In either method, an identification can be ruled in or out by matching features seen on the face with those on the skull by fading images into each other on the screen. Although positive identification has been claimed using the electronic method (Helmer, 1987), a definitive test remains to be performed.

All of these methods offer some help in the process of identification of an unknown body, but each has its limits, and it is important never to believe that any of them offers a final solution. Each one is only another step on the long trail leading to an identification.

Court Testimony

The element that makes forensic medicine different from almost every other anthropological field is that a forensic scientist must be ready to testify in court—about any case investigated, or as a witness about matters of substance involving an individual's area of expertise. An excellent comprehensive review of the forensic anthropologist's relation to the legal process is offered by Galloway and colleagues (1990). What sets the forensic scientist apart from many other witnesses is his or her status as an expert witness.

Ordinary witnesses are called to testify about what they have observed, and anyone can be an ordinary witness if he or she has seen, heard, felt, tasted, or smelled something of importance to the presentation of evidence in a court case. But that is all. Ordinary witnesses may not testify regarding their opinion or beliefs on a certain event or circumstance. The expert witness, on the other hand, is someone who has had special training and/or experience that qualifies him or her not only to recount what he or she has done and how it was done, but also to explain to the jury the significance of those observations. A forensic anthropologist might be called to explain how an identification was made or what trauma has been visited upon a skeleton in the critical perimortem interval. One's obligation as an expert witness is to explain clearly to the jury what analysis was performed. Inasmuch as the forensic anthropologist has specialized knowledge about the human skeleton, a part of that explanation may revolve around how (for example) sex is determined from skeletal remains.

Forensic anthropological findings may also be relevant to the interpretation of particular features of the skeleton as well as to the cause and manner of death. An example is cited by forensic anthropologist Douglas Ubelaker and forensic odontologist Norman Sperber (1988). In that case, a body lay in a cistern near Omaha, Nebraska, for nearly nine years, showing degeneration of bone on the front of the skull and the teeth. That degeneration indicated that a corrosive substance had been poured on the body, and that the two bleached spots on the skull were the result of sunlight briefly focusing through holes in the thick manhole cover over the top of the cistern. This was part of the evidence that led to the conviction of the nineteen-year-old woman's murderer.

Before testifying in any case, a forensic anthropologist must first be contacted by one side or the other. Most often, forensic anthropologists are involved in criminal rather than civil proceedings, though there seems to be a growing "market" for testimony in civil suits as well. Forensic anthropologists are natural witnesses for the prosecution. For many years, they were such uncommon figures in trials that anthropological testimony went largely unchallenged by the defense or any defense witnesses. Defense teams were clearly unfamiliar with the presentation of skeletal evidence and did not bone up on it in advance. However, increasingly, forensic anthropologists have also found themselves working the other side of the table, opposite a colleague.

Before any court testimony is given, the custom is to schedule a pretrial conference in which the attorney meets informally with the witness he or she is calling. This conference gives the prospective witness a chance to lay out the information needed for his or her qualification by the court as an expert witness and to present the results of his or her analysis, so that the attorney can discover what questions to ask and how to put them. Only by becoming familiar with the nature of the evidence may an attorney determine the best way to bring it to the jury. The witness can only answer the questions put, and unless those questions are carefully framed, the evidence may not be effectively presented. In a sense, this pretrial conference is the opportunity for the expert to educate the attorney. It is not a rehearsal of testimony, but is a means for discovering how to achieve maximum effectiveness in its presentation. To eschew this step robs the presentation of evidence of its value.

Forensic anthropologist Susan Jimenez was called to the scene of a buried body. Because predators had invaded the shallow grave, bones were scattered over a wide area. The excavation and search took two days, the analysis required another two days, and the completion of the report, several additional hours the next day. Called to testify before a grand jury, she repeatedly requested a pretrial conference and was assured that there would be time for one. She arrived early to go over her report—and waited. After an hour or so, she was ushered into the jury chamber and the examination began. The district attorney had apparently decided to "wing" it, bypassing the pretrial conference. Moreover, he later acknowledged that he never even took the time to read her report. As a consequence, though Jimenez was prepared, the district attorney was not. The questions came thick and fast, but lacked substance and never really got to the heart of the matter critical to the case, identification. Not having read the report, he also bungled the presentation of trauma evidence. The public is not well served when attorneys attempt to save time by eliminating this important step.

Several years ago, I was called to testify for the prosecution about the identity of a lower leg and foot found in a shoe in a dried-up riverbed in the southern part of New Mexico. The remains had also been analyzed by a physical anthropologist, who had been called to testify for the defense. Before one can begin the testimony, the court goes through the ritual of "qualification." The attorney leads the prospective witness through an examination that details one's education, special training, and experience. This may also include a recounting of offices held in forensic organizations, and casework, research, publication, and teaching experience in forensics. Its purpose is to convince the jury that the person about to testify has the knowledge and experience necessary to perform the analysis that has been done. If accepted by the court, the specialist is then qualified to testify as an expert witness.

In this instance the qualification went well, was stipulated to by the defense, and accepted by the judge. When my testimony was complete, I stepped down. Then the defense set about qualifying its expert witness. After hearing the presentation, the judge leaned his elbows on his desk, fixed his gaze on the defense attorney, and said, "Before today I never knew that there was such a thing as a forensic anthropologist, or that there was board certification in it. But if our previous witness was an expert in forensic anthropology, your witness is not. She may testify as an expert witness in physical anthropology, but not in forensic anthropology." While I was sorry that my colleague had been shot down like this, it was gratifying that the judge was able to make the distinction. Incidentally, even though the leg could not be positively identified as belonging to the missing person, its age, sex, and condition were consistent with those of the missing person. The jurors apparently believed that the leg was evidence that somebody was probably dead and that it was most likely the missing person. They convicted.

Depending upon the attorney, explanations of the skeletal material and its analysis may be brief, or detailed—including the use of slides, charts, models, or demonstration skeletal material. In fact, juries seem to enjoy a brief lesson in skeletal anatomy, particularly when it is augmented with actual demonstration skeletons (typically using none of the bones from the case under trial, which could be regarded as inflammatory). This explanation gives the jurors a nice break from the tedium of the usual expert-witness testimony, which, as the O. J. Simpson trial reminded us, can be extremely detailed, complicated, and, yes, even boring. Some experts seem to feel that they have best demonstrated their expertise when their exit from the stand is accompanied by a bevy of puzzled looks, and perhaps a few heavy-lidded eyes in nodding heads. On the contrary, their testimony has been most effective when the jurors lean forward in their seats, captivated by an interesting and well-presented summary of how the expert has discovered the facts of the case, which amounts to a semester of forensic osteology boiled down into an insightful half-hour or so. Once a jury has been given that background, the forensic anthropologist can easily explain the significance of the observations made in the case.

It is better to explain details simply so that they can be understood by the average person than to attempt to impress the jury with one's command of specialized vocabulary. After all, the function of the jury is to take this information, combine it with everything else seen and heard, and render a just verdict. The job of the expert witness is *not* to be an advocate for the side for which he or she is testifying. The attorneys are the advocates, the prosecution advocating guilt and the defense advocating innocence, regardless of the charge . . . and regardless of the evidence. The expert witnesses are there for the sole purpose of laying out for the jury the bit of evidence that falls into their area of expertise. The jury, not the expert witness, is charged with the responsibility of making the decision.

We have all heard "horror stories" from some of our colleagues about rough handling by defense attorneys, in which their abilities were challenged unkindly. This sort of hostile cross-examination can be brought on by an expert witness venturing beyond his or her area of expertise (Galloway et al., 1990). Much of it is legal maneuvering in which attorneys strive to instill doubt or confusion in the minds of the jurors. Sometimes, however, the attorneys come up on the short end. Peter V. MacDonald (1987) relates a story told to him by a Victoria (B.C.) colleague. A psychiatrist testifying for the plaintiff described those individuals who were susceptible to post-traumatic neurosis as "rigid, compulsive, and inflexible." This fit the description of the plaintiff as given by other witnesses. The defense wished to downplay the importance of this testimony by showing that such traits were rarely found in a single person. The psychiatrist insisted that whole groups of people exhibit most or all of these characteristics. The attorney challenged the psychiatrist to name even one group of people having such character traits. The psychiatrist smiled at the jury and replied, "The most obvious example is lawyers."

8
Medicolegal Investigation

The New Mexico Office of the Medical Investigator

In days of yore, the investigation of death was a good deal more casual than it is today. The important thing was that someone was dead. Nor was that particularly surprising. Death was accepted as a normal consequence of life. People were closer to the earth in those days, and the natural cycle of birth and death—a single season for most plants and a matter of a few years for small mammals—was accepted as a part of the natural order.

In human households, the extended family, sometimes comprising four generations, was the norm. One could witness the entire cycle of life being repeated time and time again. In these more remote times, when knowledgeable medical care was not routinely available, people died early and young. Well, that's not completely true. The average age at death in prehistoric and even early historic times may have been under thirty-five years, but that did not mean that when one reached that age it was necessarily all over. Many lived to ripe old ages even then. It is true to say, however, that every significant injury or disease could be life-threatening.

But it was not always easy to be sure whether someone was dead. The custom of the wake probably owes its existence to that dilemma. If you keep a body around for a few days while kinfolk and friends gather to pay their last respects, it will soon be clear enough whether the person is dead. The body will begin to undergo some of the decompositional changes discussed earlier, and before long the congregated relatives will become quite willing to conclude the exercise by burying the deceased. Even so, in the latter part of the nineteenth century, there remained enough doubt about the finality of death that some of the better coffins were equipped with signaling devices just in case the corpse awoke to find that the world had suddenly become dark and cramped. The unfortunate subterranean could then pull a lever and raise a flag to announce his or her recovery. Although clever, this device seems not to have been used very often. As the practice of embalming grew in popularity, accidental burial became a thing of the past. The probability of surviving the replacement of the blood in one's veins with what amounts to antifreeze is about as close to zero as it is possible to calculate. Occasionally, however, a story about a person regaining consciousness on a mortician's slab, having been pronounced dead, will surface. The public official most frequently charged with pronouncement of death is the coroner. When the English began their colonization of North America, they brought the office of the coroner with them. Like so many other imports, the office changed, losing a great deal of its power and prestige on its way to the colonies. Not only was the coroner no longer a royal appointment, he was forced to run for the office like a common politician in many jurisdictions. Unlike most other offices, however, the election of a coroner was not usually a hot contest. Most people were not eager to deal with dead bodies. As a consequence, the office often attracted persons with only the most marginal credentials for determining the cause and manner of death. Indeed, even today the otherwise sophisticated and intellectually advanced state of Colorado demands of its candidates for coroner only ninety days residence in the county in which they seek the office.

Morticians, service station operators, and the proverbial little old lady in tennis shoes would not seem to be particularly promising choices for such an office, yet some tennis-shoe-shod oldsters have been particularly good at the job, since they have attended courses in medicolegal investigation. They frequently exercise the coroner's option of seeking outside advice from qualified experts and arrange to have proper autopsies performed whenever appropriate.

The Medical Examiner

As the weaknesses of the coroner system became apparent, several large cities adopted medical examiner systems. In 1939, Maryland became the first state to adopt such a system statewide. Unlike the typical county coroner, who is usually untrained in medicine, the medical examiner in most jurisdictions is a licensed physician, a forensic pathologist trained in the determination of cause and manner of death. In a few municipalities, the office of coroner was combined with that of medical examiner.

The advantages of a medical examiner system are numerous. First, the selection of the chief medical examiner is based on qualifications and merit, not on political popularity, which is how most coroners are selected. Second, the system enforces a uniform handling of cases across each its jurisdiction. A system expanded to the entire state ensures that even the lowliest sharecropper who dies in the remotest part of the state will receive the same diligent investigation as the most powerful political figure shot by an indignant taxpayer. Third, with death investigation standardized at a sophisticated level, the likelihood that a murder will go undetected or that a death due to dangerous working conditions will escape notice diminishes substantially.

The first western state, and the largest one at that time, to institute a statewide system of medicolegal investigation was Utah. However, its first chief medical examiner, forensic pathologist Dr. James T. Weston, was aware of numerous shortcomings in the laws and the operation of that system. He was asked to assist the State of New Mexico in the design of an ideal system. Through his efforts and the dedicated work of many others, New Mexico's legislature passed legislation in 1973 eliminating the county coroner and substituting a centralized medical examiner system.

The New Mexico Office of the Medical Investigator

On July 1, 1973, county coroners were replaced with the Office of the Medical Investigator (OMI), a medical examiner system based in Albuquerque. (Since New Mexico already had a medical examiner who certified physicians for their medical licenses, the name "medical *investigator*" was used, even though it is a medical *examiner* system.) This new agency was charged by state law to investigate all sudden, unnatural, untimely, unattended, and suspicious deaths. Its head was to be a board-certified forensic pathologist appointed by a supervisory board made up of the dean of the University of New Mexico School of Medicine, the chief of the New Mexico State Police, the state secretary of the Health and Environment Department and the chairman of the New Mexico Board of Thanatopractice. The office thus became a state agency, supported by the state government, but operating independently of law enforcement agencies.

Upon notification of a reportable death, an investigator is sent to the scene. The appropriate law enforcement agency also responds. Jurisdiction is divided, law enforcement being responsible for the scene and the OMI for the body. This division of labor assures a death investigation that is independent of law enforcement agencies. Furthermore, while many medical examiner systems employ the police as their investigative arm, New Mexico uses lay investigators. Most of these are part-time employees (approximately 120 in the thirty-three counties). Albuquerque and the rest of Bernalillo County, the most populous area in the state, require six full-time investigators.

Weston was appointed as OMI's first chief medical investigator, and he served until his untimely death in 1981. Since then, the system has been well served by three other chiefs, two of whom—Drs. Patricia McFeeley and Ross Zumwalt—currently rotate the duties between them. The OMI is funded by the state but administered through the Department of Pathology at the University of New Mexico School of Medicine. Weston's recommendation to base the system in the university was to make it a resource for the medical school and to provide training for medical students, residents, and other medical professionals. Being a part of the university also allowed the OMI to gain access to various medical and nonmedical consultants on campus. University affiliation also assured that despite the focus on service to the community, the OMI could engage in research rather than become what Weston contemptuously called a "body shop" in which cadavers would be wheeled in and out as quickly as possible (Fig. 8.1).

THE USE OF COMPUTERS

The OMI was established to improve the determination of the cause and manner of sudden, unexpected deaths, and to upgrade and standardize the handling, analysis, and reporting of deaths throughout the state. In so doing, it would become the central repository for information compiled during the course of death investigations. To facilitate collection of the data and subsequent analysis, Weston adopted computerization, making the OMI one of the first such agencies to use electronic data retrieval as an integral part of its organization. He believed that paper records and human memories are simply inadequate to preserve the information obtained from more than four thousand deaths and over a thousand autopsies each year.

To Weston, the computer was a means to (1) improve turnaround time and accuracy of autopsy and other reports, (2) maintain control over the location of bodies and status of cases, (3) collect statistical and billing data, (4) improve response to inquiries from law enforcement agencies, morticians, families, and attorneys, (5) provide a database to be used for

Fig. 8.1. James T. Weston, M.D., the designer and the first chief medical investigator of the New Mexico Office of the Medical Investigator. (Photo courtesy of Dr. Patricia J. McFeeley)

research, and (6) improve management control (Healy, Aragon, and Weston, 1983).

During more than twenty years of operation, increasing demands for data and reports outstripped the OMI's computer capacity again and again. As a consequence, it has repeatedly upgraded its computing capability employing a series of five computer systems, two of which are currently in use. These electronic databases facilitate the rapid assimilation and digestion of information, and the reporting of investigations to official agencies and concerned members of the public in a timely fashion. In addition, statistical reports and data sets are made available to various state agencies, to the Center for Disease Control in Atlanta, and to legitimate researchers. The system was also designed to provide Boolean searches of the database for research purposes (Harris, Starr, and Smialek, 1985). Aficionados of the traditional mystery might be somewhat saddened to learn that the computer named "Sherlock" has recently given way to the more powerful and faster "Quincy."

Computer terminals providing direct access to the data are available to most employees throughout the office. The system combines both data and text files, including well-defined databases and free text describing the details and circumstances of each case. This word processing capability allows autopsy and other reports to be entered directly into the data bank (Harris, Starr, and Smialek, 1985). The word processor is also used by pathologists and others to prepare manuscripts, correspondence, and calendars and by clerical staff to handle the complex paperwork of the organization.

Services to the Public

The OMI is dedicated to the determination of the cause and manner of death, but is vitally concerned with the protection of the public from unnecessary health risks. Through the performance of an autopsy, the cause of death may be linked to a contagious disease or to unsafe working conditions. Uncovering such a link can be important in preventing unnecessary deaths. The OMI also provides information to the Medical Examiners/Coroners Consumer Product Alert Project for possible dissemination of warnings about unsafe products and equipment. Statistical data on deaths caused by controlled substances or therapeutic drugs are similarly available to public agencies. Such information is important to an understanding and controlling the frequency of drug-related deaths.

The New Mexico Sudden Infant Death Syndrome (SIDS) Information and Counseling Program, as part of the OMI, provides information and support to those families who have lost an infant to SIDS. They also provide assistance and education programs to other health professionals who deal with SIDS deaths. Out of this program has grown a Death Intervention Program, which provides support and educational services to all New Mexico families experiencing the death of a child, unrelated to SIDS, between infancy and eighteen years.

Since 1975 the OMI has conducted an annual Death Investigation Seminar. This week-long seminar features up-to-date instruction from experts in the many disciplines of forensic science. Many of the instructors are on the OMI staff, while others with specific expertise and national reputations are invited as guest lecturers. The seminar's primary purpose is to enhance the abilities of the OMI's 110 field investigators, half of whom attend in alternate years. Some of these dedicated deputies have been with the OMI since its inception. The seminar regularly draws more than half of its attendance, generally over a hundred, from law enforcement officers, death investigators, pathologists, and others. Participants come not only from around the Southwest, but from across the nation and from Canada. Each seminar provides details, new procedures, and information on death investigation, as well as a review of a wide range of topics from year to year. For example, lecturers may discuss SIDS, gunshot wounds, blunt trauma, burned bodies, recovery of bodies, odontology, anthropology, and a host of other topics.

The use of forensic anthropology in death investigation has expanded greatly in the last decade and seminars specifically devoted to the discipline have sprung up around the country. In 1995, the OMI inaugurated its own week-long seminar in forensic anthropology. The faculty consists both of local forensic anthropologists and experienced forensic anthropologists from across the country. Conducted with the cooperation of the Maxwell Museum, the seminar is kept down to fewer than thirty participants, enabling each attendee to work directly with skeletal material and receive individual attention from the faculty.

How a Case is Processed

The OMI enabling legislation requires that whenever human remains or remains suspected of being human are found within the state (except on Indian lands or military reservations, which may invite OMI's presence) the discoverer must notify either the local law enforcement agency or the OMI. The notified agency alerts the other, and both converge upon the scene. The police agency secures the scene and. in cooperation with the OMI, makes photographs and sketches, gathers evidence, interviews witnesses, and performs other relevant work. The OMI investigator, who may also take photographs and interview witnesses then takes custody of the body, seals it in a body bag, and arranges for its delivery to the OMI.

Nearly 66 percent of all deaths in any jurisdiction occur naturally. In 1995, though 12,189 deaths occurred in New Mexico, only 4,200 were reported to the OMI. Furthermore, 2,965 (64 percent) of those 4,200 cases were determined to be due to natural causes by circumstances and medical histories, so that an autopsy was not required (OMI, 1995). In each such case, an external examination of the body is conducted to rule out any possibility of injury. The clothing is inspected and the body undressed.

The body is minutely examined. Scars, surgical incisions, tattoos, and other marks are noted, blood and other fluid samples are taken, and the body is released.

In those cases where the cause and manner of death are not evident, where there are other medicolegal reasons, or where the judgment of the forensic pathologist calls for it, an autopsy is scheduled. Most forensic autopsies are complete procedures, beginning with an external examination, which is followed by removal and dissection of all organs. Tissue samples from every organ are preserved for possible microscopic and other examinations. The autopsy procedure is rigorous but flexible enough to accommodate the needs of a wide variety of cases. A full autopsy will usually involve a team of three or four people: the pathologist and his assistants. The procedure may take as little as one to two hours but, with complicated cases, may require more time and still more assistants. In the instance of multiple gunshot wounds, for example, not only must each bullet and major fragment be recovered, but the trajectory of the missile through the body should be determined, often with the aid of probes and x-rays. The pathologist dictates the details of the findings into a tape recorder. This dictation is given to transcriptionists, who enter it into the computer as a part of the case record.

When identification is an issue, the forensic odontologist may be summoned to chart the teeth, and the forensic anthropologist may be asked to determine the demographic specifics of the case. Particularly when decomposed, burned, or skeletonized bodies are the subjects, the usual means of identification and analysis cannot be used. The organs and organ systems that the pathologist is trained to evaluate have been compromised and their information content reduced. In those cases, then, the anthropologist and odontologist are of particular value. The anthropologist is also useful where analysis of damage to the bodies (and the bones) bears on establishing the cause or manner of death.

Cases not of Medicolegal Significance

On occasion, it will be evident at the scene that remains are not human, and that no further action need be taken. On the other hand, scene investigators seldom have grounding in skeletal anatomy and may not always be able to determine whether remains are human. If they are human and of undoubted medicolegal significance, they will be delivered to the main office for analysis. If the investigator can positively determine—

sometimes with the help of a field archaeologist—that the remains are too old to be of medicolegal significance (that is to say that they have been in situ for more than fifty years and the chances of finding the person or persons responsible for putting them there are therefore very slim), they can simply be covered back up and reported to the appropriate agency. Where there is any doubt, the remains will be delivered to the main office for analysis. Remains may be prehistoric or historic (including things like "trophy skulls" or specimens from teaching collections) and thus not of medicolegal significance.

In addition to prehistoric or historic human remains and nonhuman bones, another example of a case that has no medicolegal significance (in the usual sense) is the occasional buried body, or collection of body parts, which appears on the surface as the result of a prank, excavation in an area not known to contain bodies, or high water. These can usually be recognized for what they are because of the presence of embalming fluids or artifacts of the embalming process (Berryman et al., 1991). Of course, the law would have an interest in such cases if the grave was purposely and maliciously invaded.

The Forensic Pathology Team

The forensic team consists a number of individuals, each with an expertise in a different area: field investigator, forensic pathologist, autopsy technician, forensic toxicologist, forensic odontologist, and forensic anthropologist. Depending upon the nature of the case, other members could be added, such as a forensic entomologist or a forensic psychiatrist. Of course not all of these team members are required in the analysis of every case.

As previously mentioned, the OMI employs lay investigators who are neither sworn law enforcement officers nor medical technicians. Nevertheless, such positions often attract people with some law enforcement or medical experience. Rigorously trained for their scene investigation duties, they pronounce the victim dead, initiate the chain of evidence, work with police, determine whether the death will require further investigation, and take custody of the body for delivery to either the OMI or a funeral home. They also assist with completion of the death certificate and act as the primary interface between the OMI and the family.

The pathologist assigned to a case acts as the "case manager," scheduling and performing the autopsy and collecting prescribed tissue samples for analysis. The pathologist's responsibility is to ascertain the cause and manner of death, for which the office assumes jurisdiction. Additional duties may include identification of the body, uncovering a previously unrecognized crime, or the discovery of potential hazards to public health. Not all deaths require autopsies. The cause and manner of death can often be determined through a review of medical records, the circumstances of death, and an external examination of the body. The pathologist is ultimately responsible for signing the death certificate.

Autopsy technicians at the OMI are usually young people with an interest in medicine. Many of them are undergraduate students who eventually move on to medical school or to work in allied fields. Under the supervision of the pathologists, they attend to the preparation of a body for autopsy, ready the necessary instruments, produce x-rays and photographs, and assist with some routine autopsy procedures. They also take the final steps in preparing the body for release to a funeral home and keep the autopsy area safe and orderly.

The toxicologist is routinely consulted to determine whether foreign substances (i.e. poisons) are present in the body and if their concentration is high enough to bear on the person's death. The toxicologist is often asked to help interpret alcohol levels found in a body at death, but the mandate of the toxicologist extends beyond alcohol to any of the various recreational or therapeutic drugs that can affect a person's mental acuity and functions. The discovery of any such drugs in a body can greatly affect the determination of the cause and manner of death.

The most commonly found substance and the one most frequently abused is alcohol. New Mexico recently lowered its presumptive level of driving under the influence of alcohol from 0.1 percent to 0.08 percent, the level at which it is assumed that impairment of function occurs. New Mexico's motor vehicle death rate, second highest of the fifty states, has gained the state some notoriety. Toxicology shows that 50 percent of those tested who were involved in vehicular deaths had alcohol present in their bloodstreams (OMI, 1994). In fact, blood alcohol levels significantly beyond the minimum "lethal level" (0.4 percent) have been found both in drivers and pedestrians involved in accidents resulting in death.

Odontologists and anthropologists are less frequently consulted. A forensic odontologist is a dentist trained and experienced in forensic work. In most cases, pathologists can swiftly and easily identify a body, but in others identification is the prime issue at autopsy. The odontologist is frequently called upon to make those identifications, as he or she can rule in or out a putative identification by means of a dental comparison. If supported with adequately detailed antemortem records from the victim's dentist, a positive identification can usually be made.

The skills of the odontologist can be utilized for a positive identification only when there are adequate antemortem records for comparison with a body. While these are usually charts prepared by the victim's dentist, records may also consist of x-rays of the mouth and teeth, summary written records, or, on occasion, photographs that can be matched to the victim's teeth. Forensic odontologists can make very rapid identifications from such records and their input is invaluable in the processing of victims of mass disasters. Even without dental records, odontologists can provide useful information about the quality and origin of the dental care, as well as offering some perspective on the demography of the decedent.

Anthropologists are typically consulted when the remains are skeletal or partly skeletonized, when the body is decomposed or burned, or when x-rays of a fresh body's skeleton can provide some insight into identification or the nature of injury to bones. They are also useful in providing an independent confirmation of identity. Anthropologists are often consulted for assistance in excavating a body, in the reconstruction of shattered bones, in the reproduction of faces on skulls, and myriad other tasks. By this point in the book, you will no doubt have anticipated the next line: when in doubt, call a forensic anthropologist.

COURTROOM TESTIMONY

Cases cannot be considered closed simply because the final reports are filed and the data have been entered in the computer. In all cases, there is a potential for new information coming to light. These new facts could alter the cause and manner of death or some other medicolegal opinion. In addition, the family or other interested persons may request a review of the findings with the pathologist. Many of the cases handled by medical examiner systems around the country involve the attenuation of life by human or other agencies. In such cases, the final societal demands can be satisfied only when the company or person allegedly committing the offense is brought to court.

Forensic experts are thus faced with the potential of giving courtroom testimony in many of the cases they handle. In this milieu, they are subpoenaed to testify and appear in court as expert witnesses. To so testify, they must be qualified as experts and accepted by the court, as explained in the previous chapter. The expert is allowed to present evidence, interpret that evidence, and express opinions about its validity, importance, and meaning. Expert witnesses may be called both by the prosecution and the defense. In such instances, those expert witnesses may present diametrically opposed interpretations of the same case.

The Office of the Medical Investigator as a Model System

Since its founding, the OMI has been studied and visited by medicolegal authorities from around the nation and the world. Many of the practices now routinely employed elsewhere were first tried or perfected by the OMI. The citizens of the state of New Mexico have good reason to be proud of their exemplary system for the investigation of death.

Among Chief Medical Investigator Weston's early tasks was getting the OMI system up and running against a degree of local resistance. The new legislation prescribed that a deputy medical investigator be summoned to the scene of any dead body, and that the deputy should work the scene with the law enforcement people. Each sheriff or local police chief had thus to surrender some of his or her authority, and not all were delighted at the prospect of sharing a death scene with a representative of some bureaucracy in far-away Albuquerque. Eventually these problems were resolved, mainly by OMI's working demonstration of the advantages of a professional medicolegal death investigation system.

The problems of managing such a far-flung system were legion. New Mexico is the fifth largest of the United States, with an area of over 121,000 square miles. To cover adequately this vast area, the OMI initially relied upon district medical investigators (local physicians) to conduct routine autopsies in parts of the state remote from Albuquerque. Since the more difficult autopsies still required the attention of forensic pathologists, several methods were tried, including flying forensic pathologists across the state for autopsies. In the last few years, all autopsies to be done under OMI authority have been driven into Albuquerque. Transporting bodies across half the length or breadth of the state is expensive, but this has been proven to be the most effective way of conducting autopsies with consistent high quality and under controlled conditions.

There have been some problems, however. Any complex system is bound to have some unexpected glitches to bedevil it. For example, the OMI now requires that ambulance drivers be not only of sober and upstanding character, but bonded. Experience has demonstrated the necessity of such tight constraints. Several years ago, an ambulance brought a body from Gallup, near the Arizona border, into Albuquerque for autopsy. The work was finished late in the afternoon, and the body was ready to be returned to Gallup. The ambulance driver now faced the prospect of a long drive back into the glare of the setting sun. Deciding to fortify himself against the numbing drone of tires on pavement, he settled into a local beverage emporium. By the time he finally got up the will to head west, the sun was coasting down behind the west mesa volcanos, and he was a bit numb himself.

Sensibly, he checked into a motel, letting his charge cool his heels in the ambulance outside until morning. But quantities of intoxicants have a way of relaxing inhibitions, and before long he was bragging to other temporary denizens of the motel that he had a dead body in his ambulance and, by golly, he was going to show them. He jerked open the back door and whisked the gurney out into the motel parking lot so that his admirers could better observe his quiet cargo. Apparently not everyone was impressed with the display, since someone called the police.

Gathering what remained of his wits, the driver hoisted the body back into the ambulance and headed off toward Gallup, preferring the solitude of the road to that of a jail cell. He made it about thirty miles before the combination of tire hum, the lateness of the hour, and the effects of his binge all caught up with him. Somewhere in the vicinity of Laguna Pueblo, his ambulance followed its own instincts, never very good in a motor vehicle, and ended up in the borrow pit. The doors flew open, and both the living and the dead were ejected. One can readily imagine the consternation of the police arriving at the scene to find one alive, contrite, but buzzy-headed driver, and one dead, autopsied passenger.

In any large system, such problems are bound to arise, but with stern and forceful action, a recurrence can be prevented. Indeed, with six deputy medical investigators housed in the main office in Albuquerque and more than 120 others spread throughout the state, all interfacing with a variety of local, state, and national law enforcement agencies, it is amazing that the system operates as smoothly as it does.

State law specifically charges the OMI with investigation under a long list of circumstances, the final one being "suspicious." Thus, in addition to requiring investigations in specific circumstances, the OMI may also initiate one when there is any hint of wrongdoing.

As a part of the process of looking into the cause and manner of death, the OMI, like any investigative agency, must maintain the "chain of evidence," or chain of custody, a written and signed document. Every person who handles any item of evidence—whether it be a body or a vial of drugs—must sign for it. If the case comes to trial, this chain will demonstrate to the court that the evidence has been passed from one hand to another without alteration (except as specified in written records) and is the same evidence that was recovered at the scene. In this way, the jury may be certain that the autopsied body is the same one as that found at the scene and is the same one from which the testimony they hear has been derived. A clear chain of custody ensures that a drug sample has not been switched or modified, and is an additional protection for the defendant as well as for the consistency of the case.

One of Clyde Snow's Oklahoma cases illustrates the importance of maintaining the chain of evidence. When called to testify, he was told he didn't even need to bring a toothbrush, since the prosecutor planned to have him on and off the stand in the twinkling of an eye. But as the trial opened, the defense demanded to establish the chain of evidence. The victim had been assaulted by two of his fellows and had died of the beating. In their attempt to hide the body, the murderers buried (and unburied) the providentially named Barry twice. Faced with the prospect of discovery, they chainsawed Barry into pieces of a size convenient to fling out of the bed of a pickup. For days, searchers discovered bits of Barry in the eastern Oklahoma woods, whence they were relayed by patrol car to Snow's lab in Oklahoma City.

Establishing the chain of evidence meant that the presentation of the other evidence would have to wait until all of the people who had handled the various bits of Barry had been called to the stand to establish their role. Snow got a hotel room, bought a toothbrush and eventually a new wardrobe as he patiently waited day after day for the matter of the chain of custody to be settled. Proper record keeping would have eliminated this laborious (and expensive) exercise.

The key to the successful operation of such a system is to assure that deputy medical investigators are trained so that they can go to a scene, help in its analysis, and take custody of the body. The deputy must be able to ascertain whether there is sufficient information to certify the cause and manner of death, or whether it will require additional investigation. With jurisdiction of the body already belonging to the OMI, the decision of whether an autopsy is required is an essential one.

The lives of those connected with a medical examiner's office are not easy. Although those who are investigators, pathologists, and autopsy technicians have usually chosen that line of work because they find it interesting, bristling with challenges, and because it offers them an opportunity to exercise their intellect on an array of problems presented to them, nobody, no matter how detached he or she professes to be, could be unaffected by the horizontal parade of this vast army of the dead. Very few of these forensic specialists could really be considered "ghoulish," but their exchanges are often larded with humor that would be inappropriate outside the confines of their work. This humor, however, often masks some deep-seated feelings of horror and revulsion at the inert bodies daily passing before their eyes. Forensic anthropologists, who typically see only a limited number of skeletonized cases, or other remains that have lost most of their human appearance, have an easy task by comparison. Those who deal with death on a day-to-day basis deserve not only our respect but our compassion as well. They perform an unpleasant task in our society—one that is largely invisible, but essential to the public, and one which is not undertaken lightly.

THE FACILITIES

When the OMI was established, it was temporarily housed in a small steel building at the edge of the University of New Mexico's Medical School campus. There was barely enough room for the small staff, and no facilities for conducting postmortem examinations were available. Postmortem procedures were conducted in a tiny autopsy room at the Bernalillo County Medical Center (BCMC), which later became the University of New Mexico Hospital. This facility was not designed for the high volume of work generated by both the OMI and regular hospital autopsies. Moreover, like most metropolitan hospitals, BCMC had grown by leaps and bounds, and the facilities were in a constant state of flux. One round of shifting placed the autopsy room next to the cafeteria, and the rather powerful odors of decomposed bodies crept into the ventilation system and were whisked next door. The confluence of smells—decomposed bodies and hospital food—may have made the food seem more palatable by contrast, but it led to the hospital banning the autopsy of decomposed bodies there. The OMI had to contract with a funeral parlor for that period.

The low bidder was located several miles from the hospital, near the north edge of town, and decomposed bodies were shuttled there for autopsy. However, the funeral home was not pleased at the prospect of overpowering odors of the not very recently deceased drifting silently into viewing rooms, where clusters of relatives and friends gathered around the more recently departed. To accommodate them as much as possible, the OMI agreed to conduct those autopsies outdoors, weather permitting. Fortunately, the weather was agreeable in the seasons in which decomposed bodies were most likely to be found. The autopsy crew would drive out to the funeral home, extract the body from the cooler, place it on the gurney, and wheel it out into the parking lot next to the funeral home. A screen of automobiles shielded the process from traffic on busy North Fourth Street, which was also U.S. Highway 85, the old main route into town. This main north-south route from Denver to El Paso was slowly being superseded by the construction of Interstate 25, up on the then-lonely sandy mesa a couple of miles to the east.

While appearing casual, the autopsies were conducted with the same rigor and attention to detail that they would have received in a carefully designed facility. In those days, before the passage of the Occupational Safety and Health Act, autopsy personnel slipped on an apron and a pair of gloves, and settled down under the arching cottonwoods to begin the task. Most of the odor usually dissipated in the breezes, making these outdoor autopsies quite pleasant. In those remote times sunscreen was regarded as the most important autopsy protection. Donning a mask was considered a bit wimpish, though the initiates sometimes did, surreptitiously slathering a bit of camphor on the inside to block the odor. At one of these sessions, two FBI agents showed up to observe the procedure, prompting a number of humorous sotto voce comments about the strange sight they made, attired in suits, white shirts, ties, and . . . gas masks.

Weston immediately began pushing for the construction of a facility adequate to handle all the many and varied demands that would be placed upon it in the future. When construction was complete in 1976, the OMI moved into the east half of the ground floor of the new Tri-State Labs. In the west half was the Veterinary Diagnostic Services while the State Health labs occupied the upper floors. The sparkling new facilities accommodated all autopsies in a state-of-the-art facility that provided a reception area, a conference room, and office space for staff, pathologists, and investigators. A long hallway led to the autopsy suite at the rear of the building, which could also be entered from a large garage and body-receiving

Fig. 8.2. The autopsy suite at the OMI. (Photo courtesy of the Office of the Medical Investigator, Albuquerque, New Mexico)

area. There were also rooms for storage of autopsy tissue samples and other evidence and a histology lab (Fig. 8.2).

To allow for expansion, Weston's design included an unfinished area, equal in size to the office space. Before long, that space was finished and filled with new offices for the expanding staff as well as a new computer room. A second expansion added an isolation room for bodies suspected of harboring infectious diseases, a forensic anthropology lab, walk-in coolers, and new space for investigators beyond the autopsy suite.

The somewhat casual autopsy dress that was common around the country even a decade ago has given way to full protection, and the bustle of activity in the brilliantly lit autopsy suite has accelerated with ever increasing caseloads. The OMI has made every effort to isolate those who perform the autopsies from health dangers of blood-borne pathogens such as AIDS, and others like hepatitis, New Mexico's endemic plague, and hantavirus while they conduct their duties. The world of the autopsy has become ever more demanding and scientific. The susurration of cottonwood leaves no longer plays counterpoint to the autopsy.

The Downside of Forensic Anthropology

The preceding descriptions focus on the organization and operation of the New Mexico OMI. Established medical examiner offices elsewhere operate in a similar manner. However, the role played by forensic anthropology is not a consistent feature. A happy accident of circumstance established forensic anthropology as more or less an integral part of the OMI's operation almost from the start, but the inclusion of forensic anthropology in medicolegal investigative units in other parts of the country varies greatly. In most, however, there are no official appointments, no business cards or other trappings of affiliation. When a medical examiner gets a bone case, he or she may just as readily decide to work it alone as to call the forensic anthropologist.

Since most anthropologists are affiliated with universities, they can race over to look at bodies after classes are over for the day. Indeed, this points up one of the fundamental problems for forensic anthropologists. Like other academics, they must work to establish their professional reputations by hobnobbing with others in their field, conducting research, and presenting the results at meetings and in journals. Building up one's credentials in any field is a slow process, retarded by the need to concoct class lectures and exams, as well as tending to the usual department and university obligations. Still, the process may be a bit easier in forensic anthropology where there are only around two hundred people to get to know, rather than the two thousand or so in all of physical anthropology.

Unlike other academics, however, the forensic anthropologist must earn respect within the medicolegal community. While the average academic faces problems in gaining access to suitable research material, the forensic anthropologist has to interface with a group outside the academic world: the sheriffs, police, coroners, and medical examiners from whom casework must come. Unlike other researchers, the forensic anthropologist can't just go out and scare up his or her own cases. Chasing ambulances from the scene of an accident to the hospital may provide fodder for some lawyers but that approach will not work in forensic anthropology. The forensic anthropologist must go forth, rather like an artist or musician, dossier in hand, to "sell the product," forensic anthropology. Most law enforcement officials and medical examiners are probably not used to dealing with university types and must be convinced of the value of forensic anthropology. This can be a hard sell and may take years to accomplish.

Even if one can convince officialdom of the value of adding forensic anthropology to their armamentarium, the reaction is often, "Well, forensic anthropology might be helpful to us on the occasional case, but we don't have money to pay outside consultants."

This presents the forensic anthropologist with a dilemma. As forensic anthropologists know, there are a good many instances in which those unfamiliar with skeletal analysis have missed critical clues that would have been obvious to a bone person. For instance, forensic anthropologist Diane France had a case not long ago in which the coroner ("a forensic pathologist of some repute around here," she says) based his opinion of the cause of death principally on the x-ray of a skull rather than the skull itself. The damage to the skull was obscured by decomposing soft tissue, which was why he relied on the x-ray. Death, he concluded, was due to sharp force injury to the cranium. France, knowing that the best evidence of trauma was in the bones, carefully went about removing the soft tissue that stood in the way of a clear view. Once the skull was clean, the fatal evidence of *blunt* trauma was obvious to her.

She studied the nature of the defect, then told the investigator he should return to the scene to search for a blunt object that could have been used in the assault. Look, she told him, for a blunt object larger than a pipe, but smaller than a cinder block. He turned to his fellow investigator and asked, "Gee, do you suppose we should go out and pick up that two-by-four with the hair on it?"

In the rush of processing cases, even experienced forensic investigators sometimes take shortcuts or overlook what later seems obvious. The trained eye of the forensic anthropologist offers a different perspective, one that can sometimes change the way a case is viewed; in this instance, a change from a diagnosis of sharp to blunt trauma as the cause of death.

Forensic anthropologist Walter Birkby remembers when the decomposed remains of a 22-year-old female were discovered by hunters near Tucson. Excavated by law enforcement personnel, the remains were taken to the medical examiner's office. Again, without fully cleaning the bones, the pathologists concluded that her death had been caused by "probable knife wounds to the chest and back."

Birkby then cleaned the skeleton and discovered that the "knife wounds" in the ribs showed an unexpected crushing along the margins, rather than the usual sharp edges of an incision. Moreover, since the bone surfaces exposed by this damage were not discolored and undamaged surfaces were discolored, the damage most likely occurred after burial. The excavators later admitted that they had used their sharp-pointed shovels to help lift the remains from the grave and at least one had even hit the rib cage with a shovel.

This convinced Birkby that the damage was postmortem, and could not, therefore, be linked with the cause of the young woman's death. While a cause of death could never be established in this case, anthropological work demonstrated that the initial assumptions were incorrect.

These two examples illustrate the way in which forensic anthropologist's attention to bone can be useful in pointing the investigative machinery in the right direction. Every forensic anthropologist probably has had similar experiences. The forensic anthropologist thus feels an obligation to make his or her expertise available so that such mistaken hypotheses will not go unscrutinized and collateral evidence unrecognized. It is clearly in the interest of society to see that murder is discovered and that every effort is made to bring the perpetrator to justice. So what to do when the medical examiner claims not to be able to pay for forensic anthropology? Getting paid to do casework is clearly better than not getting paid, yet most forensic anthropologists conclude that their obligation to society necessitates that they offer their services gratis in order that the work be done. In addition, most believe that their validation as forensic anthropologists derives principally from casework. Casework is the primary means by which their training is put to use and their store of knowledge increased. It must, therefore, be pursued.

Half a dozen of the eldest and most experienced forensic anthropologists have established solid reputations in the broader medicolegal community. They are sought out on high-profile cases and are often handsomely rewarded for the exercise of their endeavors. Those just starting out (as well as many who have been around for a long time) do not have the "big name" that commands both respect and sizable monetary rewards. Some of our colleagues continue to have as clients small law enforcement agencies with tight budgets that can somehow just never be stretched to cover outside expertise. When faced with the undesirable alternatives of not getting cases or having to do them without payment, most forensic anthropologists opt for the latter.

Feeling the need to maintain and sharpen their skills through casework, these forensic anthropologists work cases for free, hoping that some day the medical examiner will pull them aside and say, "We appreciate the great work that you have been doing for us all of these years and would like to begin paying you for cases." While the prestige of the MD degree can bring in thousands of dollars for a case, the forensic anthropologist often feels that pulling down even as much as a hundred dollars for hours of work on a case is a rare and delightful experience.

This situation is without parallel in forensic science. In no other specialty are the practitioners so poorly recompensed for their work. It is impossible to imagine that board-certified forensic pathologists would ever be forced to handle cases simply for the enrichment of experience for themselves and their students. The same might be said for toxicologists, odontologists, accident examiners, and other areas of forensic expertise.

There are probably hundreds of examples that could be dredged up, but one will suffice. An anthropologist was unable to investigate an alleged grave for the medical examiner because of teaching obligations. He sent three graduate students to the scene, which was near a town some 120 miles to the north of his university. As they completed their work out at the remote scene, it began to snow. By the time they had returned to town, roads were drifting in and the radio was advising motorists not to travel south. Deciding that the prudent course was to procure a motel room for the night, the students called the office for permission to make lodging arrangements, but were rebuffed. Finally, the local police association rescued them by covering the cost of the motel. This incident has left those students with some resentment, since the medical examiner apparently expected them not only to donate an entire day to helping the office with a case it couldn't handle, but to pay for their own food and lodging on top of that. Graduate students typically live close enough to the poverty line that they are unable to absorb such unanticipated expenses without doing violence to their budgets.

Forensic anthropologists believe that they have a great deal to offer the world of legal medicine. They present far more professional papers than their numbers would predict. They enthusiastically pursue casework at greater personal expense and sacrifice than other forensic scientists. Their efforts are well received and have usually added materially to the cases they work on. They take baths and brush their teeth as frequently as other forensic scientists. So why is there such a reluctance to pay them for what they do? Maybe it is because they are mostly employed by universities, which are assumed to be flinging vast sums of money at them. What we have here is clearly another urban myth.

9

Nefarious Application of Force to the Skeleton

Sharp and Blunt Force Skeletal Trauma

THE ADOBE BODY

In eastern New Mexico lived a man who was not universally admired by his fellows. Born in a tiny high-plains community west of Tucumcari, he managed only a third-grade education. This effectively excluded him from the more desirable jobs. His occupation was listed as "laborer," though he began to drift into less savory lines of work. His bad reputation was enhanced by the fact that in 1965 he had been admitted to the New Mexico State Penitentiary, where he served one year of his two- to ten-year sentence for robbery.

It seems that a public-spirited group of citizens decided that conditions in their town would be improved if this person, a Mr. Mark Miracle, were to leave. He, unfortunately, seemed disinclined to migrate. In view of his reluctance, the townspeople took it upon themselves to rid themselves of this pest. Apparently concluding that he would only return if given an old-fashioned tar-and-feather sendoff, they decided on a more permanent arrangement. Some of their number repaired to a remote location (with which the state of New Mexico is generously endowed) in this nearly mile-high part of the Canadian River drainage and created a concavity in the soil. Too confined to meet the standards established by Montana Vigilantes in the last century, it was adequate for their purposes.

By some ruse, they managed to lure their victim to the scene and set upon him, shooting him, stabbing him, and dropping his body in the hollow they had created earlier. Miracle, however, did not go gently into the night, rising out of his grave and setting into his attackers. They responded with more blows, stabs, and kicks. This finally quieted him down enough to get him back in the hole, and with relief they packed him in and went on their way, leaving his mound for the coyotes to contemplate.

Three years later, one of the party, apparently afflicted with pangs of remorse, went to the local law enforcement agency and confessed to his role in the sleight of hand that made Mr. Miracle disappear. He led a group to the scene, and with mighty digging in the rocky soil, the OMI investigator and his helpers succeeded in exhuming the body, which was bagged, sealed, and delivered to the OMI. Mark Miracle had risen from his grave again.

The Autopsy

Lying on the table in the Decomposed Body Room was a large mound of dirt, about the size of a large person. The excavators had carefully dug all around the body, not disturbing a thing in the process. It was one of the neatest jobs of excavating a body ever done by an OMI investigator. If carelessly or hurriedly done, the process of excavation can both destroy and miss evidence, but in this instance the investigator had painstakingly dug around the body and delivered to the OMI a large, vaguely human-shaped block of adobe. Working with the pathologist, we carefully chipped away the hard, encrusted dirt, to reveal a rather small individual well down the decomposition pathway. Three years on the surface will lead to complete skeletonization, but three years under ground will significantly retard the process—to a degree that is proportional to the depth at which the body is buried (Rodriguez and Bass, 1985) (Fig. 9.1).

Samples of decomposing tissue were taken, but the process was so far advanced that there was literally nothing to be learned from the rather undifferentiated mass of slimy soft tissue embracing the skeleton. Hence, the real insights into the case would have to develop from an anthropological investigation. We toiled for hours, extracting bone after bone from the disgustingly gooey mass of soft tissue. It became evident that there were several interesting defects on several of the bones, and, with the pathologist's concurrence, they were taken to the lab for further processing.

Skeletal Preparation

There are a number of ways to clean soft tissue from bones and some rather heated discussions about how it should be done. No one argues, however, with the fundamental principle that bone must be clean in order to see clearly the surface details. Although some archaeologists feel that adequate cleaning can be done by flicking the dirt off with brushes, they are not the ones that have to analyze the bones. For those who study bone,

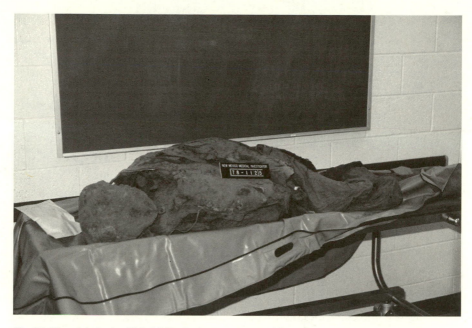

Fig. 9.1. The adobe body of Mark Miracle shown as it arrived from the burial scene.

the surface must be as clean as possible. Essential details can be completely obscured by a thin film of dirt. It is simply impossible to do a proper job of osteological analysis when bony details are concealed by grime.

For skeletons recovered from long-term burial, cleaning usually entails cleaning off as much of the dirt as possible and then scrubbing the surfaces with an old toothbrush under running water. "Scrub" here does not mean that one should attack bones with the same vigor one would use when polishing corroded brass or cleaning a bathtub. Bones, after all, are delicate things and must be handled with care. A gently pulsating stream of water is useful for flushing dirt out of foramina and various fissures and depressions, and soft toothbrushes work for most other surfaces. The water washes the dirt away and a screen over the drain will ensure that nothing small like a tooth or bone fragment gets lost. After washing, the bones can be allowed slowly to air dry, then marked with an appropriate control number and preserved.

For individuals more recently dead, there will always be a residue of soft tissue adhering to the bone, and gentle scrubbing with a toothbrush will accomplish nothing beyond clogging the toothbrush with that decomposing soft tissue. More heroic methods are required for the removal of soft tissue clinging determinedly to the skeleton. The tiny, delicate bones of infants will eventually become very clean if just allowed to macerate, where the soft tissue is softened by soaking. Adult skeletons might also come clean by maceration alone, but the process would take too long.

The cleaning of bone is begun by removing as much of the soft tissue as is practical. Then the bones are placed in a container, and submerged in water. Covered by a lid, the container is tucked away. Every few days, the water is decanted, the process carrying away strings of decomposing soft tissue with it. This ritual is repeated as often as is necessary. Forensic anthropologist Dr. Judy Suchey uses this method to prepare pubic bones for her research on skeletal aging. On the faces of these bones are etched delicate features that are important in age determination, and to make sure that they are not altered by scrubbing, Suchey has decreed that they will soak until clean. Using maceration alone will require many days—even weeks, for larger structures. Most forensic anthropology is so time sensitive that it would be impractical to wait around for weeks for things to become clean enough to analyze.

The same problem is encountered with the use of dermestid beetles to clean bone. The beetles do a very neat and thorough job, but for a mass as large as a human body, even when most of the soft tissue has already been removed, weeks will pass before the bones are clean. There are a couple of other problems with beetles. Temperature and humidity must be closely controlled for them to work most efficiently, and some separate, closed facility must be provided, for the little critters are wont to wander. Furthermore, there is a pervasive and rather unpleasant odor that accompanies the lengthy process. For these reasons, most forensic anthropologists, while admiring the end result and envying the luxury of just sitting back and letting the beetles do all the work, do not use them.

After forensic anthropologists have manually removed the bulk of the soft tissue and have macerated the bones for as many days or weeks as are necessary, they will begin the boiling process. We usually say "boil," but what we really mean is "simmer." Bringing the bones to a boil is good for making soup, but bad for making skeletons. Various people employ different chemicals to hasten the process, ranging from household detergent to a very caustic antiformin solution. What one does is dictated by the condition of the bone, whether the body has been injected with preservatives, the amount of soft tissue present, how soon the work must be finished, and what will happen to the bones afterward.

After drying, the assigned case number is placed on every bone of the specimen, an important link in the chain of evidence. With its own number, a wandering bone can always be restored to its proper home. If the bones are to be maintained in a permanent research collection, the preparation is completed by impregnating them with a preservative. For many years, the favored preservative has been polyvinyl acetate, though in a pinch a thinned satin varnish could be used. Ideally, every step should be reversible, so that a preservative can be removed should it prove necessary in the future. Preservation is important both because it helps to strengthen the bone and because it renders it less susceptible to expansion and contraction with changes in humidity and temperature (Utermohle et al., 1983).

No matter what is done, skeletal preparation is a very time-consuming and labor-intensive process. It is distinctly unpleasant, sometimes arousing ire even of people at some distance from the operation. A critical element in the process is a fume hood, the large venting structure seen in chemistry labs. With its internal blower, a fume hood will pull off most of the noxious fumes from the rotting soft tissue and exhaust them high enough in the air to dilute them sufficiently that they may drift unnoticed into the nostrils of passers-by.

In our old makeshift basement lab in the Maxwell Museum, we had no such fancy facilities. The process began innocently enough and on a very small scale, but soon grew to such a size that a rather unsavory opinion of the lab began to build. Every forensic anthropologist has at some point made his or her activity known by the pungent fumes wafted by errant breezes from the preparation vessel to some unanticipated receptor. Humans have some of the most insensitive noses to be found in the animal kingdom but not so insensitive as to be oblivious to this kind of work. In a case such as that of Mr. Miracle, we used to take the bones we wished to prepare with us from the OMI to the old Maxwell Museum Lab, a dingy basement space more suited to the storage of old tires than to the preparation and analysis of evidence. Having already removed most of the soft tissue, we plunged the bones into a bucket of water to macerate. To speed up the process, we decanted the contents of the bucket into a sink every few days. The sink was in a cramped, dark little room, which we grandly referred to as the "wet lab," a dank space that also housed a hulking antique x-ray machine.

When maceration had taken us as far as it could, we packed the bones into an inconspicuous container, trotted upstairs to the second floor in the adjacent part of the building (which could only be reached by going outside), and into the lab of biological anthropologist Dr. James Spuhler, who kindly allowed us to use his fume hood for simmering the bones. Spuhler's lab, a Stonehenge of stacks of books and papers, contained the only fume hood in the building. In an unguarded moment, he once confessed that he had even handled an occasional forensic case in years gone by. At least he appreciated the importance of what we were doing.

This sounds exactly like what it was, an attempt to do something in a situation where the facilities were inadequate. Nor is this uncommon. Most forensic anthropologists have had to be quite inventive in accomplishing their tasks with bargain-basement facilities and equipment. I once tried cleaning the soft tissue off a head fixed in formalin by blasting it with low-pressure live steam in a University of Colorado engineering lab. At the end of twenty minutes or so, there was a large circle of gloppy tissue on the floor and an even larger circle of goggling and gagging engineers. There must be a better way.

As long as our preparation work remained a small-scale operation, it did not seem to bother anyone, but as our vistas expanded, the volume of skeletal material being prepared similarly increased. Soon we moved from skulls and an occasional isolated bone to complete skeletons. But of course the facilities did not change, and before long the increased volume alerted people to the serious shortcomings of our physical plant.

Steeling ourselves for the task of pouring off the maceration products that had accumulated in the buckets, we would roll up our sleeves, take deep breaths, pry the lids off the (by this time, twenty-gallon) buckets, waddle over to the sink, tip up the buckets, and disgorge the mass into the drain. Then we would repeat the process with the remaining buckets. After three or four, we would look at each other and say, "That wasn't so bad." Either the smell of the rotting soft tissue was not as bad as we remembered, or perhaps the sense of smell truly is the first thing to go. About that time, the phone would always ring in the main lab across the hall. "Are you doing something disgusting?" the irate voice on the other end of the line would suspiciously demand.

Immediately adjacent to the wet lab was the door leading into the machine room, a large, dingy room that lay next to the wet lab, under the ground floor of the Anthropology Building. It was filled with electrical gear, a maze of huge pipes, ducting, and the climate-control apparatus for the building. This door was too short by a couple of inches, and a considerable gale was sucked out of the hallway, through that gap, and into the machine room. The greenish tinged air we created with our decantations was being pulled out of the hallway by the voracious monster blowers on the other side of the door and blasted throughout the building. The unfortunate recipient of the most direct flow seemed to be the museum gallery. On those occasions when we poured off our buckets, visitors often attenuated their museum promenades. In one instance, the fumes became so overpowering that a visitor vomited on the carpet. We tried various strategies to solve this problem, and finally resorted to decanting only on weekend evenings when the building was unlikely to be occupied by anyone. However, there would still be a lingering olfactory hint that we had been busy when the museum opened on Monday morning.

Dr. Jerry Brody, the director, an art historian and an archaeologist, suffered these outrages with surprisingly good humor but finally decreed that this sort of thing could just not be allowed to continue. As well as being able to exercise his influence as director, he had a very strong argument at his disposal—we were making disgusting smells that were impacting on the whole building. Although I made a weak attempt to counter by pointing out the importance of what we were doing, our days of macerating and boiling in the old lab were over. We eventually arranged with the OMI to do the work there. Fortunately, OMI's building expansion plans included a forensic anthropology lab equipped with two fume hoods. This arrangement allowed our preparation work to descend below the level of department consciousness. There is virtue in maintaining a low profile.

The point of all of this is to demonstrate that the lot of the forensic anthropologist is not always a happy one. Nor, to be honest, is that of faculty members compelled to coexist with such a person's preparation activities. It is sometimes difficult to win the approbation of others who can never quite understand what you are doing, why you are doing it, and especially why it has to smell so bad.

The Clean Miracle

The cleaned bones allegedly belonging to Mr. Miracle were a most interesting sight. The skull was relatively light and bore on its lower aspect a pair of extremely small mastoid processes. Despite its small size and rather delicate build, the skeleton was male. His skeletal age was about forty to forty-five years old. The features of the skull were consistent with Hispanic characteristics. According to stature estimates made from the long bones, he was estimated to be five feet five and a half inches to five feet eight and a half inches tall. According to the records we later saw, the missing Mr. Miracle was an Hispanic male whose chronological age was forty-two years. He was five feet five inches tall, and he weighed in at a mere 111 pounds.

Although he was officially listed as a laborer, his skeleton told us that Mark Miracle had not unduly taxed it. By his age, a laborer should certainly be developing some osteoarthritis on his vertebrae (Stewart, 1958), but Miracle's vertebrae showed only the slightest hint. Hence, although our Mr. Miracle was clearly not the sort of person that one would expect to see in the parlor car of a first-class train, sipping mint juleps and smoking Cuban cigars, he had not made a habit of engaging in heavy physical labor. Had he done so, those pesky little osteophytic bony spikes would have begun to grow out from the margins of his vertebrae.

The skeleton also told us that Miracle had managed to get himself into situations from which he did not emerge unscathed. Both nasal bones (which form the root of the nose) were extensively fractured and healed, so he had apparently stopped a fist with his nose more than once. His nose was strongly deviated to the left, a feature that could be seen plainly in his prison mug shot. The bones adjoining the nasals had also been fractured and, in the remodeling, had lost a considerable portion of their mass. The left zygomatic arch (the narrow bridge of bone that can be felt on the cheek just behind the eyes) had been fractured and healed. The arch was adorned with a lumpy area of healed bone. His left cheek had been smashed by the impact of a blunt object—perhaps a fist or a bottle. Thirteen of his twenty-four ribs had been broken at one time or another, the fractures on the left side apparently having occurred later than those on the right. His right elbow, greatly remodeled, had been the site, many years previously, of the impact of a blunt force of considerable magnitude. The ulna (one of the two lower arm bones) could be articulated with the humerus (the upper arm bone), and by manipulating that joint, it became clear that the arm could not be straightened. He must have had only about 15 degrees of motion instead of the normal 160 degrees or so. We later

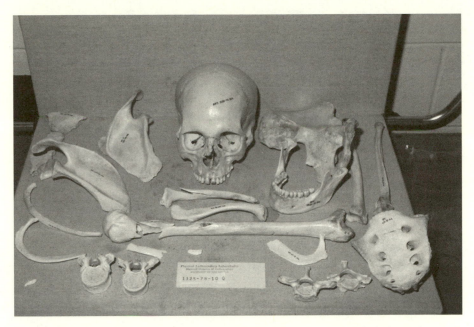

Fig. 9.2. The bones of Mark Miracle removed and retained for further study. Note the broken and remodeled base of the nose and the drastically remodeled elbow joint. Other bones show perimortem defects: a gunshot wound, as well as sharp and blunt trauma. The line seen between the upper two elements of the sacrum is lapsed union (delayed fusion), not a stab wound.

learned that, in his youth, he had been kicked in the elbow by a horse. The imperfect healing suggested that he had not been treated for the injury. Those numerous defects, all of which had healed, told us quite a bit about his lifestyle (Fig. 9.2).

Even more interesting from the perspective of discovering the cause and manner of death were unhealed defects seen on other bones. There were several fractures that had resulted from blunt trauma. Superimposed on the healed fracture of the left zygomatic described above was a trio of new fractures on that delicate arch, which had been crunched inwards by a blow. The right clavicle had a "hinged" fracture. The clavicle angled upwards, the upper surface of the bone being cleanly broken, with a tiny bit of bone holding its bottom together. The upward angle showed that the blow had been delivered from below. The most obvious explanation for such a defect is that as he was lying supine on the ground someone kicked toward his head, fracturing his clavicle. The transverse processes of three vertebrae had been fractured. This would suggest that blunt force, in at least three separate blows, had been delivered close to the center of his back, perhaps as he was lying prone on the ground. He must have been twisting and rolling in the effort to evade more injury. His right fifth rib had been fractured in the front, the result of a blow to his chest or compression of the rib cage from a blow on the back when lying on the ground.

There was also evidence that a gun had been employed in the murder of Mr. Miracle. The right proximal humerus (just below the shoulder joint) was shattered down to 11 cm (about five inches) below the top of the bone. Restoring the fragments to their antemortem positions revealed a very smooth round hole some 10 mm (just under half an inch) across in one side. It looked like a gunshot wound of entrance.

He had also suffered some sharp force injury. The manubrium of the sternum (the upper part of the breastbone) had a little crack at its lower right edge. Closer inspection showed that the "crack" resulted from the insertion of a blade into the bone, after which it had sprung closed. The blade penetrated the entire thickness of the bone and no doubt pushed somewhat into the organs beneath as well. About halfway around the fourth right rib, just in front of the arm, was found the unmistakable incision caused by a knife blow to the right side. In the middle of the blade of the left scapula was a small defect, a small gap, surrounded by uplifted pieces of the thin bone that make up the blade of the scapula. This sharp trauma resulted from someone plunging a knife clear through his chest and into the scapula from the front. The exact location of insertion could not be found, but at the proper angle the knife could have intersected the heart (Fig. 9.3).

Midway down the shaft of the right humerus, a bit of bone had been cleanly gouged out by a knife blow. One of the cervical vertebrae bore the imprint of a knife, as did two of the thoracic vertebrae (Fig. 9.4). That meant that the killer(s) used a knife long enough to penetrate the entire depth of his chest, which, allowing for some compression, would mean a blade at least four inches long. A triangular piece of bone had been snapped off the front of the lowest neck vertebra. The unkindest cut of all was one that ran across the top of his left pubic bone.

This is what an analysis of the skeleton told us, and on the basis of this information, it was possible to say that about the time he died Miracle had been hit in the left side of the head, shot in the arm, kicked in the

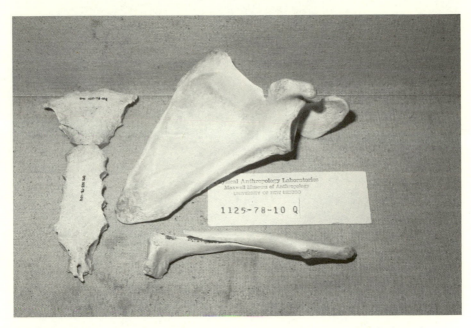

Fig. 9.3. A closer view of the sternum (on the left), showing a narrow line toward the base of the top part (the manubrium)—a stab wound. In the middle is the left scapula (shoulder blade), in the middle of which is a small defect representing the point of a knife that entered the body from the front. Below is the right clavicle (collarbone) showing a longitudinal blunt force fracture.

chest, and kicked or hit on the back. He was stabbed at least eight times: once in the right chest, twice in the neck, three times in the front of his chest, in his arm, and in his groin. The stab to the neck and at least one to the chest entered on his left side, suggesting that the knife blade was probably more like six to eight inches long. The triangular defect is an indication that either he or the knife was violently moved while the knife was lodged in the vertebra. Could he have been stabbed more than eight times? Yes, and he may have been. There are large areas—the stomach for example—where a person can be stabbed and there will be no mark on the bone. Indeed, if the knife blade is held horizontally, there is about a 50 percent chance that any given stab to the thorax will not hit a rib. It is thus possible to stab a person to death and leave behind no evidence of the act on the skeleton. Given the frenzy of violence visited on Mark Miracle, he may well have been stabbed more than eight times. However, although one can posit a whole shower of (now invisible) stab wounds,

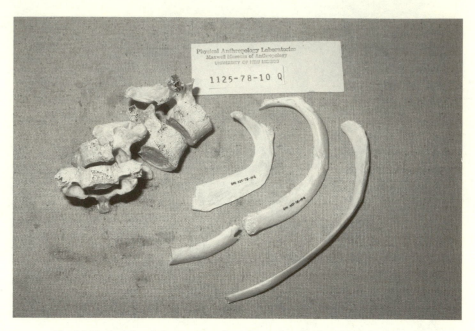

Fig. 9.4. To the left and above are two thoracic vertebrae. A slice of bone has been shaved from the lower margin of the middle one and an incised mark can be seen across the body of the upper one. Below them is a lower cervical vertebra which has had a large piece snapped off the front of its body by the twisting of a knife blade. On the right are the first three right ribs. The second one has an old but unhealed fracture.

one cannot say categorically that there were more than eight, since those are the only ones for which there is direct skeletal evidence, and the skeleton is the only evidence we have.

What can one conclude about the cause and manner of death when essentially all of the information comes from the skeleton? First, given the nature of the defects that can be seen on the skeleton, it is clear that nothing succeeds like excess. The large number and the type of defects on Miracle's skeleton, for example, made it easy to determine that his death was not a natural one. Nor was it suicide or accidental. All that is left is homicide.

If there is a general rule about homicide it is probably that a killer will not typically interrupt his attack, change weapons, and continue the assault, a forensic application of Occam's razor. If there is a combination of blunt force and gunshot wound trauma, then, one might first attempt to discern whether it was the barrel or the butt of the gun that had produced the blunt force injury before looking at other alternatives.

It seemed that Mr. Miracle had been on the receiving end of gunshot, blunt force, and sharp force trauma. Either the killer had been very, very determined and had committed some of those acts after death (of the decedent), or there were multiple assailants. In this case, the most satisfactory hypothesis is that Mr. Miracle was attacked by two or more assailants. The knife wound to the humerus suggests that he may have been twisting around in a vigorous attempt to defend himself, since the arm is not a choice target for stabbing. The same might be argued for the wound in the groin and the triangular defect in the vertebra. While the gunshot wound might have played a role in his death—and there may have been other gunshot wounds that were not visible on the skeleton—the stab wounds would certainly have been sufficient, so that his death is attributable to sharp trauma—exsanguination due to stab wounds, if you will.

There are not many instances in which the forensic anthropologist really has a chance to see the whole picture, but this was certainly one. Some, in fact, shy away from employing trauma analysis to offer insight on the cause and manner of death, but in this case the evidence from the skeleton was so unequivocal that offering an opinion was appropriate. Moreover, in view of the fact that the body was so badly decomposed as to preclude any meaningful soft tissue trauma analysis, any primary evidence had to come from the bones. After all, one of the things that makes forensic anthropology *forensic* is a focus on discovering those skeletal attributes that can be useful in ascertaining the cause and manner of death. Nevertheless, although the anthropological analysis may reveal why and how someone has died, it is important to remember that the pathologist, not the forensic anthropologist, makes the call.

Sharp and Blunt Trauma to Bones

Most texts and papers written in the field of forensic pathology concentrate on the effects of injury to the soft tissue. Pathologists have written much less on the nature of trauma to bone. Since forensic anthropologists concentrate on the skeleton, they are also interested in the effects of both sharp and blunt trauma to bone. In recent years, forensic anthropologists have begun to add documentation of skeletal injury to the forensic literature. From gunshot wounds (Smith, Berryman, and Lahren, 1987) to injuries caused by sharks (Rathbun and Rathbun, 1984) and bears (Murad and Boddy, 1987), the whole range of skeletal defects is important for forensic anthropologists to understand.

While sharp force cuts and divides tissues, blunt force tears, shreds, and crushes. Pathologists look for patterned injuries, the impacts of a weapon on the body that leaves behind an imprint which may be matched to the weapon used. They also seek out the tiny, delicate bridges of tissue across wounds that reveal the use of blunt force, and they look for bruises. Bruises may not be apparent at death and may require deep dissection into the area to reveal the pooling of blood beneath the skin from small vessels ruptured by the blow. It is important to look for a vital reaction at the injury site: bleeding that will show that the heart was pumping at the time of the injury. A lack of vital reaction shows that the defect was produced after death.

Incised wounds are cuts produced by a sharp object, producing a defect longer than it is deep, while stab wounds are deeper than they are long. Most sharp and blunt trauma is superficial, not reaching to the bone, so that a person may be badly battered or stabbed with no effect on the bone. A case like that of Mr. Miracle is thus unusual in that so much force was used and that both sharp and blunt trauma showed up on the skeleton. Nor does the forensic anthropologist commonly see defense wounds, most common on the hands and forearms, produced as a victim raises an arm to ward off a blow, or attempts to grasp the blade of the knife to protect him- or herself from it.

Still, sharp and blunt trauma do both show up on skeletons from time to time. Ribs commonly show little chips of bone missing from their upper and lower margins as a result of stab wounds to the chest. Although the ribs were fragmented and burned on some of the victims of the New Mexico State Penitentiary riot, it was still possible to see little notches on the ribs resulting from stab wounds. One of the gentlemen now residing in a box in the Maxwell Museum's Documented Collection, known to his friends as "Deadeye," was attacked many years before he took up residence in the museum by someone wielding a sharp, heavy weapon like a meat cleaver or an axe. That weapon cut into his right eye and sliced into the cheekbone beneath it. Deadeye survived for a number of years, having lost the sight of an eye, but the slightly uplifted and healed damage to his maxillary bone bore mute testimony to the injury. Museum records include no documentation of his attack, injury, and treatment, but his bones tell us a good deal of the story. Blunt trauma also leaves its signature. In one case, a man could not be identified from his teeth since he had only a few left, and there were no dental records for comparison. However, several years earlier, his lower jaw had been broken in two places and wired back together. Since an x-ray was made at the time of treatment, it could be compared with the cleaned bone. In the intervening years the jaw had healed completely, but the wires were still in place and their location, the number of twists, and their exact patterns were identical when compared with the x-ray of Abner Malody taken at the time of his treatment several years before. This highly individualistic repair to the bone made a positive identification possible.

In southeastern New Mexico lies the "oil patch." This part of New Mexico is sometimes referred to as "Little Texas," the western extension of the oil-producing Permian Basin of West Texas. With the discovery of oil in 1928, this high-plains area of the state quickly boomed with the usual assortment of pool halls, brothels, and gambling establishments. It has now settled down to a quieter existence with only an occasional wild weekend party to disturb the tranquility, but one morning an oil worker discovered the naked body of a woman, coated with a thick layer of heavy oil, lying in the sump pit of an oil well. Noting what appeared to be an impact site on her cheek, the autopsy team peeled back the layers of soft tissue to reveal a fractured and displaced right cheekbone. This unhealed injury was inflicted perimortem. It was not the cause of her death, but had probably rendered her unable to defend herself from her attacker. She was soon identified as 23-year-old Vera Lardge.

A surgical procedure can also alter the appearance of bones. Within a three-month period in 1975, two such cases arrived at the OMI. The first, Red Singer, was found in the northwest corner of the state in late spring. He had apparently fallen victim to exposure, and skeletonization was well under way by the time he was found. On the right side of his head was a gaping hole about the size of a fist. He appeared to have been killed by a heavy blow or blows to the side of the head, but as the dried and leathery soft tissue was peeled back from the aperture, it quickly became obvious that this was not so. Around the edges of the hole, the bone was smooth. There had been some kind of surgical intervention and whatever had happened, Mr. Singer had survived and lived for years afterwards. The normal process of bone repair had smoothed out the rough edges.

The cleaned skull showed not only the loss of most of his teeth, but other blunt trauma defects, including a healed fracture that ran almost all the way around his head. As it turned out, Mr. Singer had been a railroad employee who had fallen into a disagreement of some sort with a train. Such disagreements are invariably decided in favor of the train, and Singer's encounter proved no exception. He was taken to the hospital with massive skull fractures, where rather than wiring the fragments back into position, the surgeons elected to remove them, leaving him with a large open trephination in the side of his head, a very soft spot on this adult head.

Within three months of the Singer case, Harvey Davidson arrived at the lab. He had been reported missing about a year before. At the time of his discovery in the bosque next to the Rio Grande in Albuquerque, he had been reduced to a pile of bones held together by clothing and a few strings of desiccated soft tissue. His left fibula had been fractured distally years before and had been fixed to the tibia by large orthopaedic screws. (In other words, his broken left ankle had been repaired by an orthopaedic surgeon.) A full summary of this interesting skeleton would take a page or more, but in this context the most amazing thing was a fist-sized trephination on the left side of his skull. The old and almost edentulous Mr. Davidson was a virtual mirror image of the middle-aged and almost edentulous Mr. Singer. It seems to be common practice in cases of skull fracture to wire the pieces back together, or to install a plate in place of the bone, but here, within a three-month period, were two men with open trephinations. In the more than twenty years that have passed since that pair, no others have paused for a forensic anthropology examination.

Vehicular Deaths

Bone fractures are common occurrences in vehicular deaths. The incorporation of seat belts and air bags into motor vehicles, while turning many potential deaths into serious injuries, has hardly eliminated road deaths. Regardless of where one is seated in a car, the rapid deceleration seen with vehicle crashes frequently fractures bones. Although the vehicle will come to a nearly instantaneous stop as a result of running into a tree, a bridge abutment, or another vehicle, its passengers will continue to obey Newton's laws of motion, moving in the same direction they were going until stopped by the interior of the car.

For that reason, the assessment of a vehicular death must include an analysis not only of the body but of the vehicle as well. The vehicle must be shown to have been in good operating condition prior to the crash; if not, any defects discovered must be demonstrated to have had relevance—

or not—to the crash. The classic example of the impression of the gas pedal found on the sole of the shoe of a driver who had crashed into a bridge abutment is used to illustrate the way in which small clues can help establish the manner of death. Such a death obviously looks more like suicide than one in which the shoe bears the print of the brake pedal.

Vehicular deaths also include pedestrians struck by vehicles. At high speeds, the victim's body may be thrown over the top of one car to be run over or struck again by following vehicles. The headlights, hood ornaments, tires, and other projections can leave a patterned injury on the body, showing exactly where the person was struck. These patterns can later be matched to the object(s) which caused them. Similarly, for occupants of the car, the steering wheel and other objects affixed to the interior can leave their patterns on both the soft tissue and the bones. Forensic anthropologists are infrequently involved in the analysis of bodies found in automotive deaths, since the analysis of bone trauma is usually less important to the resolution of a case than that of the soft tissues. Typically, the only time a forensic anthropologist is involved is if the body is mangled or burned.

The bad-weather crash of a light plane bound for Taos from Albuquerque some years ago did call for forensic anthropology, however. Discovered within hours of the crash, the bodies were brought to the OMI for autopsy. In aircraft crashes there is generally damage to the bodies due to dismemberment as a result of the crash and to the effects of fire. Though fire had not broken out in this case, the forces unleashed by the crash had torn the bodies apart. According to the information available, the small aircraft was owned and piloted by Mr. Brown. With him were his wife, their daughter, and her husband. An entire family was wiped out in the blink of an eye. The immediate problems were, first, identification, and second, the sorting of body parts. Since the plane had been reported as missing and had subsequently been discovered with the remains of four people aboard, there were tentative identifications already. Once dental records had been obtained, it was possible to make quite satisfactory positive identifications. Sorting, more difficult, was helped by the fact that there had been two males and two females, and for each sex one was older and the other younger. All of the parts were x-rayed so that it was possible to see what the bone inside the mass of soft tissue looked like. It was sometimes easier to tell what the body part was from the x-ray of the bone inside it than from looking at the torn and sundered soft tissue surrounding it.

The parts could then be sorted by size and bone type. As a final step, the ends of fragmented pieces of bone protruding from the soft tissue were matched to each other. This became in effect a four-layer jigsaw puzzle in which bones played a significant role, even though the remains were fully fleshed. The goal was to make certain that none of Mr. Brown ended up with Mrs. Brown, and that their daughter and her husband were also properly parceled out. It would simply not do to have parts of person B buried with person A. Some considerable effort is made to assure that this sort of thing does not happen. In the long run, in this case involving family members only, it wouldn't really have made a difference to any of them, but the modern practice of forensic medicine will not allow one to do less than everything that one can.

If the relatively low speed crash of a small aircraft can be so destructive to bodies, you can imagine what high-speed crashes can do. Despite high technology and excellent training, a small error in judgment can precipitate disaster in high-performance military aircraft. At 600 miles per hour, an aircraft covers a mile in just six seconds. Flying at low altitudes at even half that speed, an aircraft meeting the ground can easily generate enough force to tear itself and its occupant(s) into pieces no larger than a fist. Even with such agonizingly pulverized remains, jaw fragments can be used for an identification by means of a dental comparison. Since boots protect the feet, footprints, recorded for military flyers, can also provide the basis for an identification. Even if an aircraft was a single-seater, a forensic anthropologist may still be called to go through the remains to ensure that the fragments recovered are all consistent with the presumed identity of the pilot and to demonstrate that only one individual was present. This routine analysis gives an extra bit of assurance that events were as they are presumed to have been.

Passengers or train crews are infrequently killed in railroad accidents. However, many people are killed by trains when they wander onto tracks or heedlessly drive across them, unwittingly providing fresh reminders of the basic physics lesson that says that two objects cannot occupy the same space at the same time. The train, with mass and velocity in its favor, is more likely to emerge from any such vehicular joust as the clear winner. A person will fare even less well than a car. This was illustrated by a case from several years ago.

The unmistakable odor of liquor hung heavy in the air of the autopsy suite. The body lying on the autopsy table was rather muddled. A few hours earlier, it had been a living being, whose judgment and muscular control had been seriously compromised by the ingestion of a generous amount of intoxicants and whose end had come not far from a fabled and perennially dry region of death.

The tracks of the Southern Pacific Railroad head south out of Corona and jog west through Ancho to avoid the Sacramento Mountains. From there, they run south, down the valley through Coyote to Carizozo, between the mountains to the east and the Mal Pais (the badlands) to the west. This is an impressive land. The jagged, jumbled black basaltic blocks of the Mal Pais remind us that the earth is constantly reshaping itself. Produced by one of the most recent of huge basaltic flows in the United States (only two thousand years ago), the sharp, hard lava flow makes up the Valley of Fires State Park a few miles west of Carizozo. Unlike the brilliant reddish orange of Nevada's Valley of Fires State Park, the stark bleakness of New Mexico's Valley of Fires is a forecast that a few miles farther west, over the Oscura Mountains that define the western border of the Mal Pais, lies the Spanish scourge, a desiccated, forbidding, and mysterious land known as *Jornada del Muerto* (Journey of Death). It was in this valley that, in 1945, the nuclear age burst into being with the explosion of the world's first atomic bomb at the Trinity site. The name *Jornada del Muerto* now took on a new and more sinister meaning.

There was also a journey of death to be played out that day on the tracks of the Southern Pacific. The locomotive crew of a freight train nearing Carizozo saw a lump between the rails ahead of them. They shut off the power, sounded the horn, and applied the brakes, and were horrified to see this lump resolve into a human who struggled to his feet and shakily held up his hand in a motion to stop. Within seconds, close to five thousand tons of freight train bore down and passed over the hapless figure. The train was finally brought to a stop as the thirty-third car passed over his now lifeless body. The impact with the locomotive and subsequent passage of many wheels had reduced him to an unrecognizable pulp, shattering bones and thoroughly churning his organs. The alcohol, thus liberated from his system, now permeated the autopsy suite where we analyzed his remains. Forensic anthropology was called in to generate a demographic profile from the mangled bones. That description eventually led us to dental records that produced an identification of the body.

In another example, two young men were riding a motorcycle down the railroad tracks just south of Albuquerque. It ran out of gas and the two of them began pushing the machine a half-mile back up the track to a highway crossing. Their effort was interrupted by the warning blast of an air horn behind them. An Amtrak passenger train was sailing around the curve, heading for its 12:55 P.M. appointment in Albuquerque, just minutes ahead at better than 60 miles per hour. The engineer applied the brakes and leaned on the horn. The two fellows looked back and kept pushing, but the rapid approach of the train led to a quick reassessment of the situation. The assistant pusher yelled at the owner to forget it and jump. Reluctant to abandon the effort and his machine, he attempted to lever his bike off the tracks. Upon arrival at the scene half an hour later, the locomotive stood stoically idling, the only clue to the misfortune being a couple of small shreds of bloody tissue hanging from projecting fittings on its nose. The motorcycle was shredded; the unfortunate owner fared no better.

Motorists insist on blasting across railroad crossings at the last moment, oblivious to the danger of the rapidly approaching train and ignoring the blaring horn and flashing lights. Each of these near misses leaves badly shaken crews in its wake, and each unnecessary death not only leaves a family bereft, but also lingers to torture the crew members with the memory of a tragedy they could only watch unfold but not avoid.

A dramatic example of a vehicular death was also a train death. Or was it? Near Las Vegas, New Mexico, a Santa Fe Railroad freight train was heading south at night when the headlight picked up a shape on the tracks ahead. The usual ritual ensued: blasting of horn, application of brakes, and the inevitable impact when the shape did not move. Brought to the autopsy suite, the odor of liquor was once again powerfully evident, but something about this accident did not seem right. Though the body was badly mutilated by the passage of numerous wheels, the internal organs did not seem to bear the expected effects of alcohol consumption. Toxicological test results later showed that despite the powerful odor of liquor emanating from the body, there was no alcohol present *in* the tissues. Pressing on into the organs, there appeared to be a couple of instances of tissue having been cleanly divided, as if by a knife, rather than being crushed and torn, as by blunt forces. Those areas displayed none of the tissue bridging previously described. A lack of vital reaction, such as bruising, showed that the victim had been dead at the time of impact. Once attuned to looking for these subtleties, other inconsistencies, though minute, fairly jump out at one. There were also some small pieces of bone sliced off the edges of ribs. The victim had clearly been stabbed. This death could no longer be treated as an accident, but homicide.

Ultimately, further police work turned up the murderers, who had stabbed their victim, doused him with alcohol to make it look as though he had overindulged, and pitched him onto the tracks to be run over by the next train. It was a nearly perfect crime, foiled by the watchful eyes of those at the autopsy table. What turned this "accident" into homicide was the discovery of the knife wounds in the ribs. The skeleton speaks in the softest of voices, but if one listens closely the bones do talk.

10

A Plethora of Bodies

Forensic Anthropology in Mass Disasters

Unpleasantness at the Pen

Saturday morning's news carried stories of a disturbance at the New Mexico State Penitentiary. The prison is it located just south of the New Mexico capital city of Santa Fe (which delights in calling itself the "City Different"), mecca for the nouveaux riches and those who aspire to that status. Back in territorial times, the government distributed its favors throughout the state, dotting the map with legislative lagniappe so that the residents of the territory would be properly rewarded for their correct attitudes and behavior. The savvy legislators sited the state's university on a lonely mesa just east of that Johnny-come-lately village sixty miles south along the Rio Grande, Albuquerque, keeping the penitentiary for themselves. Perhaps, they reasoned, inmates were a higher class of people than university professors. Or maybe the legislature wanted to be close to the prison, facilitating the shuttling of people back and forth from one institution to another as their terms at one or the other expired.

However, on this second morning of February 1980 the news from the overcrowded prison on the arid 6,000-foot-high mesa south of Santa Fe was grim. Built to house 850 men, 1,156 were crammed in there when the violence erupted (Mayer, 1980). An extended drinking session in one of the dormitories was fueled by a potion concocted from raisins and sugar, which had been liberated from the mess hall. At 1:40 A.M., guards sent in to quell the partying were overpowered. Prisoners surged out of the dorm and into the halls of the prison, overcoming other guards as they went. Access to the central control room was blocked by a newly installed unbreakable glass window, from which protective steel bars had been removed. The prisoners had apparently not been told that this thick window had been fashioned from unbreakable glass, so they picked up a fire extinguisher and smashed through it.

Within twenty minutes of the breakout, the prisoners were in the control room with access to the entire prison. They opened all the cell doors, and as Saturday morning dawned the entire facility was in the hands of the inmates. Some guards raced out ahead of the flood tide of prisoners, while others managed to hide themselves from the marauders. A few were captured and held by prisoners, but none was killed. Prisoners roamed freely throughout the facility, breaking into the mess hall and the infirmary. In the latter they found easy access to the medical supplies, some adventuresome types popping vast numbers and great varieties of pills down their gullets. Eventually, many of them found themselves being woozily transported to local St. Vincent hospital, where all miraculously survived. Prisoners raged through the now powerless and heatless facility, killing other inmates. They set major fires in the gymnasium, the Protestant chapel, and the education wing, and smaller fires elsewhere. Dormitories were ransacked, and great fun was had by many. The background and consequences of the uprising are chillingly told by Morris (1983) in *The Devil's Butcher Shop*.

The penitentiary had employed the "snitch" method, in which prisoners were rewarded for ratting on their fellows and held thereafter in isolation from the general population. The snitches were the immediate targets in this revolt, and before the smoke cleared thirty-three prisoners were dead at the hands of others. This is allegedly the largest number of prisoners killed in any prison riot in the history of the United States. The OMI's role in the resolution of the prison riot has never been fully told, and what follows here is only a general overview, concentrating on the role of forensic anthropology.

By Saturday morning, about twelve hours after the takeover, speculation was running well ahead of fact. Reporters guessed that as many as a hundred prisoners might have died. We were ready. The principals at the OMI had been alerted, and by late Saturday morning the office was humming with activity. Not knowing how many bodies there would be, we prepared for a hundred by making sure that supplies were present, folders and paperwork assembled, a refrigerator truck delivered next to the back door, and a ramp built up to it.

Late on Saturday, some prisoners carried the first bodies out of the prison and up to an opening in the fence. National Guardsmen called in by Governor Bruce King stood guard as Assistant Medical Investigator Patricia McFeeley made preliminary evaluations. Dr. McFeeley, then operating out of Santa Fe for the OMI, was called away from a baby shower being given in her honor to attend to the processing of bodies. Each body was assigned a temporary number, logged in, bagged, sealed, and turned over to the National Guard for transport. Preliminary identifications on these first few bodies were made at the scene by assistant district attorneys who recognized the battered bodies as people they had put behind those now cold and smokey bars.

In some ways, this was a slow-motion disaster. Disasters usually happen in a thunderclap. In cases involving airplane crashes, floods, fires, and bombs, which are all virtually instantaneous, the medical examiner or coroner is suddenly faced with a phalanx of the dead with essentially no warning. But here, the first word of the riot came over the news media early on Saturday, and the day was punctuated with an incessant drumroll of reports, each only slightly less breathless than the last. It was not until Sunday that the prison came back under the control of the authorities and most of the bodies were released.

THE PLAN

Based on the OMI's mass disaster plan, Chief Medical Investigator James T. Weston made a number of decisions that set the tone for the operation. First, the established autopsy facilities at the main office in Albuquerque would be the setting for all autopsies. This would be more efficient than moving all of the pathologists, autopsy assistants, support personnel, supplies, and equipment sixty miles north to a temporary morgue. The bodies were quickly brought by National Guard 6×6 trucks to Albuquerque for autopsy. Second, since each of the thirty-three deaths was clearly homicidal, a full and very detailed autopsy would be necessary for each one. Third, rather than delaying and complicating the situation by calling on his forensic pathology colleagues across the country for help, Weston decided that all autopsies would be handled by the OMI staff. They would be assisted by residents who had been through the forensic pathology rotation as a part of the affiliated medical program at the university hospital next door to the OMI. They would work alternating twelve-hour shifts until the autopsies were finished. Fourth, since there was insufficient cooler space at the office, arrangements were made to bring a refrigerator truck up to the back door to handle the overflow. Fifth, each body would have to be extensively photographed. Many of the dead were hated snitches, and because of their unpopularity among their fellows their bodies bore evidence of the venting of much frustration with a variety of weapons. In the case of multiple stab wounds, vinyl sheets would be placed over the body and defects traced on the sheet. (In some instances, an entire twelve-hour shift would be required for completion of a single autopsy by one team.) Sixth, forensic odontologist Homer Campbell would assemble a crew of odontological assistants to take oral swabs, perform extensive dental examinations, and chart all teeth for identification purposes. Seventh, Albuquerque Police Department specialists would fingerprint all bodies for comparison with penitentiary records for identification. Eighth, a forensic anthropology team would be sent into the prison to search for remains. Lastly, he decided that upon completion of the work the autopsies would be reviewed by outside experts.

THE AUTOPSIES

The first few bodies arrived on Saturday afternoon and autopsies were begun immediately. The bulk of them arrived on Sunday and were initially assigned one of the spaces marked out in the OMI garage. A folder containing all the necessary paperwork was placed with each and accompanied the body through initial processing. Each body was then assigned a case number, weighed, and placed in the inside cooler or the refrigerated truck outside. A master chart showed the location of each body and the status of the work done on it. One by one, the bodies were removed from the inside cooler and passed down an "assembly line."

The first stop was adjacent to the cooler. Investigators photographed each intact seal and the number adjacent to it, broke the seal, opened the body bag, took fingerprints, and removed, bagged, and numbered trace evidence. The body was then rolled down the hall toward the autopsy room to the dental team, whose members took mouth swabs and, with portable lights and magnifiers, charted the teeth. They also took fingernail clippings, hair combings, and recovered any trace evidence missed by the first team. From there the body went to an autopsy team that followed the standard OMI autopsy protocol, augmenting it with x-rays, photographs, drawings, and tracings as necessary. Upon completion of each of these steps, the corresponding square on the master sheet would be checked off. When the autopsy was finished, the body was trundled out to the refrigerator truck. In the meantime, empty cells in the indoor cooler would be restocked with bodies from the truck to assure an uninterrupted flow. Late on the Wednesday following the retaking of the penitentiary, the autopsies were finished.

The Forensic Anthropology Excursion

By the time the penitentiary was retaken on Sunday, the prisoners had wrought extensive damage throughout the facility, turning over beds and lockers, destroying cabinets and equipment, throwing food around, and setting numerous fires. Walls were scorched and blackened. Most of the windows had been shattered, while others had melted from the fierce heat and sagged drunkenly out of their frames. Fires still sputtered in the education wing, the Protestant chapel, and the gymnasium. The heat had reduced telephones to amorphous black blobs with dials protruding from them. All that remained of a piano in the chapel—an iron plate with strings hanging lifelessly from it—was covered by a foot of powdery gray ash. Electricity and heat had been cut off, and water from fire sprinklers mixed with fallen ceiling tiles had formed a gray-white mush that gurgled ankle deep through the halls. Chaos reigned.

Although the facility was once again in the hands of the law, there was much confusion about who was who, who was still there, and who was dead. Head counts proved frustratingly inadequate. Given the previously demonstrated porosity of the prison walls, it was considered most likely that some prisoners had escaped at the height of the confusion. Others were being shipped off to facilities in other states until the prison could be restored to what passed as normal. Were there bodies lurking under piles of burned rubble and debris in the gymnasium, the Protestant chapel, the education wing, or elsewhere? Were there, as prisoners said, bodies "stacked like cordwood" on the stage of the gym before the fire was set? Were there, as rumors had it, bodies hanging off meathooks next to overripe sides of beef and greenish tinged eggs in the meatlocker?

By Monday, the decision had been made to send in the anthropology team. Many students and former students had already called to offer their help, and before long we had nearly twenty people who were willing to take time away from their jobs or from classes. This would be a difficult situation for most forensic anthropologists. Most of us are affiliated with academic institutions, and our prime responsibility is therefore to the students in our classes. Usually, if someone calls to tell us that there is a body or a pile of bones to look at, a response can be delayed until classes are over for the day; sometimes a quick look can be fitted in between classes. However, there is an understandable reluctance to cancel classes except under the most unusual and demanding circumstances. The search for bodies clearly fell into this latter category. Since we would have to spend Wednesday and Thursday at the prison, there was no alternative to canceling Wednesday's two classes.

On our arrival at the prison, small fires still smoked fitfully in the gym, whose far wall appeared very insubstantial through the haze. Fire inspectors had determined that accelerants were spread around before the fire was ignited. Large air supply ducts along the walls fed the flames, turning the wood-floored gym into a veritable volcano of fire that belched out through the windows. The conflagration twisted and displaced the huge steel beams supporting the roof, which sagged perilously toward the floor, the law of gravity remaining unaffected by the rampant lawlessness of the past days. The fire inspector met us at the door and said, "We think the roof will hold up, but if you hear creaking sounds, run for the walls and try to get out." He stayed safely under an overhang at the rear of the dark, cold, cavernous room (Fig. 10.1).

Three bodies had been recovered from the gym floor on Monday by OMI investigator Paul Condon and our task was to discover whether there were any more. We did this by carefully raking through some 15–20 cm (6–8 inches) of ash and partly burned ceiling tiles. A portion of the crew was thus engaged for both days. Three dark smears marked the places from which the bodies had been removed by OMI investigators accompanied by armed guards on Sunday. Numerous additional bone scraps were recovered from those areas.

In the meantime, another group raked and shoveled its way through the much smaller education wing and Protestant chapel. While this work was going forward, at intervals I was conducted through the meatlocker and through offices, hallways, and other areas that sustained lesser fire damage, looking for more bodies. We all eventually returned to the gym to finish the work there. At the end of our two days of raking and searching on hands and knees, we had found only a small amount of fragmented bone from the floor where the three bodies had been. No such fragments were found anywhere else in the prison. We concluded that there were no additional bodies anywhere in any of the areas we had combed. We

Fig. 10.1. The gymnasium at the New Mexico State Penitentiary when the forensic anthropology crew arrived to search for bodies. Small fires are still burning and the roof beams are sagging dangerously.

also concluded that even under the best of conditions, the penitentiary was not a place we would like to spend any more than those two days.

As with any disaster, there was intense media interest. During our two days in the prison, we looked up occasionally to see media representatives being conducted through on one of their several tours. The state legislature was also in session at the time. It seemed that every lawmaker was so vitally interested in what had transpired in the prison as to leave the Zia-shaped state capitol building ("the roundhouse" in local parlance) and drive out for a look. Curious law enforcement types from around the state also managed to talk their way in. Every time we ventured out into a hallway, we encountered a throng of people, some with cameras and tape recorders, others in natty three-piece suits, and still others attired in cowboy hats, Levi's, and badges, wandering around and gaping at the disorder. All slogged through the mess in high rubber boots thoughtfully provided by the prison. This agglomeration of visitors met, mingled with, and moved on from the shambling crowd of prisoners, the prison guards, National Guards-

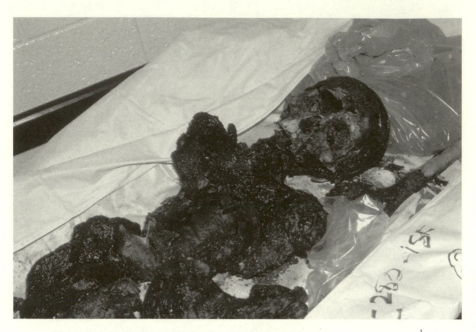

Fig. 10.2. One of the burned bodies from the penitentiary riot.

men, and other law enforcement types struggling to get things running normally again. Alice could not have tumbled through her looking glass into a more bizarre world.

The Analysis

Back at the OMI, our next task was to begin the process of identification of the burned bodies. All six had been burned "beyond recognition" as the phrase has it, the least damaged body intact but blackened and singed by the flames. Three were exposed to the prolonged and intense gym fire that burned limbs off to within a few inches of the shoulders and pelvis. Only stubs of ribs protruded from the vertebral column. The skulls were shattered and blackened, but the skull vaults were mostly intact, revealing that they had probably been damaged by blows to the head before the fire started as pointed out in the discussion of the effects of fire on bone in chapter 1 (Fig. 10.2). One of the other victims had barricaded himself in his cell, but his vengeful attackers shot him in the head with a tear-gas projectile and set fire to his corpse with an acetylene torch.

Since bodies in such an advanced state of destruction by burning have

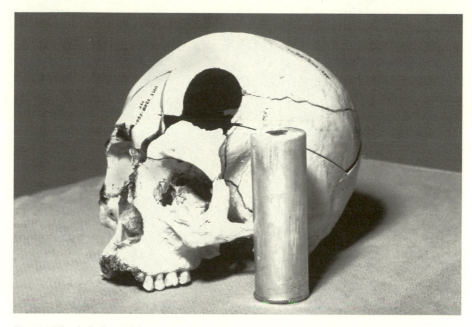

Fig. 10.3. The skull of one of the victims, shot with a tear gas gun (projectile shown in foreground) that produced the very large entrance wound seen on the forehead. Due to the low velocity, there was no exit wound. The body was subsequently set afire.

very little information to pass on to the pathologist, the autopsies were relatively brief. Each of the autopsied burned bodies was then passed on for anthropological examination. Starting on Friday, after our return from the penitentiary, these burned bodies and the fragments of bone recovered with them were removed one by one from the cooler. Each body bag was carefully searched to recover each small fragment of bone. These were laid out according to size and shape on benches in the room used for the autopsy of decomposed bodies. The fragments were gradually glued back together to form complete bones. With that done, measurements were taken and the usual anthropological assessments made. This demanding process consumed many days (Fig. 10.3).

Arriving home just in time for the 10 P.M. news on Saturday night a week after the riot began, I heard Governor Bruce King solemnly opine that six bodies had been burned so badly that they would never be identified. He did not know that by careful sorting and reconstructing of bone fragments we had already achieved positive identifications on two of them.

Fig. 10.4. Bone fragments from one of the burned bodies being sorted and reconstructed.

A final positive identification on the others was only a couple of days away. The identifications were based on a combination of anthropological and dental evidence. We were able to determine age, sex, race, and stature for each of the bodies from carefully reconstructed bones (Fig. 10.4). We were also able to discover useful skeletal anomalies on some, and secured x-rays for comparison for some and dental records for all. Although prison records had been destroyed, investigators found arrest records and medical records upon which to base the identifications. OMI's odontologist Homer Campbell also put in many long, late hours to resolve problems of identification. We were confident that the identifications were much more secure based on these multiple anthropological and dental grounds than is usually the case in any similar disaster, and none has ever been challenged.

THE FINAL RESOLUTION

All of the autopsies were completed by the Wednesday after the penitentiary had been secured. We finished our identifications of the burned bodies by the middle of the next week. The bodies were then washed again, prepared, and released to the next of kin, and the OMI soon settled back into its accustomed routine, having managed to handle its normal case-load while this operation went forward. However, the tidal wave of battered and burned bodies left its mark on some of the staff, who required counseling to regain their equilibrium. Even those used to dealing with a continuous river of dead bodies can be impacted by such a flood.

Since each of the thirty-three deaths was a homicide, the OMI's work was not over, however. The autopsies and all of the photographs were extensively reviewed by the pathologists in preparation for upcoming trials. They were then reviewed by an outside panel of forensic experts. Many additional days of effort were put into analyzing wounds and linking them to weapons recovered from the prison. Months later, the trials of those charged with the murders required detailed testimony from many of the OMI staff. Finally, after a couple of years, testimony was complete, the case files were closed, and the operation was finished, but for anyone who participates in that kind of work, or other such mass disasters, it is never really over.

The Challenge of Mass Disasters

It is the nature of mass disasters that they cannot be predicted. The policy of every medical examiner and coroner, therefore, should be to have a disaster plan ready. The OMI was lucky in a number of respects with the penitentiary riot. First, the scene was contained within the prison walls, so determining the area to be searched and establishing its security were not issues. Second, since the first body was not delivered for autopsy until more than half a day after the first notice of the event, there was ample time for preparation. Third, the medical investigator's facility had been well planned and was running smoothly. With enough room and good equipment available to process and autopsy the bodies, procuring another location and moving supplies and equipment there was unnecessary. Fourth, a large pool of diverse local forensic talent mitigated the need to bring in outside experts and the attendant delays in negotiations and expense that so doing would have entailed.

Twenty-seven of the victims were handled by using standard autopsy techniques. Only six of them required extraordinary (i.e. forensic anthropological) analysis. Without the input of forensic anthropology, identifications of those six bodies could eventually have been made on dental grounds alone. Similarly, without dental work, the identifications could have been made on anthropological grounds alone. Yet, with both, those identifications were made with the security that multiple grounds afford.

The OMI also benefited greatly from the many selfless students and former students who racked up hundreds of hours of volunteer time to help search the prison, assist in the effort of moving bodies around, and help in piecing fragmented bones back together. A note of thanks to them is in order here. The task could not have been accomplished without them. As is all too common in the field of forensic anthropology, all of these people volunteered their time, expecting to gain nothing but experience and the satisfaction that derives from a job well done. Each of them did, however, get a letter of appreciation from Jim Weston.

The Meaning of "Mass Disaster"

At intervals, the country is rocked by news of a mass disaster. A traditional definition for "mass disaster" was that it was any event resulting in six or more deaths at the same time and in the same place from one basic cause. A more recent definition is attuned to local conditions: a mass disaster is an event that causes such a number of essentially simultaneous deaths in the same location that the facilities and personnel available to handle and process them are overwhelmed. Thus, what would be a disaster in Dinosaur (Colorado) would probably be an average day in Albuquerque and a languorous day in Los Angeles. In our business, we sometimes forget that such disasters are also usually accompanied by a large number of injuries, and that the injured must be speedily removed from the scene, stabilized, and transported to medical facilities for further treatment. All of this must be done while the law enforcement authorities secure the scene to block access to looters, those who would "just like to help," and the morbidly curious.

A probably apocryphal story concerns a good samaritan who happened upon a multiple vehicular crash that had strewn bodies around the landscape. To ward off potential looters, he walked from one body to the next, removing wallets and purses. When the police arrived, he proudly presented his identification booty to them, having never given a thought to remember what he took from which body. Of course, no self-respecting forensic scientist is going to base an identification entirely on pocket contents, but it would have been nice to have had a little hint of a place to start.

Disasters can take many forms. They can be of natural origin, such as floods, forest fires, earthquakes, hurricanes, tornados, tsunamis, and many others, or they can be of essentially human origin, for example transportation accidents, building fires, or structure collapse due to engineering deficiencies. Even more philosophically devastating are those disasters that are deliberately instigated by humans for the purpose of demonstrating their personal disdain for the status quo. Airplane bombers, building bombers, and others unfeelingly and indiscriminately slaughter innocent humans by the score. Their motives may be fathomable, but their means are—there is no softer word—insane.

The impact of disasters can be moderated somewhat by extensive and careful advance planning. By this means, it is possible to ameliorate some of the widespread confusion that descends like a blanket when disaster strikes. Every medical examiner knows that a disaster can occur in his or her jurisdiction and has a plan in place for that event.

Disaster in Reno

One of the finest examples of advance planning is that put in place by the coroner of Washoe County, Nevada, Vernon McCarty. The tall, trim McCarty, sporting carefully managed short, wavy hair and neatly attired in boots, is true to his western upbringing. His appearance, his quiet and modest demeanor, echoes his no-nonsense approach to forensic work. He is a careful, precise fellow who leaves little to chance. He takes the matter of determination of cause and manner of death very seriously— so seriously, in fact, that his keen sense of humor and engaging smile may not be evident on first meeting. Upon his arrival at the Coroner's Office in Reno in 1979, he prudently set about designing a disaster plan.

At 1:04 A.M. on January 21, 1985, a Lockheed L-188 turboprop operated by Galaxy Airlines carrying sixty-five passengers and a crew of six left Reno-Cannon International Airport. The pilot was on the radio almost immediately to report an unusual vibration and request clearance for an emergency landing. A left-downwind landing was approved, but the plane banked slightly to the right, lost altitude, and crashed into a field about two miles from the runway from an altitude of 100 to 200 feet. The tail-section struck the ground first, and the aircraft skidded about a quarter of a mile across a frosty field. It then hit the embankment of an irrigation ditch and broke apart about a third of the way from the nose, hurling some passengers, baggage, and debris for another two hundred feet. A portion of the fuselage skidded into a recreational vehicle sales lot and came to rest across the northbound lanes of U.S. Highway 395. Flames quickly engulfed the entire area.

Racing down Highway 395 in response to an unrelated call, a sheriff's officer witnessed the crash and immediately called for reinforcements. Emergency and Fire personnel, alerted at the time of the pilot's distress call, were on the scene within five minutes. The force of the crash ruptured the full fuel tanks, spreading a sheet of fire over the wreckage. Indeed, though three passengers had been thrown far enough away from the flames to remain alive for a short period, only one, a seventeen-year-old male, survived the crash. The fire was under control in less than thirty minutes, but the aircraft was incinerated and all of the remaining victims, found in or near the fuselage, were extensively charred.

Coroner McCarty was at an FBI-sponsored seminar in Washington, D.C., at the time, but he had left his meticulously organized disaster plan behind in his office. It was necessary only to open the book and start calling the telephone numbers listed to put the plan into operation. Arrangements were made to set up a temporary morgue in two sixty-feet-square rooms at the Nevada State Fairgrounds; refrigerated trucks were ordered to hold the bodies; telephones were installed; a previously designed accounting mechanism went into operation to allocate disaster costs. By the time McCarty was able to return to Reno, the system was functioning smoothly.

A grid pattern was laid out over the scene at 7 m (23 foot) intervals with wooden stakes and plastic tape. Each square was numbered, and bodies and personal effects were measured and numbered so that their exact location could be discerned later. Two teams, each consisting of a deputy coroner, a photographer, a recorder, measurement takers, and litter bearers systematically recovered all the bodies, which were then removed to one of the three refrigerated trucks.

At the temporary morgue, the bodies were removed from the trucks and placed on a table in numerical sequence. Beginning with the first victim, the examination team started a case file, assigned a case number, described the body, determined the sex of the victim, and entered this information on a wall chart along with the crash scene recovery number. Next, a second team, which consisted of three pairs of dentists, removed the teeth and surrounding bone from the faces of all the victims. Each set was tagged with the case number, cleaned, charted, and placed in numerical order on a table. Then a team of FBI Disaster Squad fingerprint specialists removed, cleaned, inked, and rolled charred fingers.

The fourth step was to perform an autopsy on each set of remains. These were conducted by three teams comprised of a forensic pathologist and a technician. A standard protocol directed the conduct of each autopsy to assure uniformity in handling. Property inventory teams accompanied the pathologists to collect and label the various tissue specimens and property associated with each body. Over $52,000 in cash, $115,000 in jewelry, and all luggage were recovered and eventually returned to the next of kin (McCarty et al., 1987).

Caskets and embalming supplies were quickly delivered to the temporary morgue. Dental records of all but eight victims arrived in Reno within four days. Positive identifications were made for fifty-nine victims from those records in two hours. The names of all those identified were then released. The refusal of the coroner to release names until bodies were positively identified gave rise to some controversy, but by delaying, the team was able to detect any inconsistencies in the airline manifest and to narrow down the search for those bodies that, lacking records, proved difficult to identify. Careful, meticulous procedures assured that no misidentifications were made. News conferences were held at frequent intervals, including conducted tours of the crash scene itself. Media telephone inquiries were directed to the next news conference.

Determination of the cause of death for each victim was made on receipt of the toxicology results by the coroner and forensic pathologists. Twenty-seven of the victims (40 percent) died from blunt force trauma. Eight (11 percent), showing soot in their airways, perished from flash fire but with low concentrations of carbon monoxide. The remaining thirty-three (49 percent) succumbed to a combination of smoke inhalation and thermal injury. Virtually all of those ejected from the aircraft died from injuries, while those trapped inside survived the crash only to die of smoke inhalation and fire (Salomone et al., 1987).

The entire operation from recovery to release of the bodies was completed five days after the crash without any significant disruption of normal community services. The rapid and smoothly executed management of this disaster illustrates the value of a well-designed disaster plan. The handling of other, better-known airline crashes, has suffered both from inadequate advance planning and the all-too-human tendency to make snap decisions that were later regretted.

Forensic Anthropological Work in Other Disasters

Although many disasters have been handled without the help of forensic anthropologists, their ability to analyze and identify human remains from skeletal evidence has often been recognized as being of value. For example, the recovery and identification of the shattered and scattered parts of victims of a massive fireworks factory explosion in Tennessee (Bass and Rodriguez, 1986) is an operation that could not have been accomplished without the aid of forensic anthropology.

Forensic anthropologists have long been involved in the recovery and identification of bodies in aircraft crashes. Some are crashes of military flights, such as the Arrow Air DC8 chartered by the U.S. Army that went down in Gander, Newfoundland, on December 12, 1985. While most of the 256 bodies could be identified by dental work and fingerprints, a number remained unidentified until forensic anthropologist Madeleine Hinkes arrived from the army's Central Identification Laboratory in Hawaii to work on sets of remains. Ellis Kerley was the forensic anthropologist member of the team identifying the bodies from the explosion of the space shuttle *Challenger*, witnessed repeatedly in agonizingly slow-motion video replay. Sometimes forensic anthropologists are called in to assist in the identification of bodies found in the wreckage of crashes on foreign soil. Such was the case in early 1996, when the aircraft carrying Commerce Secretary Ron Brown and his party went down over the former Yugoslavia. However, most of the crashes that forensic anthropologists have worked on have involved civil aircraft.

For many years, the investigation of aircraft crashes was undertaken by the Federal Aviation Administration (FAA). Richard G. Snyder, an aviator and anthropologist, was hired by the FAA in 1960. He quickly hired Clyde Snow and others to flesh out the Physical Anthropology section of the Civil Aeromedical Research Institute. This institute also rostered engineers, physicians, physiologists, and others, whose task was to investigate the structural failures of aircraft and people.

The FAA investigated major crashes under the auspices and guidance of the National Transportation Safety Board, which had a skeleton crew "go team" consisting of about a half-dozen persons—specialists in weather, airframes, power plants, and human factors—who could be at a crash scene within hours. The anthropologists were assigned to the Human Factors

Group charged with interviewing survivors as well as the identification of human remains.

In the mid-1960s Snyder left the FAA to set up a biomechanics lab for the Ford Motor Company but soon migrated to a joint appointment at the Highway Safety Research Institute (at the Institute of Science and Technology) and the University of Michigan, where he taught and did some forensic work. He eventually retired to a busy life of forensic consultation developed from his comprehensive understanding of the ways in which human bodies react to the stresses produced by aircraft. Snow remained at the FAA, conducting crash investigations, handling forensic anthropology work for Oklahoma and other states, and conducting research into crashes. His last crash investigation for the FAA was one of the deadliest, the 1979 American Airlines Flight 191, DC-10 crash in Chicago, in which 273 perished. Within a few days, the majority of the bodies had been identified, but a residual pool of difficult remains resulted in a call for Snow to help. He recalls that the force of the crash left about twelve thousand body parts to keep track of. He worked with an airline computer programmer to devise a program that would track remains and search data for potential matches. He believes this to be the first time that a computer was employed in mass-disaster victim identification (Turcica, 1995). Snow took early retirement in 1979. He was immediately pounced upon by forensic pathologists across the country to assist in identification work. He went on to achieve wide renown for his use of forensic anthropology to document human rights abuses throughout the world (Joyce and Stover, 1991).

Thus, by 1980 the FAA's anthropological focus in aircraft crash investigation had dissolved. But by this time, forensic anthropology had grown to the extent that experts were available across the nation for this important work. In recent years, National Disaster Medical System Disaster Mortuary Teams (fortunately generally referred to as "D-MORT") have been increasingly involved in organizing responses to mass fatalities. Teams including forensic anthropologists, dentists, and pathologists have been in the field since 1993, dealing with disasters ranging from cemetery floods to the Alfred Murrah Building bombing in Oklahoma City in 1995.

There are many recent examples of forensic anthropological work with mass fatalities. For instance, in the 1994 American Eagle Flight 4184 crash, forensic anthropological work was accomplished by Bruce Anderson, a forensic anthropologist from the Central Identification Laboratory in Hawaii, Anthony Falsetti and William Rodriguez from the Armed Forces Institute of Pathology in Washington, D.C., Robert Sundick from Western Michigan University in Kalamzoo, and Beth Murray from the College of St. Joseph in Cincinnati. Positive identifications were made for fifty-one of the victims, the remainder being established on the basis of personal effects (News, 1994). Sundick says that their ten-hour days were filled with an unbroken procession of body bags. In the USAir Flight 427 crash near Pittsburgh in 1994, forensic anthropologists Dennis Dirkmaat from Mercyhurst College, and William Rodriguez and Paul Sledzik from the AFIP were able to process the remains in a little over a week, identifying bone fragments, isolating teeth and jaws for identification and re-associating fragments of children. Of the 132 persons killed in the crash, 125 were quickly identified (Sledzik, 1994b). As pointed out earlier, forensic anthropologists across the country have also assisted in identification following a number of military aircraft crashes. In each of these instances, and many others, they were instrumental in recovery, separating commingled remains, and the identification of victims.

But forensic anthropologists are also involved in many other kinds of mass disasters in which recovery, or identification, offers problems. For instance, in the early 1970s in northern Colorado, the Big Thompson River, already swollen with heavy rains, was hit with a torrential downpour around Estes Park. A wall of water scoured the steep canyon, leaving more than thirty dead. With the aid of forensic anthropologist Michael Charney, all were identified. In this flood, some bodies were carried miles downstream and badly battered, adding to the difficulty of identification.

In the summer of 1993, great floods again ravaged the Midwest, disrupting transportation, communication, and people's lives. An unexpected side-effect was what might be thought of as a historical mass disaster. High waters had washed nearly eight hundred sets of human remains out of a cemetery near Hardin, Missouri. While eight hundred bodies ought to qualify as a mass disaster in anyone's book, the fact that they had been dead and buried for thirty to seventy years prior to the disaster took a little edge off of the urgency that normally attends such affairs.

These "bodies" ranged from isolated single bones to virtually complete bodies in coffins. They were dated by the type of coffin and the artifacts found with them. In under two weeks, the seven-person anthropology team examined 407 individuals, making two positive identifications and finding many examples of diseases both of bones and soft tissue. They found not only skeletonized but mummified remains and bodies with soft tissue still left, but could get no correlation between time of interment and the condition of the body (Sledzik, 1994a).

On Thursday, July 7, 1994, a forest fire burning furiously at the edge of Glenwood Springs, Colorado, was fanned by high winds, causing it to change direction abruptly, trapping twelve firefighters. While the bodies were being recovered, the ten-member Colorado Body Identification Team was called to the scene. A temporary morgue was set up in the double garage of a funeral home in Glenwood Springs. The team worked until 1 A.M. on July 8 to complete the autopsies. Since the remains had been recovered by other firefighters and (as is often the case) positive identifications could quickly be made on dental grounds, the more detailed and time-consuming anthropological analysis was unnecessary. Inclusion of a forensic anthropologist on the team, however, was important, since it is always impossible to know in advance precisely what one will encounter at the scene of a disaster or what the condition of the bodies will be (France, 1994).

After the fire at the Branch Davidian compound near Waco, Texas, a team of ten forensic anthropologists from the Smithsonian Institution, the Tarrant County Medical Examiner's Office, and the University of Tennessee, as well as the FBI were summoned to assist in the recovery and examination of the burned remains. Bodies were transported to the Tarrant County Medical Examiner's Office in Fort Worth for analysis. Douglas Ubelaker (1993) writes that the anthropologists were particularly "useful in recovering the remains, establishing information that contributed to identification, sorting out commingled remains and identifying trauma."

As can be seen by these few examples of the work of forensic anthropologists in the recovery and identification of bodies in multiple death situations, the circumstances vary widely, but what they all share is a large number of people dead at one time in a single location. In many of these instances, bodies have been burned, sometimes have been dismembered, and are always difficult to identify. Almost every time a mass disaster occurs, reporters will solemnly conclude that (at least some of) the bodies will never be identified. As the abilities of forensic anthropologists become more widely appreciated, they are more frequently being brought in to assist. It is certainly fair to say that in every instance in which forensic anthropology has been brought to bear, bodies that would otherwise not have been identified have been.

Afterword

Clyde Snow's visit to the Maxwell Museum's lab in the early 1970s, discussed in the preface, provided a pleasurable break in the tedium of skeletal preparation, yet after the passage of several months I had almost forgotten about Snow's promise to tell the medical investigator there was an anthropologist on campus who would like to work on forensic cases. Then the phone rang. It was Chief Medical Investigator Weston. He had just received a skeleton from California to identify. Was I interested? Within minutes, his chief deputy and another investigator were at the lab door with a box of bones and some x-rays they had taken.

After a bit of picking and sorting, it became clear that the skeleton was a white female in her late twenties, about five feet six inches tall. The basics of determination of age, sex, stature, and race out of the way, I turned my attention to the x-rays. There were two of them, both of a rib. Ribs are uncommon subjects of radiographic attention and I could see nothing that suggested a reason for this intense interest. It was necessary to inspect the ribs carefully to see what was there. About halfway around the upper edge of the left second rib was a little ding. A chip of bone was missing. What could cause a little tiny fragment of bone to be dislodged from such a protected location? Moreover, might an associated defect be seen on the adjacent structure? Pulling out the first left rib, it was immediately obvious that another chip had been broken off the lower border of that rib.

Those familiar with skeletal anatomy are probably rising out of their easy chairs to say what I said then: "What about the clavicle?" (It acts as a strut to hold the shoulder in position, curving sinuously but gently over the first couple of ribs, and a defect in both the first and second ribs would suggest that there may be another linked defect on the clavicle.) Sure enough, incised into the back side (the posterior surface) of the clavicle were three shallow, roughly parallel scratches. The hypothesis that most efficiently explains all of these observations is that a sharp-edged object, like a knife, was inserted into the upper rib cage of the young lady, perhaps penetrating her heart.

I wrote a report setting forth my findings, concluding that this young lady had likely been killed by a stab wound (or wounds) down into the left shoulder next to the head. A short time later, Weston called to say that while he had hoped for a determination of age and sex, he had not expected to get a suggestion on the cause of death as well. He decided that this forensic anthropology was pretty nifty, and from that time on, the cases began to flow in increasing numbers.

A number of the cases recounted in the previous pages attracted no small amount of publicity, but most of that centered on the police, the suspects, and—to a much lesser extent—on the mechanisms that generated information about the case. In other words, in most instances, the OMI and those associated with it, worked quietly in the background, probing gently but insistently into why and how a death occurred, using the best evidence available—the body itself.

I once interviewed a prospect for a position in forensic pathology at the OMI. In response to a question about his forensic goals, he responded with charming honesty that he hoped to craft a glistening reputation as a result of work on high-profile cases. He believed that these cases would also line his pockets quite satisfactorily. Such aspirations are quickly deflated in practice, since most cases offer few occasions to chat up the media or to buff one's reputation to a deep gloss and they provide only modest opportunities for adding to the store of knowledge or challenging a commonly held view. By the way, he didn't get the job.

The vast majority of cases handled by any forensic anthropologist are routine: excavations of "dry holes" that produce nothing but dirt, the discovery of nonhuman remains, and the appearance of skeletons of individuals too long dead to be of medicolegal significance. In addition to these, there are the complete, the badly burned, the decomposed, and the skeletonized bodies for which the issues and the analyses are straightforward and the results clear cut and unambiguous. Such cases sound entrancing, but oddly enough they too become routine. Though each of them does present its own lessons, cases bristling with potential for major enlightenment are infrequent.

Occasionally I am asked what is the best, or most memorable, case that

I have worked on. The stock answer has always been, "The next one," but now, with the leisure to contemplate past cases more fully, a revised answer might be in order. The best case is not the one that brings reporters to the door; nor is it the one that holds out the thrill of being able to get more in dollars out of it than one has spent. It is the case that, because of the sort of material recovered, its incompleteness, or the evidence of violence visited upon it, pushes one to probe further into the nature of human skeletal variability. It is the case that sends the forensic anthropologist knocking at the door of the unknown. There is a real thrill that comes with discovering something that no one else has, or very few others have, known before. It is, in short, the same delight of discovery that pervades and is the very essence of science. It is that element of human nature that compels us to go where no one has been before.

Most of those who got started in forensic anthropology in the 1960s and 1970s could tell similar stories about their early work in forensic anthropology. Most of them backed into forensic work, having been introduced to it by one of the pioneers mentioned earlier. As their workload increased, they began to teach forensic anthropology themselves, and by the 1980s the first people trained specifically to be forensic anthropologists began to emerge from the universities.

Now, with the retirement and pending retirement of many of those with the brightest reputations (as well as some of the rest of us who have been around long enough), programs offering forensic anthropology have disappeared or have been de-emphasized. A lack of appreciation in the broader field of anthropology continues. Many—practitioners and students—have been concerned that these circumstances foretell the demise of the field. Over the past three or four years, there has been a great deal of agonizing about this, both orally and in print, at the national as well as the regional level.

Still, a coterie of able and conscientious forensic anthropologists, with just the slightest trace of premature gray in their hair, is performing work with all of the patience and skill required. Our short-term perspective may be robbing the community at large of a longer view. Many younger forensic anthropologists, cognizant of the despair felt by some, have stepped into the breach to build new laboratories and to establish new programs. Those whose visions encompass only the past may own the past, but those with sufficient wisdom, faith, and commitment to build the future will own that future.

While education of forensic anthropologists may thus appear bleak to some, the undeniable trend is for forensic anthropologists to become busier with casework and for the discipline to become better known. The inherent fascination with what the forensic anthropologist does has pushed forensic anthropology into the limelight. It has become so popular that courses taught by non-forensic anthropologists are springing up across the land.

While the general public—and perhaps some of our esteemed colleagues in other forensic specialties—may believe that the field consists of only a half-dozen famous specialists, the bulk of the important work of forensic anthropology is being done throughout the country (and around the world) by scores of dedicated people whose names are hardly household words. You have met some of them here, but it is worth remembering that every time you see television coverage of an aircraft crash or of a body being recovered and every time that you pick up a newspaper with an article regarding discovered remains, yet another forensic anthropologist could be involved. Perhaps the readers who have made it this far will now have a heightened appreciation for who forensic anthropologists are, what they do, how they do it, and even why they do it.

Glossary

ADIPOCERE—The saponification, or transformation of soft tissue into a fatty, soaplike substance through long exposure of a body to cold water. The extent of the development of this process may be helpful in evaluating the *postmortem interval*.

ANTEMORTEM—The time prior to the death of a person. An injury to the skeleton happening before death will not bear directly on the cause of death. The extent of the healing of the bone will correspond to the amount of time that has elapsed since the injury. See also *perimortem, postmortem*.

ANTHROPOMETRY—Measurements taken of a body or its parts. Expressed in the Metric system, such measurements (of bones, technically called osteometry) can be used to estimate stature, the age of infants, aspects of body shape and proportions, and population affinity.

ANTHROPOSCOPY—The observation of "discontinuous traits," those things which cannot be measured, such as variation in number and placement of *foramina* and other features that vary between sexes and populations.

AURICULAR SURFACE—The ear-shaped surface on the inside of the innominate, part of the sacroiliac junction where the *sacrum* and its associated spinal column attach to the pelvis.

AUTOPSY—The regular, deliberate dissection of a body, its organs, and organ systems in order to ascertain the *cause* and *manner of death* for medicolegal purposes.

BASIOCCIPITAL SYNCHONDROSIS—The area on the base of the skull, or spheno-occipital synchondrosis, sometimes incorrectly called the "basal suture," where the occipital and sphenoid bones touch and, in the teens, begin to fuse together. Apparently the most regular of fusion events in the skull, it is useful in assessing the age of younger individuals.

BLUNT FORCE INJURY—Injury to either soft or hard tissue resulting from the application of an object so shaped as to compress, bruise, and tear the skin, rather than to incise it (see *incised wound*). If sufficient force is used, the underlying bone may also be fractured.

BROW RIDGE—The superciliary arch (the bony bar directly above the eyes). More pronounced in males, this trait is sometimes used as one of several criteria for judging the sex of a skull.

CADAVER DOG—A dog trained specifically to respond to the odor of decaying flesh. One of the means used to locate bodies when a general area where the remains might be found has been identified by an informant or other means.

CALLUS—A lumpy deposit of bone at the site of a fracture or other injury to bone. Composed of woven bone, a callus can be discovered by palpation (feeling by hand), or x-ray of a body.

(continuation of Callus)

As the injury heals, the callus is resorbed, but it leaves sufficient trace that its existence can be seen many years after the injury took place.

CANCELLOUS BONE—Sometimes called trabecular bone, it is a spongy-looking bone found between layers of *compact bone* in the skull, pelvis, or ribs, and in the middle of the shafts of long and short bones. It adds greatly to the strength of a bone without adding significantly to the weight because of its architecture.

CARNASSIAL TOOTH—The molar tooth of animals belonging to the order Carnivora, including such familiar domestic animals as dogs and cats. The action of the lower against the upper tooth is like that of a pair of pinking shears, slicing meat into pieces small enough to be swallowed.

CARNIVORE—Any member of the order Carnivora, a group of animals that occupies ecological niches in which the principal food is meat. Such animals are typically equipped with large canine teeth, claws, a keen sense of smell, binocular vision, fleetfootedness, and other characteristics designed to produce effective sensing, stalking, killing, and consumption of prey animals .

CARTILAGE—A somewhat pliable connective tissue that holds bones together, lines the surfaces of joints, and in some cases provides a template from which bone forms, spreading out from the *center of ossification*, the region in which transformation from cartilage to bone begins.

CAUSE OF DEATH—The agent or effect resulting in a physiological derangement or biochemical disturbance that is incompatible with life. This agent or effect may be set in motion in a vast number of ways. See also *manner of death*.

CHAIN OF EVIDENCE—Also called chain of custody, this is the written documentation of the passage of evidence from one person to another. By this means it is possible to demonstrate in court that a piece of evidence offered in testimony is the same as the one recovered at a scene.

CLAVICLE—The slightly S-shaped, rounded bone with flattened ends (a part of the shoulder girdle) that attaches the skeleton of the arm to the skeleton of the trunk. It is sometimes called the collarbone, and keeps your shoulder from dropping down into your pocket.

COMMINGLED—Remains of two or more individuals intermixed. Mixing can occur either as a result of careless recovery of bodies, or by dismemberment and jumbling due to forces involved in an aircraft crash or other such event. Such mixing must be sorted out before any analysis can take place. Criteria for sorting could include difference in size, sex, age, stature, disease, nutrition, and so on.

COMPACT BONE—Alternatively called cortical bone, this is the dense, hard outer (and inner) layer of a bone that isolates it from its surroundings and to which muscles and tendons attach. See also *cancellous bone*.

CREMAINS—The intentionally incinerated remains of a body, produced by a commercial cremation retort, which burns off organic matter, leaving behind calcined and fragile bones and other inorganics such as dental fillings, appliances, and prosthetic devices. (The bone is usually ground to a powder before being returned to the family.)

DECOMPOSITION—The breakdown in tissues that commences with the cessation of life (see *vital reaction*). Along with decrease in temperature, an early stage of decomposition is *rigor mortis*. This is accompanied by *livor mortis*. The extent of decomposition may be used as a guide in establishing the *postmortem interval*.

DERMESTID BEETLES—Beetles used to remove soft tissue from bones in the preparation of skeletons. They are also part of a succession of insects that visit a body after death. Through a study of forensic entomology data bearing on the *postmortem interval* may be generated.

DOCUMENTED COLLECTION—A collection of skeletons from known individuals, incorporating information on the age, sex, race, stature, cause of death, *antemortem* defects, and other matters useful for research on skeletons.

ECTOCRANIAL—On the outside of the skull, or the outer surface of the skull. Gunshot wounds and *blunt force* trauma, for example, leave different marks on the outside of the skull (the ectocranial *compact bone*). See also *endocranial*.

EDENTULOUS—Without any natural teeth.

ENDOCRANIAL—On the inside of the skull, or the inner surface of the skull. The endocranial surface of the skull responds differently to different kinds of stresses, so that its evaluation is necessary to assess the damage that has occurred to a skull. See also *ectocranial*.

EPIPHYSIS—Characteristic of mammals, it is the bony cap at the ends of long, short, and irregular bones that provides a smooth joint surface and muscle insertion, yet allows for growth through an increase in bone length.

EXTENSOR MUSCLES—Those muscles that cause joints to straighten out (to extend). For instance, the extensors for the hand are located on the upper side of the arm, with tendons running down through the wrist to bring about the motion. See also *flexor muscles*.

FACIAL REPRODUCTION—Sometimes called facial reconstruction (which it really is not) or facial approximation, it is the process of applying clay to a skull or a cast of a skull. Conforming to established standards for different populations, the process can be used to create leads for an identification. However, it cannot by itself be used for identification.

FACIAL SUPERIMPOSITION—The process of merging (either electronically or mechanically) the images of a skull and a photograph in order to rule in or rule out possible identities on the basis of compatibility or incompatibility of features.

FIBULA—The small bone of the lower leg that is said to bear around 12 percent of the weight of the body. (The large lower leg bone is the *tibia*).

FLEXOR MUSCLES—The muscles that cause joints to bend (flex) from the straightened position. In the hand, for example, though there are small intrinsic muscles, the major muscles of flexion are located on the bottom of the forearm. Since they are more massive than the *extensor muscles*, the drying and contraction caused by fires will bring about joint flexion, producing in a burned body a *pugilistic attitude*.

FORAMINA (plural of foramen)—The holes in bone for the passage of blood vessels, nerves, etc. They can be as large as the foramen magnum on the base of the skull, through which the spinal cord passes, or as small as the mental foramen on the mandible near the chin.

FORENSIC ANTHROPOLOGY—The application of the findings, procedures, and practices of osteological physical anthropology to medicolegal matters.

FORENSIC ODONTOLOGY—The application of the practice of dentistry to medicolegal matters, principally the identification of unknown bodies.

FORENSIC PATHOLOGY—The application of analytical methods (including the *autopsy*) in order to discover the *cause* and *manner of death* of a deceased person so that proper action can be taken in a medicolegal context.

FORENSIC TOXICOLOGY—The evaluation of various bodily fluids for the purpose of discovering whether a person was under the influence of any drug at the time of death.

FRONTAL SINUS—A cavity in the frontal bone in the space between and above the eyes. It is regarded as idiosyncratic and thus to be of use in the identification of unknown bodies by x-ray comparison .

Homo sapiens—The standard binomen (genus and species) of modern humans.

HUMERUS—The large bone of the upper arm. It is useful for estimation of age, sex, stature, muscularity, and other features of the skeleton.

ILIUM—One of three bones (ilium, ischium, and pubis) that fuse together in youth to make up the innominate. Left and right innominates, which contain the hip socket and the *sacrum*, make up the pelvis and are useful for determination of age, sex, parity, and many other factors.

INCISED WOUND—A cut wound, which is by definition longer than it is deep.

LAMELLAE—The concentric rings surrounding the *osteon*, which make up the Haversian system, the unit of bone growth and blood circulation in bones.

LIVOR MORTIS—A bluish purple discoloration on the lower (dependent) parts of a body after death, resulting from blood settling under the effects of gravity. The blood cannot flow into parts of the circulatory system that are compressed by the body being in contact with a surface. These areas are blanched. If a body is moved before livor is fixed (before about twelve hours), a secondary livor will form, indicating that the body has been tampered with. An early part of *decomposition*.

MANNER OF DEATH—The agent responsible for causing death. There are five types: natural, accidental, homicidal, suicidal, and undetermined. Fixing on the *cause* and manner of death is a critical function of forensic medicine.

MASTOID PROCESS—The lump of bone (larger in males) which may be felt behind the lower part of the ear), into which some of the muscles that move the head insert. The conformation of the air cells may be used for identification purposes.

MEDICAL EXAMINER—An official charged with investigation into deaths and the determination of the *cause* and *manner of death*. The office generally replaces that of the coroner and is usually occupied by a physician with special training in *forensic pathology*.

MUMMIFICATION—Natural mummification is the process of desiccation that can take place in cold, dry environments, or in very hot, dry ones, where the usual agents of decay and *decomposition* are not in play.

OSSIFICATION (CENTER OF)—A point, approximately in the middle of the cartilagineous precursor (see *cartilage*) of bone (or *epiphysis*) in which the transmutation to bone begins. Since these centers appear at different times in different bones, their clear visibility in x-ray is useful as a means of helping to establish the age of fetal and infant remains.

OSTEOMETRIC BOARD—Sometimes called a "bone board," this is a device for precisely measuring long bones (bones of the arms and legs) and other bones for stature estimation or other calculations.

OSTEON—The bone cell active in the growth of bone. As an individual ages, osteons die, eventually to be replaced by others. Observation of the growth of new cells is the basis of a technique for the microscopic estimation of age from bone samples removed from a skeleton.

OSTEOPHYTE—An extra growth on bone, this is a spur or lip that extends from the edge of a bone across a joint space toward another bone. Osteophytes develop not only as a normal part of aging, but also in response to injury and some diseases. Analysis of their development is useful in evaluating the age of a skeleton and also in determining how a person's function may have been affected, which is potentially helpful in establishing the identity of the remains.

PATHOLOGY—The study of disease. The study of diseases of the bone is osteopathology, and the growth of new bone or the loss of bone is a manifestation of that disease. Diagnosis of the disease is on the basis of the age of the individual, the location of the defect, and whether it is bone gain or bone loss. An anomaly is not a disease, but an idiosyncratic feature peculiar to that person. A description of both anomalies and pathologies can be useful in helping to narrow down possibilities for an identification.

PERIMORTEM—The period around the time of death. An injury to a bone that has not had time to begin to heal or that occurred not long after the death (perhaps in the recovery or transportation of a body) is said to be perimortem. Since such an injury is taken to occur at about the time of the death, it may have a bearing on both the *cause* and *manner of death* and must be investigated fully. In some cases, such as those where defects are consistent with gunshot wounds, sharp, or blunt trauma, the damage to the bone is such as to suggest that the underlying soft tissue structures could not have survived the injury. It is thus likely that the defect is linked with the demise of the individual. See also *antemortem, postmortem.*

PHALANGES—The bones of the fingers and toes. With fourteen in each hand and foot, the total of fifty-six phalanges makes this the largest category of bones within the 206 found in the human skeleton. Alas, they are among the least informative of the bones, but they must still be evaluated in any forensic anthropological examination.

POSITIVE IDENTIFICATION—An identification based on such solid, incontrovertible physical evidence as to be highly probable to be correct.

POSTMORTEM—The time period after the death of an individual. An injury to a bone that was inflicted well after the time when an individual died is characterized by color differences between the inside and outside of a bone due to its contact with soil or the lack of dynamic response by the bone to the force. Under most circumstances, then, such defects have no medicolegal significance and do not bear on the person's death. See also *antemortem, perimortem.*

POSTMORTEM INTERVAL—The time since death. The earlier after death that a body is found, the more precisely the time since death can be fixed by a variety of observational and chemical testing. If skeletonized or nearly skeletonized remains are found, generally the only means for establishing postmortem interval is the experience of the investigators in knowing how long it takes in that geographical locale to produce the observed state of the remains.

PUGILISTIC ATTITUDE—The slightly curled-up, almost fetal position assumed by burned bodies. The bodies appear to lie in a crouched position, legs and arms bent rather like those of a boxer, as a result of the drying and shrinkage of muscle tissue caused by the fire. See also *flexor muscles.*

RADIUS—One of the two bones of the forearm, the radius rotates around the *ulna*, allowing the hand to be supinated (palm up) or pronated (palm down).

RIGOR MORTIS—A state of stiffness throughout the body, which is an early part of the process of *decomposition*. Rigor begins in the smallest muscles first—those of the hands and face—progresses to the larger muscles, reaches its maximum about twelve hours after death, and passes off after about twenty-four. Development of rigor may be used to help determine the *postmortem interval.* Contrarily an inconsistency between the development of rigor and

(continuation of Rigor mortis)

the time since death (established by other means) may indicate that the body had been moved from one location to another before being found.

ROBUSTICITY—An expression of the heaviness and muscular development of a skeleton. In general, males are more robust than females. Muscle hypertrophy and, thus, skeletal robusticity are enhanced by exertion, so that (for example) weightlifters, runners, and cowboys all have differently developed skeletal robusticities. Analysis of skeletal development can be helpful in suggesting certain activities the decedent may or may not have habitually engaged in.

SACRUM—A roughly triangular bone (point down) made up of five fused vertebrae, which with the innominates makes up the back third of the pelvis. The movable part (or suprasacral) vertebral column joins the sacrum at its broad top.

SKELETAL AGE—Age of a skeleton as shown by the state of its *centers of ossification, epiphyses,* dental development, and other markers including the development of *osteophytes.* This may not always correspond exactly with the chronological age (the age of an individual in years since his or her birth), since there are many factors that can accelerate or decelerate skeletal maturation. Severe malnutrition, for example, can retard the rate at which a skeleton matures, leading to a younger skeletal than chronological age. The use of birth control pills, on the contrary, can accelerate skeletal maturation, leading to an overestimate of skeletal age. The forensic anthropologist must attempt to correct for any such contingencies in making an estimate of the chronological age of a skeleton.

STAB WOUND—A wound in either soft or hard tissue caused by a sharp bladed instrument. While an *incised wound* is longer than it is deep, a stab wound is deeper than it is long. Stab wounds to bone are not generally deep, but in where the bone is thin—the blades of the innominates, the scapula, or the ribs—a knife can completely penetrate, the resulting defect being longer than it is deep. It will be obvious if that is the case.

SUBPUBIC ANGLE—The angle made by the pubic bones as they spread laterally below the pubic symphysis, on the front edge of the innominate. A narrow angle such as that between the splayed-out index and middle fingers is more typical of males, whereas a wide angle like that between the splayed-out thumb and index finger is more typical of females. This angle, along with the surrounding architecture of the pubic region, is extremely valuable in assessing the sex of a skeleton.

TAPHONOMY—The breakdown (including *decomposition*) of animal remains subsequent to death, and their modification by terrestrial, avian, and aquatic predators, including carrying off of body parts by animals, movement of bones by streams, washing, and climatic and weather phenomena.

TIBIA—The largest bone of the lower leg, the "shinbone." Next to it is the smaller *fibula.*

TOXICOLOGY—An analysis of bodily fluids in the search for "poisons." See also *forensic toxicology.*

TREPHINATION—The surgical technique of cutting into and removing a part of the skull bones, typically to relieve internal pressure building up from a hematoma, an accumulation of blood in the brain as the result of a head injury. Trephination, though for apparently different purposes, has been done for hundreds of years, accomplished at one time with sharpened stone tools. Survival rates in earlier times were not too good.

ULNA—One of the bones of the lower arm, around which the *radius* rotates.

VERTEBRA—An element of a segmented backbone, common to all animals of the subphylum Vertebrata. In forensic anthropology, vertebrae are useful both for age determination and as an element of the identification procedure.

VITAL REACTION—The sort of response generated by a live person, including the production of bruises, which are caused by the rupture of capillaries resulting in bleeding under the skin. Once the heart stops pumping, bleeding from wounds ceases. Therefore, wounds administered after death lack a vital reaction.

VITREOUS HUMOR—The fluid of the eye. As a part of the postmortem sampling procedure, vitreous humor is withdrawn from the eye by syringe for toxicological examination. See also *forensic toxicology.*

ZYGOMATIC ARCH—The delicate arch that may be felt on the cheeks just behind the eyes. These arches provide space for the temporalis muscles to pass under from their origin on the top of the skull to the top of the mandible. (The muscles can be felt bunching up when chewing.)

References

Adelson, L. 1974. *The Pathology of Homicide*. Springfield: Charles C. Thomas.

Angel, J. L. 1974. *Bones Can Fool People*. FBI Law Enforcement Bulletin No. 43.

Anonymous. N.d. *Internal Descriptions of the OMI Written for General Information and OMI Reports*. N.p.: n.p.

Baby, Ray S. 1954. *Hopewell Cremation Practices*. Ohio Historical Society Papers in Archaeology No. 1: 1–7.

Baker, Roger P. 1967. *Postmortem Examination*. Philadelphia: W. B. Saunders and Company.

Bass, William M. 1984a. Is it Possible to Consume a Body Completely in a Fire? In *Human Identification*, edited by Ted A. Rathbun and Jane E. Buikstra. Springfield: Charles C. Thomas.

———. 1984b. Time Interval Since Death: A Difficult Decision. In *Human Identification*, edited by Ted A. Rathbun and Jane E. Buikstra. Springfield: Charles C. Thomas.

———. 1987. *Human Osteology*, 3d ed. Special Publication No. 2. Columbia: The Missouri Archaeological Society.

Bass, William, and William C. Rodriguez, III. 1986. The Place of Forensic Anthropology in a Mass Disaster: The Benton Fireworks Explosion. Paper given at the meeting of the American Academy of Forensic Sciences, February, New Orleans.

Beck, W. A., and Y. A. Haase. 1979. *Historical Atlas of New Mexico*. Norman: University of Oklahoma Press.

Belshaw, Jim. 1996. Bring Your Identity Card. *Albuquerque Journal*, July 10.

Bennett, K. A. 1992. *A Field Guide for Human Skeletal Identification*. Springfield: Charles C. Thomas.

Berryman, Hugh E., William M. Bass, Steven A. Symes, and O'Brian C. Smith, 1991. Recognition of Cemetery Remains in the Forensic Setting. *Journal of Forensic Sciences* 36 (1): 230–37.

Bradtmiller, B., and J. E. Buikstra. 1984. Effects of Burning on Human Bone Microstructure: A Preliminary Study. *Journal of Forensic Sciences* 29 (2): 535–40.

Brooks, S. T. 1955. Skeletal Age at Death: The Reliability of Cranial and Pubic Age Indicators. *American Journal of Physical Anthropology* 13: 567–97.

Brooks, S. T. 1975. Human or Not? *Journal of Forensic Sciences* 20 (1): 149–53.

Brooks, S. T., and J. M. Suchey. 1990. Skeletal Age Determination Based on the Os Pubis *Human Evolution* 5 (3): 227–38.

Brues, Alice M. 1958. Identification of Skeletal Remains. *The Journal of Criminal Law, Criminology and Police Science* 48 (5): 551–63

Burdett, William H., Elaine Cheser, Martha Davis Kipcak, and Amy Bridges Suttle. 1990. *The Roads of New Mexico*. Fredericksburg, Texas: Shearer Publishing.

Byers, S. N., Bryan Curran, and K. Akoshima. 1989. The Determination of Adult Stature From Metatarsal Length. *American Journal of Physical Anthropology* 79 (3): 275–79.

Chilton, Lance, Katherine Chilton, Polly E. Arango, James Dudley, Nancy Neary, and Patricia Stelzner. 1984. *New Mexico, A New Guide to the Colorful State*. Albuquerque: University of New Mexico Press.

Cornwell, Patricia. 1994. *The Body Farm*. New York: Charles Scribner's Sons.

Cuthbert, W. L., and F. M. Law. 1927. Identification by Comparison of Roentgenograms. *Journal of the American Medical Association* 88 (May 21).

Di Maio, Vincent J. M. 1985. *Gunshot Wounds*. New York: Elsevier.

Eisele, J. W., D. T. Reay, and Ann Cook. 1981. Sites of Suicidal Gunshot Wounds. *Journal of Forensic Sciences* 26 (3): 480–85.

Eiseley, Loren. 1969. *The Unexpected Universe*. New York: Harcourt, Brace.

El-Najjar, Mahmoud Y., and K. Richard McWilliams. 1978. *Forensic Anthropology*. Springfield: Charles C. Thomas.

Elkins, Aaron. 1987. *Old Bones*. New York: The Mysterious Press.

Fazekas, I. G., and F. Kosa. 1978. *Forensic Fetal Osteology*. Budapest: Akademiai Kiado.

Finnegan, Michael, and Daniel Kysar. 1996. Demography, Pathology, Trauma and Other Results of the Jesse James Case. *The Connective Tissue* 12 (2): 8–9.

France, Diane. 1994. Mass Fatality Incident Response in Glenwood Springs, Colorado. *The Connective Tissue* 10 (3): 3.

Galloway, Alison. 1988. Estimating Actual Height in the Older Individual. *Journal of Forensic Sciences* 22 (1): 126–36.

Galloway, Alison, Walter H. Birkby, Allen M. Jones, Thomas E. Henry, and Bruce O. Parks. 1989. Decay Rates of Human Remains in an Arid Environment. *Journal of Forensic Sciences* 34 (3): 607–16.

Galloway, Alison, Walter H. Birkby, Tzipi Kahana, and Laura Fulginiti. 1990. Physical Anthropology and the Law: Legal Responsibilities of Forensic Anthropologists. Yearbook of Physical Anthropology 33: 39–57. New York: Wiley-Liss.

Gantner, George E., and Michael Graham. 1990. Quality Assurance and the Medicolegal Autopsy Protocol. In *Handbook of Forensic Pathology*, edited by Richard C. Froede. Northfield: College of American Pathologists.

George, Robert M. 1987. The Lateral Craniographic Method of Facial Reconstruction. *Journal of Forensic Sciences* 32 (5): 1305–30.

Gerasimov, M. M. 1971. *The Face Finder*. Philadelphia: J. B. Lippincott Co.

Gilbert, B. Miles. 1973. *Mammalian Osteoarchaeology*. Columbia: Missouri Archaeology Society.

Giles, Eugene. 1996. *Frederick Seymour Hulse, 1906–1990*. Vol. 70 of *Biographical Memoirs*. Washington, D.C.: The National Academy Press.

Giles, Eugene, and Oliver Elliot. 1962. Race Identification from Cranial Measurements. *Journal of Forensic Sciences* 7: (1) 147–56.

Gill, George, and Stanley Rhine. 1990. *Skeletal Attribution of Race.* Anthropological Papers No. 4. Albuquerque: Maxwell Museum of Anthropology.

Gill, George, Susan S. Hughes, Suzanne M. Bennett, and B. Miles Gilbert. 1988. Racial Identification from the Midfacial Skeleton with Special Reference to American Indians and Whites. *Journal of Forensic Sciences* 33 (1): 92–99.

Glassman, David M., and Rodney M. Crow. 1996. Standardization Model for Describing the Extent of Burn Injury to Human Remains. *Journal of Forensic Sciences* 41 (1): 152–54.

Goff, M. L., and M. M. Flynn. 1991. Determination of Postmortem Interval by Arthropod Succession: A Case Study from the Hawaiian Islands. *Journal of Forensic Sciences* 36: 607–14.

Haglund, William D., Donald T. Reay, and Clyde C. Snow. 1987. Identification of Serial Homicide Victims in the "Green River Murder" Investigation. *Journal of Forensic Sciences* 32 (6): 1666–75.

Haglund, William D., Donald T. Reay, and Daris R. Swindler. 1989. Canid Scavenging/Disarticulation Sequence of Human Remains in the Pacific Northwest. *Journal of Forensic Sciences* 34 (3): 587–606.

Haglund, William D. and Marcella H. Sorg, eds. 1996. *Forensic Taphonomy.* New York: CRC Press.

Harris, Anna Burke, Marsha Robinson Starr, and John E. Smialek. 1985. *The Sophisticated Data Base: Unique Information in Text Form.* Proceedings of the 18th Annual Hawaiian International Conference on System Sciences.

Healy, Gael D., Kathy M. Aragon, and J. T. Weston. 1983. Computer Support for Medicolegal Investigative Systems. *Medicine and Law* 2: 239–47.

Helmer, Richard P. 1987. Identification of the Cadaver Remains of Josef Mengele. *Journal of Forensic Sciences* 32 (6): 1622–44.

Henssge, Claus, Bernard Knight, Thomas Krompecher, Burkhard Madea, and Leonard Nokes. 1995. *The Estimation of Time Since Death in the Early Postmortem Period.* Edited by Bernard Knight. Boston: Little, Brown and Co.

His, W. 1895. Johann Sebastian Bach's Gebeine and Antlitz nebst Bemerkungen uber Dessen Bilder. *Abhandlung durch Matematik und Physik* 22: 380–420.

Holland, Thomas Dean. 1986. Race Determination of Fragmentary Crania by Analysis of the Cranial Base. *Journal of Forensic Sciences* 31 (2): 719–25.

Howells, W. W. 1973. *Cranial Variation in Man.* Papers of the Peabody Museum of Archaeology and Ethnology. Harvard.

Hunt, Charles B. 1967. *Physiography of the United States.* San Francisco: W. H. Freeman and Co.

Ilan, E. 1964. Identifying Skeletal Remains. *International Criminal Police Review* 264: 76–80.

Iscan, Mehmet Yasar. 1988. *Rise of Forensic Anthropology.* Yearbook of Physical Anthropology 31: 203–29.

Iscan, Mehmet Yasar, and Kenneth A. R. Kennedy, eds. 1989. *Reconstruction of Life From the Skeleton.* New York: Alan R. Liss, Inc.

Iscan, Mehmet Yasar, Susan R. Loth, and Ronald K. Wright. 1987. Racial Variation in the Sternal Extremity of the Rib and its Effect on Age Determination. *Journal of Forensic Sciences* 32 (2): 452–66.

Johnston, F. E. 1962. Growth of the Long Bones of Infants and Young Children at Indian Knoll. *Human Biology* 23: 66–81.

Joyce, Christopher, and Eric Stover. 1991. *Witnesses from the Grave.* Boston: Little, Brown and Co.

Kennedy, Kenneth A. R. 1996. The Wrong Urn: Commingling of Cremains in Mortuary Practices. *Journal of Forensic Sciences* 41 (4): 689–92.

Kerley, Ellis R. 1965. The Microscopic Determination of Age in Human Bone. *American Journal of Physical Anthropology* 23: 149–63.

———. 1977. Forensic Anthropology. In *Forensic Medicine.* Vol. 2, C. G. Tedeschi, William G. Eckert, and Luke G. Tedeschi, eds. Philadelphia: W. B. Sauners Company.

———. 1978. *Recent Developments in Forensic Anthropology.* Yearbook of Physical Anthropology 21: 160–73.

Klepinger, Linda L., and John A. Heidingsfelder. 1996. Probable Torticollis Revealed in Decapitated Skull. *Journal of Forensic Sciences* 41 (4): 693–96.

Knight, Bernard. 1983. *The Coroner's Autopsy.* Edinburgh, U.K.: Churchill Livingston.

Kollmann, J., and W. Buchly. 1898. Die Persistenz der Rassen und die Reconstruction der Physiognomie Parhistoricher Schadel. *Archiv fur Anthropologie* 25: 329–59.

Krogman, Wilton M. 1939. Guide to the Identification of Human Skeletal Material. *FBI Law Enforcement Bulletin* No. 8.

———. 1962. *The Human Skeleton in Forensic Medicine.* Springfield: Charles C. Thomas.

Krogman, Wilton M., and Mehmet Yasar Iscan. 1986. *The Human Skeleton in Forensic Medicine.* 2d ed. Springfield: Charles C. Thomas.

Lundy, John K. 1988. A Report on the Use of Fully's Anatomical Method to Estimate Stature in Military Skeletal Remains. *Journal of Forensic Sciences* 33 (2): 534–39.

MacDonald, Peter V. 1987. *More Court Jesters.* Toronto: Stoddard Publishing Co., Ltd.

Mann, Robert W., Steven A. Symes, and William M. Bass. 1987. Maxillary Suture Obliteration: Aging the Human Skeleton Based on Intact or Fragmentary Maxilla. *Journal of Forensic Sciences* 32 (1): 148–57.

Mann, Robert W., William M. Bass, and Lee Meadows. 1990. Time Since Death and Decomposition of the Human Body: Variables and Observations in Case and Experimental Field Studies. *Journal of Forensic Sciences* 35 (1): 103–11.

Maples, William R., and Michael Browning. 1994. *Dead Men Do Tell Tales.* New York: Doubleday.

Mayer, Robert. 1980. 36 Hours in the New Mexico Prison. *Rocky Mountain Magazine,* May/June, 23–32.

McCarty, Vernon O., and J. Stanley Rhine. 1995. A Premature Funeral. Paper presented at the Last Word Society session of the 47th Annual Meeting of the American Academy of Forensic Sciences, February, Seattle.

McCarty, Vernon O., Anton P. Sohn, R. S. Ritzlin, and Joseph H. Gauthier. 1987. Scene Investigation, and Victim Examination Following the Accident of Galaxy 203: Disaster Preplanning Does Work. *American Journal of Forensic Sciences* 32 (4): 983–87.

McKern, Thomas W., and T. Dale Stewart. 1957. Skeletal Age Changes in Young American Males. Technical Report. Natick: Headquarters Quartermaster Research and Development Command.

Merbs, Charles F. 1980. *Catalogue of the Hrdlicka Paleopathology Collection*. San Diego: San Diego Museum of Man.

Micozzi, Marc S. 1991. *Postmortem Changes in Human and Animal Remains*. Springfield: Charles C. Thomas.

Miller, Peter S. 1996. Disturbances in the Soil: Finding Buried Bodies and Other Evidence Using Ground Penetrating Radar. *Journal of Forensic Sciences* 41 (4): 648–52.

Montagu, Ashley. 1964. The Concept of Race. London: Collier-MacMillian Ltd.

Morris, Roger, 1983. *The Devil's Butcher Shop*. Albuquerque: University of New Mexico Press.

Morse, D., J. Duncan, and J. Stoutamire, eds. 1983. *Handbook of Forensic Archaeology and Anthropology*. Tallahassee: Rose Printing Co.

Murad Turhon A., and Margie A. Boddy. 1987. A Case With Bear Facts. *Journal of Forensic Sciences* 32 (6): 1819–26.

Nelson, Russell. 1992. A Microscopic Comparison of Fresh and Burned Bone. *Journal of Forensic Sciences* 37 (4): 1055–60.

News Item. 1994. American Eagle Flight 4184. *The Connective Tissue* 10 (4): 8.

Noguchi, Thomas T., and Joseph D. DiMona. 1985. *Coroner at Large*. New York: Simon and Schuster.

Office of the Medical Investigator [OMI]. 1989. *Annual Report*. Albuquerque: Office of the Medical Investigator.

———. 1994. *Annual Report*. Albuquerque: Office of the Medical Investigator.

———. 1995. *Annual Report*. Albuquerque: Office of the Medical Investigator.

Ortner, Donald J., and Walter G. J. Putschar. 1985. *Identification of Pathological Conditions in Human Skeletal Remains*. Washington: Smithsonian Institution.

Owsley, Douglas W., Davor Strinovic, Mario Slaus, Dana D. Kollmann and Malcolm L. Richardson, 1996. *Recovery and Identification of Civilian Victims of the War in Croatia*. Cultural Resource Management 19 (10): 33–36.

Rathbun T. A., and B. C. Rathbun. 1984. Human Remains Recovered From a Shark's Stomach in South Carolina. *Journal of Forensic Sciences* 29 (1): 269–76.

Rathbun, Ted A., and Jane E. Buikstra, eds. 1984. *Human Identification*. Springfield: Charles C. Thomas.

Reichs, Kathleen J., ed. 1986. *Forensic Osteology*. Springfield: Charles C. Thomas.

Rhine, Stanley, and Kris Sperry. 1991. Radiographic Identification by Mastoid Sinus and Arterial Pattern. *Journal of Forensic Sciences* 36 (1): 272–79.

Rodriguez, W. C., and W. M. Bass. 1983. Insect Activity and its Relationship to Decay Rates of Human Cadavers in East Tennessee. *Journal of Forensic Sciences* 28 (2): 423–43.

———. 1985. Decomposition of Buried Bodies and Methods That May Aid in Their Location. *Journal of Forensic Sciences* 30 (3): 836–52.

Rodriguez, William C., and Wayne D. Lord. 1993. Forensic Entomology and its Use in the Determination of Time Since Death. In *Spitz and Fisher's Medicolegal Investigation of Death*, edited by Werner U. Spitz. 3rd ed. Springfield: Charles C. Thomas.

Royte, Elizabeth. 1996. 'Let the Bones Talk' is the Watchword for Scientist-Sleuths. *Smithsonian*, May, 83–90.

Salomone, Jeffrey, III, Anton P. Sohn, Roger Ritzlin, Joseph H. Gauthier, and Vernon McCarty. 1987. Correlations of Injury, Toxicology and Cause of Death to Galaxy Flight 203 Crash Site. *Journal of Forensic Sciences* 32 (5): 1403–25.

Shipman, Pat, Alan Walker, and David Bichell. 1985. *The Human Skeleton*. Cambridge: Harvard University Press.

Simpson, Keith. 1978. *Forty Years of Murder.* 1988 edition. New York: Dorset Press.

Sledzik, P. S. 1994a. Hardin, Missouri, Cemetery Disaster. *The Connective Tissue* 10 (1): 11.

———. 1994b USAir Flight 427 Crash. *The Connective Tissue* 10 (4): 8.

Smith, O'Brian C., Hugh E. Berryman, and Craig H. Lahren. 1987. Cranial Fracture Patterns and Estimate of Direction from Low Velocity Gunshot Wounds. *Journal of Forensic Sciences* 32 (5): 1416–21.

Smith, Sir Sydney. 1959. *Mostly Murder.* New York: David McKay Company, Inc.

Snow, Charles E. 1948. The Identification of the Unknown War Dead. *American Journal of Physical Anthropology* 6: 323–328.

Snow, Clyde Collins. 1982. *Forensic Anthropology.* Annual Review of Anthropology 7. Palo Alto: Annual Reviews Inc.

Snow, Clyde C., Betty Pat Gatliff, and Kenneth R. McWilliams. 1970. Reconstruction of Facial Features from the Skull: An Evaluation of its Usefulness in Forensic Anthropology. *American Journal of Physical Anthropology* 33: 221–27.

Spitz, Werner U. 1993. The Medicolegal Autopsy Report. In *Spitz and Fisher's Medicolegal Investigation of Death.* 3d ed., edited by Werner U. Spitz. Springfield: Charles C. Thomas.

Spitz, Werner U., editor. 1993. *Spitz and Fisher's Medicolegal Investigation of Death*, 3rd ed., Springfield: Charles C. Thomas.

Steele, D. Gentry. 1970. Estimation of Stature From Fragments of Long Limb Bones. In *Personal Identification in Mass Disasters*, edited by T. D. Stewart. Washington: Smithsonian Institution.

Steele, D. Gentry, and Claud A. Bramblett. 1988. *The Anatomy and Biology of the Human Skeleton*. College Station: Texas A & M University Press.

Stevens, Boyd G., and Patricia J. McFeeley. 1987. Time of Death Determination. Breakfast Seminar, American Academy of Forensic Sciences, February. San Diego.

Stewart, T. D. 1958. The Rate of Development of Vertebral Osteoarthritis in American Whites and its Significance in Skeletal Age Determination. *The Leech* 28: 144–51.

———. 1970. *Personal Identification in Mass Disasters*. Washington: Smithsonian Institution.

———. 1979. *Essentials of Forensic Anthropology.* Springfield: Charles C. Thomas.

Stout, Sam D. 1988. The Use of Histomorphology to Estimate Age. *Journal of Forensic Sciences* 33 (1): 121–25.

Todd, T. Wingate and D. W. Lyon. 1924. Cranial Suture Closure: Its Progress and Age Relationship. *American Journal of Physical Anthropology* 8.

Trotter, Mildred, and Goldine C. Gleser. 1952. Estimation of Stature from Long-Bones of American Whites and Negroes. *American Journal of Physical Anthropology* n.s. 10: 463–514.

———. 1958. A Reevaluation of Estimation of Stature Based on Measurements of Stature Taken During Life and Long-Bones After Death. *American Journal of Physical Anthropology*, n.s. 16: 79–123.

Trotter, M., and R. R. Peterson. 1955. Ash Weight of Human Skeletons in Percent of Their Dry, Fat-Free Weight. *Anatomical Record* 123: 341–68.

Turcica, Stella. 1995. Forensic Anthropology and Aircraft Accidents. *The Connective Tissue* 11 (1): 6–7.

Ubelaker, Douglas. 1984. Positive Identification from the Radiographic Comparison of Frontal Sinus Patterns. In *Human Identification*, edited by Ted A. Rathbun and Jane E. Buikstra. Springfield: Charles C. Thomas.

———. 1987. Estimating Age at Death from Immature Human Skeletons: An Overview. *Journal of Forensic Sciences* 32 (5): 1254–63.

———. 1989. *Human Skeletal Remains*, 2nd edition, Washington: Taraxacum.

———. 1993. Well Done: An Anthropological Analysis of Human Remains from Waco, Texas. *The Connective Tissue* 9 (2): 3.

Ubelaker, Douglas, and Henry Scammell. 1992. *Bones: A Forensic Detective's Casebook*. New York: HarperCollins.

Ubelaker, Douglas H., and Norman D. Sperber. 1988. Alterations in Human Bones and Teeth as a Result of Restricted Sun Exposure and Contact with Corrosive Agents. *Journal of Forensic Sciences* 33 (2): 540–48.

Utermohle, Charles J., Stephen L. Zegura and Gary M. Heathcote, 1983. Multiple Observers, Humidity and Choice of Precision Statistics: Factors Influencing Craniometric Data Quality. *American Journal of Physical Anthropology* 61 (1): 85–95.

Warren, Michael W. and William R. Maples. 1997. The Anthropometry of Contemporary Commercial Cremation. *Journal of Forensic Sciences* 42: 417–23..

Weaver, David S. 1980. Sex Differences in the Ilia of a Known Age and Sex Sample of Fetal and Infant Skeletons. *American Journal of Physical Anthropology* 52: 191–96.

———. 1986. Forensic Aspects of Fetal and Neonatal Skeletons. In *Forensic Osteology*, edited by Kathleen J. Reichs. Springfield: Charles C. Thomas.

Welcker, H. 1883. Schiller's Schadel und Todtenmaske, nebst Mittheilumgen uber Schadel und Todtenmaske Kans, Braunschweig.

———. 1888. Zur Kritik des Schillerschadels. *Archiv fur Anthropologie* 17: 19–60.

Wienker, Curtis W., and Joan E. Wood. 1988. Osteological Individuality Indicative of Migrant Citrus Laboring. *Journal of Forensic Sciences* 33 (2): 562–67.

Wienker, Curtis W., and J. Stanley Rhine. 1989. A Professional Profile of the Physical Anthropology Section Membership, American Academy of Forensic Sciences. *Journal of Forensic Sciences* 34 (3): 647–58.

White, Tim D., and Pieter A. Folkens. 1991. *Human Osteology*. San Diego: Academic Press.

Wilder, H. H. 1912. The Physiognomy of the Indians of Southern New England. *American Journal of Physical Anthropology* 14: 415–36.

Wilder, Harris Hawthorne, and Bert Wentworth. 1918. *Personal Identification*. Boston: Richard G. Badger.

Willey, P., and A. Heilman. 1987. Estimating Time Since Death Using Plant Roots and Stems. *Journal of Forensic Sciences* 32 (5): 1264–70.

Willey, P., and T. Falsetti. 1991. Inaccuracy of Height and Weight Information on Driver's Licenses. *Journal of Forensic Sciences* 36 (3): 813–19.

Index